BUSH-PILOT
IN
DIAMOND
COUNTRY

Donald Haack

Pure Heart Press
Main Street Rag Publishing Company
Charlotte, North Carolina

Cover design by Todd Haack

Acknowledgement

My thanks and appreciation to: Dr. Robert Fulton for excellent editing and technical advice on fishing, hunting and firearms. Anita Strauss LaRowe for first round editing and keeping me to a time table. My son, Todd Haack for editing script and designing the front and back book cover and Julie Kral, my daughter, for editing advice. Jan for editing and proofing. Brian and Aminge Thomas for introducing us to John Steinbeck whose advice and encouragement planted the seed of this book. All my friends who were supportive and had to bear with the birth of this first book.

Library of Congress Control Number: 2004109700

ISBN: 1-930907-49-4

Pure Heart Press/
Main Street Rag Publishing Company
4416 Shea Lane
Charlotte, NC 28227
www.MainStreetRag.com

To my wife, Janet Mills Haack
For her heroic, adventurous spirit
and unending support.

Contents

NE South America: Brazil, Venezuela, and Guyana (formerly British Guiana).

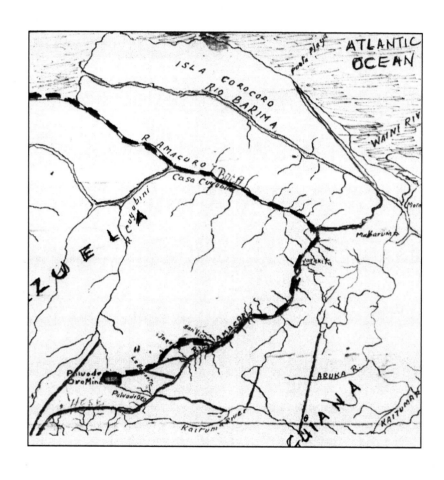

Map used on first Expedition on Orinoco and Amacuro
rivers to gold area, Polvo de Oro.

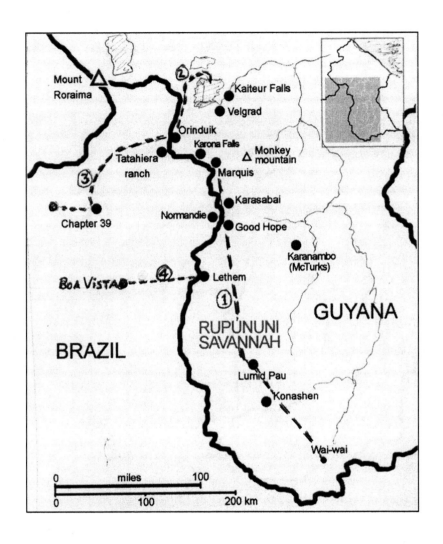

Haack's diamond trading and missionary flights:
(1) Chapter 22, Wai Wai
(2) Chapter 37, Box Canyon
(3) Chapter 39, Ambush
(4) Chapter 24, Jail

INTRODUCTION

There was a time when I read everything available on South America. The indigenous people were fascinating, the jungles hid amazing animals, and the rivers transported raw gems. The big difference between Don Haack and me? He didn't stop at reading; he *went* into the "heart of darkness." With the help of his sharp-shooting bride, he built a home, started a family, and hunted diamonds in a beautiful yet hostile land, where the nearest "neighbor" was 75 miles distant.

The characters, including the author and his wife, are as diverse a group as one would expect to find on the outskirts of civilization; yet they are described in a most human and insightful way. Though airplane crashes, floods, near drownings, arrests, and assassination attempts make for a lively narrative, the respect and fondness Haack has for the people he meets and works with is the lynchpin in his surviving to write this book.

Flying a bishop of the Catholic Church to people who've never seen a plane land, taking a nurse on a life-saving mission to remove a deadly candiru from an Indian girl, locating and rescuing a party of downed businessmen from a remote region, and managing to get an important politician to the polls in time are some of the deeds that endeared Haack to the locals. And he is effusive in his appreciation for them.

Whether sharing the excitement of meeting John Steinbeck, the glitz of being a guest on "What's My Line" TV show in New York, or how the shaman's little herbal pellets saved the author's life, *Bush Pilot* demonstrates what determination, people skills, and luck can accomplish.

Robert Fulton, Ph.D.
Monroe, NC
June 13, 2004

PROLOGUE

A Frenchman named Maurice lived in Normandie, a small settlement in northernmost Brazil across from Good Hope, a cattle ranch in British Guiana. Ten years earlier he had come overland from the infamous French prison on Devils' Island off the coast of French Guiana where convicts were sent from France. Some were hardened criminals and others were in for minor offenses. It was the island of no return.

No one ever escaped except the man made famous by the book, Papillon. Worldwide bad publicity forced France to shut down the prison and pardons were given to the inmates who had minor offenses. Maurice was one of those lucky ones. He struck out overland through French Guiana, Brazil and worked his way north to Normandie, a settlement of 30 people, situated at the foothills of the diamond bearing Pakaraima Mountains. He'd heard stories about diamonds and decided to try his luck.

He worked for six months, saved his money for a grubstake and borrowed a little more to give him supplies for one month's prospecting. He couldn't afford a boat so he traveled by foot across the Karasabai Savannah then headed west to the Ireng River, the border river and to the only major valley in the area. Without diving equipment, he worked the quarter mile wide shallow swift water areas along the bend in the river as it came out of the mountains.

He spent the first week moving rocks into a primitive dam enabling him to work in three feet of water. Picking the hardpan gravel that remained undisturbed for thousands of years and moving large rocks by hand, he scraped the loose gravel into a burlap sack held open with a vine sewed into the bag. There in shallow water along the bank he worked the gravel with his suruku, a diamond sieve. With the swirling gravel plunging up and down, the heavier material settled to the bottom. The sieve was then flipped upside down onto the bank with the heavier material concentrated at the top and center. He opened the center gravel carefully while keeping track of indicators, the heavier black ilminite and tantalite minerals concentrated in the middle.

When the ring of indicators grew from a few stones to an eight inch circle, he discovered a bright and shiny octahedron diamond. As he proceeded upstream, the indicators increased in size and were accompanied by diamonds in every sieve.

At the end of three weeks his corked carved quill was full. He emptied an aspirin bottle, which he half filled with diamonds as his rations ran out. The last day he carefully placed the diamonds into his shirt pocket and sewed it shut.

He returned to Normandie where he traded a few diamonds, paid up his debts and set out for Boa Vista, the only town in the Rio Branco territory. After selling his diamonds he returned to Normandie, stocked his shop with trade goods and his newly acquired land with fifteen head of cattle. Maurice became a man of stature, a man of wealth and a stalwart in the community.

The area he mined was named after him. Several eager young men followed Maurice's tales and directions. A few were lucky to find diamonds and Maurice Mines came to be known as a place to make a grub stake, not the million dollar hit but enough to make a difference in a standard of living. This mining, unlike tunneling in the earth, was alluvial—from the water.

The very shallow river areas had been worked for years but the more difficult deep areas remained virgin territories.

It was in Maurice Mines that we made our first diamond strike.

1958. Flying home in our Piper TriPacer, over uncharted Brazilian bush country, I became aware my life had merged with the stories of the books I once read. The jungle of South America was no longer a far-away fantasy—it was below me. No longer figments of my imagination formed by descriptive verse, the characters from the books were real. I met, lived and became friends with them.

Several of the books I read described the life of the famous bush pilot, Jimmie Angel. Others were written by the explorer and author, Leonard Clark. The Lost World, written early in the century by Sir Conan Doyle was fiction set in a South American location so remote as to be unreal. I had entered into their worlds. These books were read in my youth and I assumed the authors and characters were long dead. I was astounded to meet two of them in person and had the adventurous fortune to build a house and live in the Lost World area.

I flew Jimmie Angel and his geologists to the British Guiana-Brazilian border where they were surveying gold claims. I rescued Leonard Clark from a plane crash in the jungle. Both men became my friends and we spent time and shared adventures together. They died in separate accidents on our joint projects. I closed the last chapters of their lives—a profoundly emotional experience for me. To add to these strange coincidences, Jan, my wife, and I were living in the shadow of Sir Conan Doyle's Lost World where I was managing a diamond mining company.

When I met John Steinbeck, he had learned some of my background and offered an interesting perspective: after I'd read those books, my life was pre-destined and would run its course accordingly. As I look back, I wonder about the validity of his theory on predestination. There were many events beyond mere coincidence including that meeting with John Steinbeck, which planted the seed of this book.

Donald Haack

MEETING A LEGEND
Grenada: 1968

The picture of John Steinbeck and the announcement of his death spread across the cover of Time magazine. Jan had just finished pouring tea and glanced up at me with a pained look, then back to the magazine. The photo showed a younger man than we met. But still, the image brought back a flood of memories.

We were also sitting down to tea in 1967 when Jan mentioned that Aminga and Brian Thomas, owners of the exclusive Calabash hotel on L'Anse Aux Epines Bay, north of where we lived, had invited us for dinner. That got my attention. Besides being the most attractive tropical hotel on the island, the Calabash featured a gourmet menu. Such an evening would provide a welcome break in our routine.

"Aminga said, besides the invitation, she would tantalize us even more. They have a special guest with them. He's one of 'ours', meaning an American, I guess."

We knew Brian was not fond of Americans and in fact

discouraged their coming. He didn't include us in that category, because, as he put it, having been out of the States so many years, we were not typical American tourists. My curiosity was aroused. It was rare to find an American at the Calabash. The last one we could recall was Walter Cronkite.

We entered the Calabash front hall and enjoyed both the delicate fragrance of blooming frangipanis bursting forth from a series of alcoves along the wall and Humphrey, the three-foot Macaw parrot whose loud and piercing squawks announced the arrival of guests. He was splendid with his brilliant green body and wings, blue tail feathers and black beak that emerged underneath a bright bulbous nose. His pink eyes were alert to every movement. No one entered without a greeting from Humphrey.

We stepped down into the spacious tropical dining room. Candles in red pottery with diamond-shaped openings highlighted the artistic array of flowers and the varied crystal glasses on each table. The low ceiling rafters were covered with hanging white flowering thunbergia that danced to and fro in an undulating rhythm orchestrated by the gentle breezes from the bay. Half walls of flowers surrounded the dining area, which had two elevations so that everyone had a spectacular view of the bay a hundred feet away. On the beach, a steel drum band played soft melodious calypso music, which, at first, could barely be heard. As dinner progressed, the band moved closer to the dining room and by the last course, the seven steel drummers were playing alongside the outermost tables. They increased the tempo into powerful, pulsating calypso beats, persuading even the old and most staid diners to the dance floor. There the hanging thunbergia further teased the senses of the dancers as it brushed against their bobbing heads responding to the calypso. Brian did a masterful job of immersing his guests in a tropical paradise.

Aminga waved us to her table. Brian moved from table to table, making his guests feel at home and to confirm that every detail was orchestrated perfectly. Godfrey, our waiter and a smiling giant of a man who drove our four children to school in the hotel mini bus, greeted us with a grin that split his shining black face.

"Evening Mista, Missa Haack. Nice to have you with us tonight." Hoisting the big three-gallon basket of wine onto his shoulder, he filled our white wine glasses for the first courses.

Aminga leaned over, "John Steinbeck and his wife are staying with us. He's not at all well…asked not to be made a fuss over. Brian struck up a conversation with him yesterday and mentioned your adventures in South America. He was intrigued and asked to meet you. His wife doesn't know if he will feel up to it, though. We'll play it by ear and see what happens."

During the second and subsequent courses, Godfrey served a red wine from a similar sized jug, again delicately and dramatically balanced on his shoulder. This was the Christmas season when Brian wore a tuxedo, but no shoes. Not wearing shoes was a normal Grenada thing, but the tux with bare feet—strictly Brian. On the third course he rejoined us at our table. Brian, tall, thin, and quintessentially British, sported a reddish-brown handlebar mustache and a slightly unruly crop of matching hair. He was smiling, with twinkle wrinkles around his eyes. He exuded an air of expectation that magically infected the patron's tables he visited.

"Come, I'd like you to meet someone," he whispered as he steered us over to Steinbeck's table.

"I told him you were a bush pilot and a refugee from a revolution in South America. He would like to say hello to a fellow American. We'll keep it short, he's looking tired."

He truly didn't look sprightly. He and his wife sat along the outside wall at a small table for two. Brian introduced them to Jan and me. She looked younger but perhaps only because his illness was taking a toll on him. His face was puffy, added evidence of a health problem. He forced a smile, followed by a grimace. I wondered how much pain he endured and what an effort it must have been for him to travel. I silently hoped he could enjoy some of this surrounding beauty.

He extended his hand. I took it… not a firm grip. Brian motioned he would slide a couple of chairs over.

Donald Haack

"Thanks, but no chairs" I said as I squatted down alongside their table. Jan stood next to Mrs. Steinbeck. "The Steinbecks will think we're camped out here and I certainly wouldn't do that with Aminga's superb desserts coming up. As long as I'm still able to bend over, we can talk face to face." I sensed relief from Mrs. Steinbeck, who, I presumed, feared we might linger too long; a common situation that celebrities experience.

There was still a bit of a tense atmosphere. I hoped a bit of levity would help. I blurted out, "You know, I've read most of your books but I didn't have much of a choice...they were required reading." I looked straight at him. He looked at me more intently with a slight hint of a scowl. I don't think he was used to hearing comments like that. I waited a moment, and then smiled broadly. "But they were the most memorable books I ever read. Thank you for that. May I ask you something? Your character "Lennie" in *Of Mice & Men*, was he a real character or a composite? The reason I ask is because I actually met a character like him in the Marine Corps and I had an immediate recall of your Lennie." Because of time, I didn't relate that experience.

He spoke quietly but deliberately. I moved closer to hear.

"All of my characters were based on people I met but in some I used composites, a poetic license you might say. I could do that, you know. After all, mine were novels, just that— fiction! *You* can't do that in recounting your adventures and your life stories. Describe the people just as they are. You don't have to embellish. When you were a young boy and opened the first book on South America, you were destined to live in that part of the world, meet the people in those stories, and to become involved with them by living out the final chapter of their lives— *predestination*. You have some good stories. Write them all down. Make your reader see, feel, smell just like *you* experienced them... better than fiction any time."

Interesting, I thought. He really doesn't want to talk about himself or his books and in one sentence turned the conversation back to what he wanted; more background on our life story. The phrase, "Choice of words and control of subject" went around in my head. But what else could be expected from the legendary John Steinbeck?

Brian had apparently related quite a number of adventures to him earlier. Steinbeck referred to several specific flying and mining stories and how best to write them up, something I hadn't considered at that time. As he talked I remembered his books alluded to supernatural forces, "predestined events" he called them. And listening to him reminded me that with so many unexplainable coincidences, my own life struck a parallel to his stories. He picked up on that immediately. His debilitated physical condition had not impaired his keen memory or sense of perception.

His wife was concerned he was becoming too tired. I could see it too. She moved to rise. I indicated for her not to as I stood up. We wished them a good stay.

"Good luck on your stories."

I thanked him. We returned to our table.

"Certainly an epic evening meeting the famous John Steinbeck. I didn't even know he was still alive. We're pretty lucky, Jan."

Aminga raised her hands, signing, "So? How did it go?"

I bowed at the waist, extending my hand in a sweeping motion. "Aminga, my dear, your cuisine is to die for but tonight it will be a bit diminished by the awesome experience of meeting *the* John Steinbeck, my favorite author. Thank you, thank you. However, now I will partake of your elegant dessert.

Back home in bed, I couldn't sleep. Besides trying to recall our conversation, I had a hundred questions running around my head. He never did give me a precise answer to my question about his character, Lennie. Thinking of him brought back vivid memories of his counterpart "Raul," whom I met at Parris Island, the U.S. Marines Corp boot camp.

I was drawn into more than one fight a day, my first week. At the beginning of the second week, a monstrously large man called Raul tapped me on the shoulder. His size took me by surprise.

I wondered why I hadn't noticed him before. He must have purposely stayed in the background.

"You've been lucky so far but you can't keep this up. That big black guy, Greene, who took you on yesterday, he's smartin', and plannin' on gettin you back when you're not lookin. He's a dirty fighter, no holds barred. Not your kinda' fight. And there are others. You're the college guy here, the only one. They don't like that. C'mere a second." He took me aside and handed me a broom.

"Grab it," he ordered. I recognized this as a game played among the men. The broom was held horizontally between two opponents, who grasped it with their hands. The game is that after a side is chosen, you try to force the broom to that side. Your opponent tries to force it down to the other side. First one down wins. We grabbed the broom. I indicated my side, and said, "Okay."

His end went down in less than a second, so fast I never knew what happened.

"I guess I wasn't ready," I muttered. "Again." Same thing happened, only quicker. "Okay," I conceded, "you made your point. Uh…what is your point? I'm glad you didn't pick a fight with me." I added. "Seems you're the only one who didn't this week."

"Just what I said, you've been lucky, but you can't go on fightin every guy out there and keep comin out on top." He put the broom aside. I didn't know what to expect. In spite of his rough features and numerous scars, his face was like an open book: no guile, no intrigue, only an expression of honesty that came through as a plea. He came closer and looked around to make sure no one else could hear.

"Look," Whatever it was he wanted to say was not coming easily. "I gotta problem. Can't read. Can you help me? Can't pay but I'll make sure you don't have 'nother fight the whole time you're here. Everyone sez how hard boot camp is, and for most mebbe that's true. That's why all these fights. I come from hell. This is the best time I've had in years, but I know they'll kick me out when they find I can't read or write. If that happens, I gotta go back, finish my sentence—Alabama chain gang."

Whether in disbelief or surprise, I frowned. He took it as disbelief.

He raised his trouser leg and rolled down his sock. My mouth dropped open. There were crude scars, one on top the other. Angry, purple scar tissue raised over a half inch in some places, flesh missing in others.

"That's from the chains," he said casually. I didn't know what to say. Finally gaining some wits, I asked, "How did you get there in the first place, jail I mean?"

"I was drunk, stole a train. Pushed the engineer off in Alabama where I started, so that's where they sent me... back to Alabama. Took it through three states before I ran out of coal and sobered up. Didn't put up a fight. They had police, FBI and the army waitin' for me. Got sent right to the chain gang. No stops. Been there three years. Let me off for good behavior if I enlisted in the Marine Corps. If I don't make it here, I gotta go back and serve 'nother year, mebbe more. Don't ever want to go back. Can you help me?"

During the course of our conversation, he placed his hand on my shoulder. His touch was very gentle for a man his size. The hand on my shoulder, the furrowed brow and parted, questioning lips combined into a plea for help I couldn't refuse.

I agreed. The next few weeks we spent nights sitting against the wall in the head after lights out, the only place in camp lighted after dark. From 8 to 11:30 P.M., we worked together. He slowly but steadily learned the alphabet, pronunciations, and forming of words. He was ecstatic when he put his first full sentence together. We both laughed. I shook his hand and congratulated him on that accomplishment. He caught on fast, but then, he had great motivation. The Drill Instructors had their own head so they never knew we were there. Guys from our platoon came in, looked at us, shrugged, did their business and left...no comments, no wisecracks. We were pretty much left alone and made good progress.

The day after Raul's broom test another guy picked a fight with me. Before I knew what was going on, Raul picked him up by the back of his collar, swung him in a circle, and flung him like a discus. He landed ten feet away against the Quonset hut. It took a long time before he struggled to his feet. Nothing was broken, except his spirit. He moved on. Later that afternoon I heard a ruckus behind me. Raul was holding Greene and another black guy by their necks.

"They tried to jump you from behind," he said, talking to no one in particular, but I knew what he meant. Before I could say anything, he took their two heads and knocked them together, like two coconuts. It was a sickening sound. They dropped like two sacks of flour. After a few minutes, Greene stirred, pulled himself up to a sitting position, shook his fist at me, and said something I didn't understand. I don't think he was all with it yet. But it was another mistake for Greene. Raul reached down, grabbed Greene's upraised fist and slowly squeezed.

Greene tried to pull back. Raul held on, no emotion, no smile, no anger. He squeezed. Greene cursed. Raul squeezed. Greene yelled. Raul squeezed. Greene screamed, sweat pouring over his big nose, eyes wide, almost pop-eyed, and mouth open with a tongue wagging like a snake. Then there was no sound. He passed out. Raul dropped the hand. It was mangled. All I could think of was "Lennie" in Steinbeck's *Of Mice and Men.* Lennie, who was stronger than he was smart.

My mind raced on. I thought of my Aunt Lil who gave me books every Christmas and birthday. One in particular started it all: Sir Arthur Conan Doyle's *Lost World.* I first read it when I was ten. It described a lost civilization that existed on a mountain plateau two miles above the jungles in a remote region of South America. The story was fiction but the remote plateau, Mount Roraima, Lost World, Devil's Mountain, or *Awon Tepui*, as the natives called it, was real. It formed the tri-boundary of Brazil, British Guiana and Venezuela.

Discussing those strange coincidences was not something I wanted to do; they defied logic to the point of sounding ridiculous. For me the feeling was like vertigo, falling into big black voids, a vortex sucking me into another world where I became an integral part of the books I read. What was real? What was imagined? Where's the fine line of reality I wondered.

There was an exception to my reticence. I remembered one evening after dinner at the Calabash, Brian and I indulged in a good bit of wine during the meal. Afterwards, feeling quite mellow, we moved to his house next door and continued the evening, savoring his exceptional Five Star Courvoisier brandy in large snifters. We rolled the brandy in a swirling motion, as we sniffed...and a half bottle disappeared. Deep in our brandy, Brian and I shared many stories. He confided that in his days after college, he went to America, selling encyclopedias and vacuum cleaners door to door. That's why he couldn't stand Americans. But it was a great education.

I, in turn, confided to him all those innermost thoughts of reading books, later living in the plot of those stories, meeting the characters, and ultimately sharing in their lives and adventures. Then, unfortunately, closing the last chapter of their lives.

I started by telling him that after Jan and I arrived in South America and had settled in our new home, Marquis, my first morning flight was a revelation. To the north, Mt. Roraima, the *Lost World,* cast shadows far into the hinterland of Venezuela. That scene brought a total recall of Sir Conan Doyle's book and the first of the feelings that I was becoming a part of it.

I described the meeting with Jimmy Angel, bush pilot and main character in numerous books on gold and diamonds in Venezuelan and what a surprise it was to find he was still alive. Afterwards, we flew together for several months while I helped him establish a base and company. A few months later, he died of complications from a plane landing accident in Panama. I helped arrange for his body to be shipped to his family in Texas.

Six months later, another startling coincidence—I rescued Leonard Clark, author of *Rivers Ran East*, and *Wanderer 'till I Die*, books that I read years earlier. I presumed that he, like Jimmy Angel, was long dead. After I rescued him and his friends from a plane crash, we spent time together in British Guiana and later Venezuela, where he joined us in our mining operation and met his untimely death in a boating accident. Adding to my sense of closing chapters of peoples' lives, I buried him along the La Paragua River in southern Venezuela.

Brian seemed fascinated and asked many questions. The next morning, I felt stupid and embarrassed at having shared such intimate thoughts. Thankfully, we never alluded to that less-than-sober, story-telling evening. I hoped he had forgotten. Apparently, he hadn't. He discussed it all with John Steinbeck who remembered those and other stories in detail.

THE BEGINNING
March 1955

A few days before being discharged from the Marine Corps at Cherry Point, NC, I received a phone call from my brother, Bob. "Hey, McGee, my nickname, I know you're planning to go to Bogota in a couple of months, but would you consider a fully-paid expedition into Venezuela for a couple of weeks?"

"Could be, what's up?"

"Frank Russell wants to organize an expedition into South America."

My enthusiasm dropped immediately. Six months earlier, on a weekend leave, I brought a Marine Corps friend, Charlie Heath, home and introduced him to my brother and his diamond supplier, Frank Russell. Frank was fascinated by Charlie's South American stories, particularly those concerning Colombian emeralds. He convinced Charlie and me that if we bought them directly from the mines, they could be sold for a big profit...for all of us. When we returned to Cherry Point, I sent Charlie to Bogota on two Marine training flights. Charlie was assured by his friends that the emeralds were the finest quality. He bought several. To our untrained eyes, they looked beautiful. When all transactions were complete, Charlie and I made no profit.

Anticipating what I was thinking, brother Bob went on to say,

"Even though the emerald business didn't make a profit, there may be a positive side. That emerald project piqued Frank's interest in South America and now he wants to go into the interior of Venezuela to buy rough diamonds from the Indians. After reading up on it, he's convinced we could organize an expedition to buy diamonds from the natives. Being in the diamond business, we know how and where to sell them, which we didn't with emeralds. The three of us would go: you, Frank, and me. Are you in? It will all be paid for by Frank."

He said the magic words, "paid for by Frank," so I agreed. If I had more smarts than enthusiasm, I would have thought twice. Our past dealings with Frank were not profitable.

They wanted me to organize the expedition. Venezuela required permits, visas, and tax solvencias. We would need current maps, shots, medicines, water purification kits, clothes and a myriad of other equipment for a jungle expedition. The list was endless. I began immediately.

This expedition wasn't the best-kept secret; Frank and Bob told everyone about the pending jungle expedition into the Lost World area. The *Milwaukee Journal* requested an interview, printed a feature story and soon all Milwaukee knew our plans.

Frank Russell's wife, Faye, also researched the Orinoco area. Seven weeks into the planning and five weeks before departure date, she confronted Frank.

"If you think you're going to go down on that expedition into unknown territories on uncharted rivers, rapids and waterfalls and expect to buy diamonds from uncivilized Indians two hundred miles from any civilization...well, don't bother coming back. There won't be a wife or *our* business to return to." The straightforward ultimatum was not open for discussion. Three days passed before Frank summoned the courage to break the news to Bob and me. We were stunned. We plunged into this project with a wild enthusiasm that built up as we went along. Now, suddenly it was over.

We were still caught up in the momentum of planning. Our biggest stumbling block: no money. Bob had just started his jewelry business and I was fresh out of the Marines. We barely had two nickels to rub together.

"What if we changed this expedition from a buying to a prospecting trip?" my brother, the eternal optimist, asked.

Enthusiasm always outshines common sense and I picked up on it quickly. "We could capitalize on all the publicity, possibly getting some sponsors."

We put out queries. Schlitz Brewing Co. responded first by providing us with a WWII Schlachtboot, an inflatable rubber raft designed for an outboard. Dad placed a call to his boyhood classmate, Ralph Evinrude of Evinrude Outboard Motors. Two days later his secretary called inviting me to Evinrude's office.

"Mr. Evinrude is looking forward to meeting you, go right in." A distinguished looking man with white hair and a friendly, smile-wrinkled face came around his desk and extended his hand.

"Ralph Evinrude." We shook hands. He didn't waste time on small talk. "We've got a new state-of-the-art outboard engine, the best there is, not even on the market yet. I'm going to give you one. Your father told me all about your venture. Get me a story and some good pictures and we'll call it square. Bob Webb, our foreman wants you in our shop on 27th street to learn how to strip down the engine and put it back together. Won't be any repair shops where you're going so you'll have to be totally self-sufficient. Webb will give you all the spare parts you'll need. Good luck and remember…good pictures of our engine, lots of them."

Herb Schreiber, my uncle and vice president of Johnson Compressor Company, called to tell me his company supplied compressors for Desco Diving, manufacturers of portable *hookah* diving equipment: a small engine, compressor, air hose and a mask. It gives a diver unlimited time underwater and great maneuverability.

"Could you use that for your expedition?"

I explained that in South America, all prospecting was done in rivers. It's what we needed, but couldn't afford.

"Never mind, I'll arrange it, somehow."

He came through with a complete portable diving rig, as OEM, Original Equipment Manufacturer, for experimental purposes. Free!

Abercrombie & Fitch in Chicago picked up on our *Journal* story and offered us camping equipment. They also wanted good photos and a story. I agreed. We were on a roll. I called my old commander, Col. Kirkpatrick, at Cherry Point Marine Base and told him what we were planning.

"Do you know where I can get outdated C and A rations that wouldn't cost a fortune?" I hoped he could help, or steer me in the right direction, but I hardly expected his answer.

"I've got a half-ton going out of date in a few days. Send me ten bucks and I won't have to dump it. It's yours. I'll schedule a training flight to Venezuela with one of our flying boxcars and we'll drop it in Caracas for you, compliments of the Marine Corps. Semper Fi!"

First and foremost on my mind was my upcoming marriage to Jan Mills. We had been engaged for two years and the wedding was scheduled for July.

July 1954

In the midst of all the expedition plans, we were married and went on a two-week honeymoon. Considering what Faye Russell said to her husband, Frank, I was amazed Jan supported this somewhat wild adventure. But then, I was twenty-five years younger than Frank, and didn't have an established business to risk.

The end of December was our new departure date, a few busy months away. The dry season in South America begins in January, the prime time to prospect low water rivers.

With Christmas celebrations over, we said our farewells and departed on what was to be a "three-week" diamond expedition.

It lasted over three months. I attribute three factors to the saving of my marriage: an extraordinary wife, a unique addition to our family, and the pile of diamonds we brought back.

Bob and I landed in Milwaukee's Douglas Airport, greeted by Jan and his wife, Audrey, waiting at the bottom of the Eastern Airways ramp. I was thinking, *How well do I know this lady? We've been married nine months and I've been gone three.* I didn't know what to say. I reached into my pocket.

"I brought something for you," were the first words that came out and I handed her *Chibi*, a baby tiger cat of the ocelot family. A tiny furry ball, her eyes had just opened. I took Jan's hand and put Chibi in it. That broke the ice. We hugged. It was great to be back.

The next day was spent relating the expedition highlights to Jan. I glossed over the myriad of red tape we experienced and kept to the highlights she would want to know. With "old fashioneds" in hand and before a roaring fireplace, I began the story.

"Some of the equipment we shipped by boat was lost and took days to locate. The delays in Caracas were frustrating and it was a week before AeroVensa delivered us to Ciudad Bolivar on the Orinoco River. We bought a sixty-foot dugout, fitted our new Evinrude, and tested our diving equipment. We purchased two, fifty- five gallon barrels of gasoline, rope, tackle, diamond sieves, and local rations. Our rooms in the Hotel Bolivar were filled with equipment, challenging the maids to clean or make the beds.

The hotel bar was *the* meeting place for prospectors and miners and it was there we met the Venezuelan Consul to British Guiana, Henry Stoll, a short, dark complexioned East Indian, with curly white hair flattened on his head. He was a soft-spoken wiry old man with an aura of sincerity. I took an instant liking to him.

He explained that his partner and he had a proven gold concession that required a formal assay for Kennicott Mining Company, but no means of getting their geologist, Fred Hanson into the area. Hanson arrived two days ago and was about to return. Time was running out. Stoll's partner, Blackie Davis, was to have arranged the expedition, but never showed up. Stoll understandably, was visibly upset.

When he learned that we were here to prospect for diamonds, he confided that the Arawak Indians living around their gold claims in the Amacuro River basin had found several crystals they believed were diamonds but they didn't know for sure and didn't know how to prospect for them.

My brother and I, fully equipped for an expedition and recently returned from a week in New York identifying and grading rough diamonds, were the answer to his problems.

As I described the incident to Jan, I began to re-live the vivid details. I could hear Mr. Stoll's gentle voice, "Would you be interested in joining forces?" He pointed to the tall thin man next to him, Fred Hanson, the geologist from Kennicott. After discussing the possibilities, we were offered diamond claims in the Amacuro. Stoll and group would retain gold rights and pay half the costs of everything: boat, motor, fuel, supplies, rations and *all* expenses along the way."

Short of funds, we accepted. To have a specific destination and the possibility of diamond claims were incentives too good to refuse. We shook hands, wrote up a short legal agreement, and the next morning at daybreak were on the dock ready to go. Blackie Davis, Stoll's partner, showed up in time to jump on board.

The Evinrude started on the first pull and with no idea what we were getting into we began our Orinoco adventure. Stoll and Davis, who had both been there before, would be our guides. If we had known what lay ahead, we wouldn't have left.

On constant vigil, we spent seven sun-scorching days and cool nights navigating the Orinoco. Using binoculars by moonlight at night, we took turns scanning the river for partially submerged logs and floating trees, but what really terrified us were the stories of whirlpools three-hundred feet across that could easily suck our sixty foot dugout into their vortexes.

Our first stop, Tucupita, a government outpost, was a necessary half-day detour for permits to enter the Amacuro district. Next destination, Curiapo, a tiny village squatting on fifteen-foot stilts in the severe tide-changing Orinoco mouth, was to be our jump-off point before the open ocean crossing to the Amacuro River.

But first we had to find Curiapo, located somewhere in the maze of the delta's numerous tributaries. On our first try we picked the wrong creek and were nearly run over by two high-speed Trinidad-to-Venezuela whiskey smuggling boats. We pulled into a side creek to await daylight.

The next morning, much to our chagrin, we found ourselves surrounded by an impenetrable mat of floating hyacinths. Without open water and unable to run our engine or use paddles, we were trapped in our dugout for twenty-four hours, drifting aimlessly at the vagaries of our captor plants. Then miraculously, as quickly as they engulfed us, the hyacinths split apart and disappeared.

We eventually found Curiapo, a few houses and a trade store. We spent part of the night sleeping in one of the stick-built houses. At midnight the local Indians woke us up to tell us it was high tide and the right time to cross the mouth of the Orinoco.

Bad advice, we were to find out. Still packed, we were up and gone within minutes. It was as if we couldn't jump fast enough from one dangerous situation to another.

An hour out and without warning, we ran into what we learned later was one of the roughest storms in months. After the squall hit, we were committed and couldn't change direction. Waves continually broke into the boat, but we knew if they hit us head on or from an angle, we would slice through and swamp immediately. We stayed in the parallel wave troughs hoping to reach the Amacuro mouth before we were forced onto land. For two hours we battled our way across open ocean in our ill-equipped dugout. Early on it became obvious the boat was filling up and we would have to bail regardless how badly we were being tossed about. Sinking was imminent.

Bob was on the Evinrude. I crawled over the gas drum and started bailing. I used one arm until it went numb then switched to the other while Bob jammed his foot on my back to keep me from being washed overboard. No one else bailed, they were either too sick or scared. Two terrifying hours later, totally exhausted, almost out of fuel, and more by luck than navigation, we entered the calm water of the Amacuro River.

We came up on an Amerindian hut, secured the dugout, crawled up the ladder and slept alongside the surprised Arawak Indians. They looked at us, didn't say a word, and thankfully went back to sleep. I thought that was the epitome of great hospitality. We awoke at noon with the bright sunlight pouring in and a circle of curious Indians around us. Arawaks were supposed to be friendly and they were in spite of our strange intrusion in their life. Stoll translated their broken Spanish. They couldn't believe we crossed the ocean during the storm in that boat! They kept pointing at our dugout in disbelief. Stoll convinced them we did, after which we thanked them, exchanged pleasantries, gave them some C rations and went on our way.

In the flat water, we made good progress going as far as we could with the long dugout, then tied it along the bank and transferred to the schlactboot, which was easy to haul over rocks and fallen trees. After a few miles, the stream narrowed to a small creek even too small for the rubber boat and we hauled it onto the bank. From there on would have to be on foot. I looked from Mr. Stoll to our pile of rations and equipment and raised my hands as if to say, *now what*? He smiled and motioned with his nose. Two Arawak Indians were standing alongside of me. I didn't hear them approach; they just suddenly appeared. In Spanish, they introduced themselves, Juan and Waddi. I estimated their ages at twenty. They were about five foot six, bronzed skin, stocky build, barefooted and wearing khaki shorts. As most Indians I would meet, they kept their hands at their sides, weight on one foot, and head slightly cocked to one side as if asking a question. Good-looking young men. Blackie, who had been cutting lines along the claims, had worked with them and when he left explained that he would return with a group in a fortnight. They expected us a week earlier. As we spoke, two more Arawaks stepped up. Within minutes and a little supervision our equipment was carefully stowed in their *Warashis*, backpacks of woven vines.

Knowing we had to hike the last few miles through bush with our supplies and equipment, Blackie arranged to have the Indians meet us. I asked Mr. Stoll how they knew where we would be. He smiled.

"They've been following us for hours."

Blackie never ceased to amaze me. I disliked him at first because he let Mr. Stoll down in arranging the expedition and showed up only in time to board our boat. As time went on, I found it difficult to keep a grudge. From the first day, he made a point to meet every person: miner, storekeeper, or Indian, shake their hands, talk with them at length and make them feel like they were the most important persons on earth. The same with government workers, except he'd slip a ten Bolivar note ($3 U.S.) into their pocket while telling them to have a Cerveza, beer, on him.

"Never can tell when you might need a favor," he'd whisper to one of us.

When they met him a second time, not surprisingly, they responded like family friends.

He described himself as a *tramp* mining engineer from Denver. The last one in the mine, the tramp supervised clean up, removal of all the mine tailings, the residue of any value, then made sure nothing was left behind before closing down. The description was interesting and I thought the word *tramp* fitted Blackie to a T but more because he looked like one. His dress was sloppy, he seldom shaved, and his shirt usually hung out in several places as if he just crawled out of bed. His eyebrows were black and bushy and hair unkempt, but seldom noticed, because it was covered by his dark blue baseball cap, always on while he ate, slept, and bathed. It looked a hundred years old and never washed.

We took off on a steady pace with Juan and Waddi in front cutting the trail through thicker bush with their machetes. It was a stark contrast leaving the sunlit river for the darkened jungle with its thick upper tree canopy reaching over two- hundred feet high. It would be many days before we saw the sun again. While on the move, we ate the C rations. At night our meals consisted of dried fish that had been on the bottom of the dugout and stepped on for most of the trip. If I had known we were going to eat the fish, I would have treated it with more respect. when we were walking over it.

Waddi shot a Powis, a local turkey, two monkeys, and an iguana. He was very proud of his double-barreled 16-gauge shotgun. He was an excellent marksman as evidenced by the fact that when he hunted with two shells, he returned with two birds or animals. Esthetics was a different matter. After skinning or plucking, everything was hacked up, put in a pot with herbs and greeneries found around camp, then boiled. With the strenuous pace on the trail all day, we worked up quite an appetite, probably the reason everything tasted reasonably good.

With daily showers soaking equipment, our hammocks, and us we were constantly wet. The weather near the coastal area wasn't aware it was supposed to be *dry season.* For a full two weeks we never saw the sun. We kept mosquito nets over our hammocks when the mosquitoes and other bugs became intolerable. One night to relieve myself I slipped out of my hammock and onto a sea of army ants. When I felt the first stinging bite, I shined the flashlight down onto what looked like a red river coming through the jungle. Staring at the thousands of ants making a path four feet wide, I had the impression of an enormous snake slithering through the grass. Terrified, I jumped back in the hammock. Too late. Hitting, swiping, scratching, I had hundreds of bites before I removed most of the ants. The poison from the bites caused infections, swelling feet, ankles, and legs for months. On the second night after we had settled in, we heard the rustle of leaves and twigs made by an animal moving around inside the circle of our hammocks. Worse, we could hear heavy breathing along with low guttural growling. No one moved or made a sound though I was certain everyone was awake. Moments later the quiet of the night was shattered by the jarring blast of a shotgun.

In the morning, Waddi proudly showed off *el tigre,* a large ocelot he shot a few feet from our hammocks. It had been around his village for weeks. A fortnight ago it killed a young Indian boy carrying water from a stream. When his family found him, he was half eaten.

Donald Haack

"Tigres rarely attack humans, but once they lose fear of man, they must be killed." he explained.

It wasn't a comforting feeling to know a man-killing ocelot came a few feet from our hammocks.

Early the next morning we reached the claim *Polvo de Oro*, powder gold, though for me it was hard to tell; all jungles looked alike. We unpacked while the Indians made camp before we settled down to prospect. Most of my time was spent with Fred Hanson, helping him while learning how to assay gold and searching for any signs of diamonds. Gold was everywhere; in streams, leaves, rocks, and ten feet down in pits dug by the Indians. Fred said it was the richest gold deposit he'd tested in forty years as a geologist. Mr. Stoll and Blackie were ecstatic. Bob and I were not.

I found several quartz crystals. Were those what the Indians believed to be diamonds?

After Fred completed his gold testing, we packed up and headed back to Ciudad Bolivar. Not burdened with supplies or equipment, we made the trip back in a relatively easy three days. We received the agreed-upon funds from Kennicott. Stoll and Hanson felt further indebted to us; their trip was hugely successful while we didn't find a single diamond. In appreciation, they had their Caracas attorney, Dr. Alzaibar, apply for a mining concession in the middle of a known diamond-bearing territory on the La Paragua River, a tributary of the Caroni. It would take months to process the claim and until then, we couldn't prospect it. We didn't have months. We were long past our planned stay; we had no diamonds and we didn't want to return empty handed.

Back at the hotel, Blackie Davis told us he was flying to neighboring British Guiana, affectionately known as *BG* the next morning.

"There's this Ireng River along BG's border...been producing diamonds for years. Could be worked right away. Being a British colony, it doesn't require a long wait for claims. Could get in there and start prospecting immediately. Could introduce you to the right people. You guys sure helped me and Stoll. Like to see you go home with some diamonds. I can get your prospecting licenses, permits in one day...know all the government people. Should... paid 'em enough. What do you say? Wanna join me?"

I had mixed feelings about Blackie. He screwed up at the beginning, but his explanation was that he was helping out a family in Ciudad Bolivar, got carried away and forgot when Kennicott's geologist was due. Probably true. The guy had a big heart. He always carried his pack of goodies, as he called them, and like a local Santa Claus, he doled out cigarettes, candy, medicine, Swiss knives, and unobtrusively slipped ten and twenty Venezuelan Bolivar notes to government officials and widows. I didn't have much time to consider Blackie's offer before Bob joined us at the bar. I could tell from the look on his face that something had happened. He showed me a telegram.

"Came a week ago," was all he said.

I quickly read it. Bob's mother-in-law died. I told Blackie what happened and we'd get back to him shortly.

Bob anguished over the news, trying to sort out what to do. "Too late to do anything, the funeral was last week. If we return now chances are we'll never get back here again."

I knew he had made up his mind. He told Blackie he would join him. I decided to return to the U.S.

That night I couldn't sleep. I tossed and turned with the decision to return home weighing heavily against Bob going to British Guiana with Blackie Davis. I'd never forgive myself if anything happened. Bob had a wild hair. I was the conservative who kept him from going too far. Knowing he was determined to come back with diamonds, and with the added pressure of time, I wondered what risks he might take.

I decided to stick with him, if for no other reason than to make sure he came back. I unpacked my suitcase that morning and re-packed it for the flight to B.G.

Two days later, via Pan Am, we touched down on British Guiana's Atkinson Field, an airstrip built by Americans. During World War II it was the jump-off point for ferrying American planes to Africa in the fight against the *Desert Fox*, German field marshal Erwin Rommel. Blackie, as promised, eased our way around the usual entry red tape by deftly distributing the pretty blue twenty-dollar B.G. bills, along with much backslapping and hugging. Everyone knew Blackie.

The Americans had done a beautiful job building an airfield, but nothing was done to the fifteen-mile road to Georgetown, the main city. We spent the next hour bumping, swerving, dodging cattle, people, dogs, donkeys, children, and potholes. Chickens weren't so lucky. The dust and smells were overwhelming and it was pure relief when we pulled up in front of the wooden three-story Woodbine Hotel, where Mac Wilshire the owner greeted us. Blackie gave instructions to Mac, "Take care of these boys. They wanna prospect for diamonds. Thought they might do well in the Rupununi and you could tell 'em how to get there. Any chance Caesar's in town? Could have 'em meet him and he'd take 'em back. Just treat 'em right, Mac. They helped out Stoll and me in Venezuela. I owe 'em big. Thanks."

He left in the taxi and that was the last we saw of Blackie. I wondered what the hell we were doing here.
Mac, the hotel owner, turned out to be very helpful. He introduced us to half of Georgetown's elite while we tried to formulate our plans. We were finishing breakfast when Mac came to our table. He was accompanied by a tall distinguished looking gentleman dressed in a dark business suit.

"Boys, meet Caesar. Has a cattle ranch in the interior."
It was difficult picturing this person as a rancher.

"Used to be in diamonds and he's the best one around these parts to give you good advice. Caesar, come here and meet these two young Americans. They want to prospect for diamonds."

If he had on khakis, Caesar would look like he stepped out of an African safari ad. He lit up a French Galois cigarette; held it in his teeth. It was an image that a cigarette company would pay a fortune for. He was square jawed, self-assured with a charming twinkle. His eyes narrowed as though summing us up.

"Nice to meet you," he said in a low, heavily-accented Russian voice. "What are your plans? How did you come here?"

We told him about Blackie Davis. He winced visibly at the name, reinforcing my impression that Blackie didn't enjoy the best of reputations in civilized circles. He wanted to hear the whole tale. I summarized our disastrous Venezuelan expedition as he puffed on his cigarette, but he perked up when I described our portable Schlactboot, state-of-the-art Evinrude, and portable diving rig.

"Not surprising you didn't find diamonds there. Not any in that area within five hundred miles. But you're here now."

Two hours of drinking later, he came up with an offer. Caesar later confessed he never did a business deal with anyone until he found out what the prospect was like after he had a few drinks.

"That's when you see a man's real character, when his defenses are down."

He didn't get us drunk, but pretty close. Apparently, we passed his test.

"How'd you like to come back to my ranch? It's near good diamond territory in the Pakaraima Mountains. With that portable boat you could get there in a couple of days. My nephew could be your guide and he can find a good Macusi diver to break you in. I know that country well. Used to mine it with Jimmy Angel. Made some good diamonds and that's how I bought my ranch."

He seemed straight as an arrow and had a good recommendation from Mac and other people we talked to in town. The next day we were winging our way by DC-3 into the interior to Caesar's *Good Hope Ranch* near the Brazilian border. None of the airstrips in the interior were paved. They were all dirt.

We met his wife, Nellie—tall, handsome, half Wapashani, half Scot. She opened her house to us as if we were family. We spent two days checking our equipment and Evinrude while waiting for his nephew, Harry Hart, and Domingo Galvao, the Amerindian son of Caesar's Brazilian neighbor. They arrived in a flurry of dust the third day by jeep.

Harry, a six-foot tall, thin, wiry young man unwound himself out of the jeep. His khakis were sun-bleached, and his Aussie hat partially covered his narrow, dark sun-tanned face highlighted by a small trimmed mustache and black shining eyes. His father was American, but Harry had the rugged Amerindian features of his Wapashani mother. After introductions, Harry quickly related his interest in this expedition. Our destination, *Maurice Mines* on the Ireng River, was a rich diamond area, but difficult to reach because of its remote location.

Maurice Mines was named after the Frenchman, Pierre Maurice whose trade store, garden, chickens, and cattle supplied most of region across the river from Good Hope. Years earlier Maurice came overland and, without apologies or excuses, explained where he came from: Devils' Island, the infamous French prison off the coast of French Guiana.

I told Bob that Harry was so excited about going to the mines, he told the story to encourage us. We didn't need it, we were already eager to go to any diamond bearing area to try our diving equipment.

We waved to Nellie and Caesar as we took off up the Ireng in our Schlactboot with Harry and Domingo. We were an eager foursome.

After three hard days of fighting rapids and portages with our fifteen horsepower Evinrude and Schlachboot we arrived at Maurice Mines. We wasted no time, diving in the deeper, less accessible areas. But we were new to prospecting. Harry had asthma and couldn't dive so he taught us the theory, Domingo the practical. After a few tries, we discovered Bob had claustrophobia when he attached the mask to his face. Domingo and I ended up doing the diving. We dived all day everyday and were almost too exhausted to eat.

Our food consisted of tasteless C and A rations along with some very welcomed fish that Harry caught. Sometimes we ate because we felt we had to for the nourishment, other times because it tasted absolutely delicious...the fresh fish. Domingo fried it in a skillet in butter with heaps of onions and a few local spices.

After a week of diving, I learned about Ilminite and Tantalite, shiny black minerals heavier than the surrounding gravel that were showing up in our diamond sieves. Domingo called them indicators and as they became more abundant, we started finding the first few small diamonds. We followed the indicators to the deeper areas and behind large boulders or rock outcrops that formed turbulent eddies, forcing the passing gravel to suspend for a few seconds before settling down. As they dropped, heavier particles separated first, lighter ones were swept further downstream. We were searching for those first deposits. As the days went on, Domingo and I found more and more Ilminite and Tantalite in the sieves. Every throw of the sieve produced at least one diamond. And then we got lucky.

Early that same morning a Macusi Indian from Tipuru village shot a *tigre* in our valley. After breakfast we walked over to see it and discovered she had just delivered a cub and they were going to kill it.

I stopped them, asking if I could keep it. They said it wouldn't live…too young, but they agreed to let me have it. In return, I gave them some C and A rations, which they thought was a great exchange.

I kept the tiny Ocelot cub alive by feeding it from our medical kit eyedropper, using half Carnation canned milk and half boiled water. No one expected it to live. *Chibi,* little diamond in Macusi, was more of a fighter than anyone could have known.

Our new mascot proved to be both aptly named and a good luck charm. It was that afternoon I came up with a bag of almost pure black Ilminite and Tantalite. Domingo was excited and couldn't wait to sieve. Every time he threw the Surukus, the Brazilian diamond sieves over he pointed to the cluster of diamonds in the center. We had hit a small mother lode. The rest of the day and most of the next we worked at a frantic pace until we were satisfied there were no diamonds left in that area. We had cleaned it entirely.

Bob and I were ecstatic…we counted over five hundred diamonds. The next day we folded camp and headed back to civilization with our new family member, *Chibi.*

As Jan lovingly held Chibi, who was nuzzling her cheek, I said, "That's the story of the diamonds, Chibi, and how we adopted her." And silently, I said, *And that's how we saved our marriage.*

Donald Haack

THE RETURN TO SOUTH AMERICA

The diamonds and our photogenic Chibi were the highlights of our expedition, which produced a flurry of publicity in the Milwaukee Journal, Sentinel and local radio and TV shows. Everybody wanted to be part of the story. Three of Bob's business associates talked us into forming a private company to extract diamonds on a commercial scale.

Bob had his new jewelry store. I was unemployed. Jan had a great job as county agent, wrote her own newspaper column and appeared weekly on the popular Ester Hotton radio show and as a Friday morning guest on Breta Greem's TV series. It wasn't an easy choice to leave her job but she thought it might be a once-in-a-lifetime adventure to oversee a South American diamond mining company.

After her decision and until we left, Jan stayed on her job and still found time to help me with the numerous projects: researching and buying dredging equipment, seeking markets for rough diamonds, shopping for a bush plane and learning to fly.

Donald Haack

We decided on a P22 Piper Super Cub, a tandem two-seater with short takeoff and landing capabilities. As part of the purchase, Midwest Airways agreed to flying lessons. I had to be licensed and Jan, if not licensed, at least qualified. In an emergency, she could fly to a civilized area.

In the rush to beat the British Guiana rainy season, we scheduled the shipping of our equipment and plane to Georgetown on the one available ship; it was to leave New Orleans just two months after we purchased our Super Cub. That meant that besides Jan's full time job and my organizing the mining company, we had to learn to fly and get a license.

Every night, we picked up a hamburger and milkshake on our way to Mitchell Field where our instructor gave us lessons. I flew for 45 minutes while Jan ate, and Jan flew while I ate. Four days before our departure date, I completed my cross-country flight, passed the written exam and received my license while Jan continued to hone her flying skills. The last day was spent fueling the plane, doing last minute inspections, and checking maps. That evening we packed—which consisted of sorting and eliminating baggage until the weight was reduced to fifty pounds. We finished at midnight.

At 6:00 the next morning we were at Timmerman field saying good-byes to my mother, father, Bob and Audrey while doing our pre-flight inspection. This would be our first long cross-country flight. We had to make New Orleans by evening. That would leave only 24 hours to dis-assemble, crate and load the plane on board ship…not much room for error.

For the first eight hours, the flight was uneventful except for the unexpected headwind of 15 knots, a big handicap for a 110 mph plane. Our five o'clock fueling stop was 200 miles short of our destination. This presented a serious challenge: our first night flight, in new territory, to an unfamiliar international airport. We anticipated the worst and weren't disappointed.

I knew we had to stay in radio communication for all available help. New Orleans approach picked us up 50 miles out. They were real pros, immediately recognizing a new pilot and staying in constant contact the next hour. I'm convinced they gave us a direct line of flight and diverted all international, commercial and private traffic out of our flight path. We had our hands full flying and wondering where we were. Jan with flashlight in hand navigated. We didn't always agree as to where we were, but even when we did it seldom was where the tower operators indicated.

They vectored us to the international airport along Lake Ponchintrain where the weather deteriorated into intermittent rain squalls. By flying low and slow we were able to recognize a few map points along the lake. I advised New Orleans we were in contact with the local tower and thanked them profusely. They turned us over to the tower frequency and wished us well. Just before switching, an unofficial voice asked, "How many hours do you have? When did you get your license?"

"Forty five and two days ago." There was a long silence followed by what sounded like a soft whistle.

"All the way from Milwaukee…at night? Quite a first cross country…again, *Good Luck*!"

I switched over to the tower frequency and advised them I could see landing lights. They dimmed their lights several times to confirm the visual sighting.

"Negative on seeing you dim the lights. I have on one set of landing lights. Can you see us?"

"Negative, continue approach. We'll let you know when we have you in sight."

I figured it was rain and bad visibility. We were approaching the runway lights for a straight-in final.

"Jan, turn on the other landing lights. They shine straight down, should give us a better sense of height." I pulled on half flaps for landing. The lights illuminated the area below revealing large waves with whitecaps breaking off the top—a few feet below.

"My God, this is a seaplane strip, not a landing field!" I pushed the throttle in full. We needed enough speed to go around. A horn blared indicating we were close to a stall. Our hearts were in our throats, or somewhere. Neither of us spoke as we watched the airspeed slowly increase and the rate of climb indicator confirm we were going up not down. I looked out the window. The angry waves receded below us. With flaps off, we gained altitude and our airspeed increased to a comfortable margin. I picked up the mike to answer the calls ignored during our moment of panic. I explained our situation.

The voice came back loud and clear, "29 Bravo, that was a seaplane site you almost landed on. Continue up the shore. Keep your landing lights on. We have you in sight."

My first inclination was to say, "No kidding, Dick Tracy" but the wonderful message, "have you in sight," overshadowed any sarcasm.

"Roger" was all I could say.

It was a helluva good feeling. They dimmed the airport lights twice. This time I acknowledged seeing them. We landed inelegantly with several bumps that might have qualified as multiple landings. Night landings will do that, especially the first ever. I thought of a line out of Wolfgang Langewiesche's *Stick & Rudder*; "If you can walk away from a landing, it ain't so bad." We were on terra firma. and thankful for it. Someone came out with flash sticks and directed us to a stopping point. I shut down the engine. Jan and I looked at each other. We were physically and mentally exhausted. The door opened and a head appeared.

"Hi, I'm Gardener, your freight forwarder. Are we ever glad to see you. We have a standby crew waiting to start on the plane immediately. We have to have it in the crate and on the ship by ten in the morning."

The kind Mr. Gardener likened himself to a one-man tourist board and would not listen to our plea of retiring to our room. He dropped us off at our hotel and insisted on picking us up a half hour later to see New Orleans. Our *tour* ended at 5:00 am and included the Olde Absinthe House, Brennans, and any establishment where he knew someone to introduce us, which turned out to be everyone. We returned to our hotel as it was getting light, took a shower, picked up our bags and left for the Pan Am flight; the beginning of our South American venture that was to last over twenty years, three businesses, and two revolutions.

Donald Haack

When we made the decision to start a business in a less-developed country, we knew it wasn't going to be easy. I just didn't expect the trial-by-fire would start so soon .We overnighted in Trinidad where the Guardian headlines read, *Janet arrives*. At first blush we appreciated the welcome but quickly realized it was *Hurricane Janet* they were referring to. That night our cabbie wanted us to see the night life which would have taken most of the evening, except we questioned his choice of places after barely avoiding a mob fight by climbing over tables and exiting over the stage and a half wall. Jan, in her first three months of pregnancy, didn't think that qualified as one of her best evenings. That would be the second night of our new life that she would look at me as if to say, "Why are we doing this?"

The next day we arrived in Georgetown and checked into the Woodbine Hotel. We collapsed but not before another incident. Jan walked ahead of me and as she entered the room I heard her shout and jump back into the hall, almost knocking me down.

"Look at that monster on the door jamb." She pointed up. "What is it? Get it out of here. I'm *not* sleeping here. Let's go! Now!" She started down the stairs. I looked at where she pointed.

"Come on back. It's only a little lizard. They're all over and they're good. They eat mosquitoes and flies. People want them in their houses; they're almost like pets. They don't hurt anybody."

"I don't care what you call them. I don't care what they do. They are not *my* pets. For God's sakes, they look like prehistoric animals. I am out of here. Don't unpack my bags. I'm going home…on the first plane out!" She stomped down the steps with me following. Fortunately, she ran into Mac, the owner, who persuaded her to have a civilized tea with him. Before it was over, they were laughing about the situation. I suspected it wasn't the first time Mac was faced with a North American encountering *wild* animals in his hotel. If someone told him that in less than a year, this woman would let loose a wild Ocelot in her room in hopes of taming it, he would be the last to believe it. So would I.

The first week was spent with our town representative, Winnie Chung whom we'd met through Caesar on the first trip. We set up an office applied for a phone, which they said would take six months. Winnie offered to let us use hers. We were introduced to Georgetown's social set and their high teas. On Sundays they escorted us to the Church of England followed by house gatherings awash in alcohol. It appeared that many people had little to do…of value. Of course, that was our opinion.

To clear our personal pieces, plane and equipment, we hired a customs agent, who called a week later to inform us our ship arrived. Good news. Bad news; a big hole in the side of the crate. "There's damage to the plane. Better come down. We'll have to make a report to the insurance company."

We were escorted through the customhouse and given a ladder to look in the hole. The wing apparently took the brunt of the damage; several broken ribs exposed under the ripped fabric. I brought along John Rix, a B.G. Airways engineer with an American Mechanics License to assemble the aircraft as required by our insurance company. He had allotted two weekends to do the job but this was another matter.

"You better get it out of here as quickly as possible so we can determine the extent of damage. May have to order parts from the States, could take weeks."

We were off to a great start, I thought. Within two hours we had a truck on the dock. Two cranes lifted the huge crate onto the truck. The driver moved a few feet and stopped amidst a great deal of commotion. The Customs Inspector came over.

"Can't get it out. Too high to clear the ceiling…by almost two feet. Unload and put it back where it was."

"What are we supposed to do?" We have to get it out for repairs."

"Not my job, sorry." was all he could say. I went to the head of the department. Same answer. "Not my job." No help. No suggestions. One of them shrugged and said it should have unloaded at a different dock, one without a roof—a useless bit of information. The ship departed and there was no way to move it from one dock to another.

I felt a tap on my shoulder.

"Excuse me, couldn't help but overhear. These people rank as the most unhelpful persons in the universe. I know. I come in here every three weeks... captain of that Dutch ship alongside. I hate the bastards. Want to get your plane out?"

I didn't have to say a word, my face said it all.

"Okay, get the truck back here at five, closing time. There won't be many of these mental giants around. You be right here. I'll tell you what to do. At ten after five, we'll get your plane out, or it'll sit here till Christmas. They really don't care. See you at five."

He turned and left. I had no idea what the hell he was thinking of and I wondered if he was just a nut case running around loose. Seemed like they have their share of them around these parts. I watched where he went, up the ladder on the ship where some crew members treated him with the respect due a captain. He looked over to see if I was still there. He waved and went into his cabin.

We came with the truck a half-hour early. There were comments from the driver, his helper, and my agent on the futility of it all. The plane wasn't going anywhere. A few dockworkers agreed and thought it was funny. I thought it was funny enough to hang them by their fingers. I was damned mad at the indifference. My custom agent wanted an explanation. I told him to shut up and wait. I was in good spirits. I kept thinking, in rough times you grab at straws, which is what this seemed to be. I heard a shout and looked up. It was the captain.

"I've lowered my winch line, a few feet to your left...the one with the big 'S' hook on it. Wrap it twice around the big post in the middle, tight as you can and hang the hook around the top cable. Give me a hand signal when you have it secured."

I waved up to him when I had the cable in place. He raised his hand to the crane operator. The engine revved, the line took up slack, followed by a much louder noise from above. The roof was rising. I glanced down. The roof support was torn off the floor, a foot above and rising. The roof rattled and shook, dust fell everywhere. I moved outside. I thought the building was about to collapse.

"Tell the driver to try it now. Looks like there's enough clearance. Get him outta there!"

Donald Haack

I shouted to the truck driver, immobilized by what he saw but quickly jumped into action when I yelled at him the second time. In seconds the truck was out of sight. We had just removed the biggest cargo without clearing customs. We'd handle that mess in the morning when they discovered the plane was missing.

"I'm going to let the winch down. Guide that pillar to the original spot." He gave more slack. "Now unhook the cable and get the hell out of there. That'll give the buggers something to think about in the morning!" and he laughed uproariously. I tried to shout my undying thanks. He would have no part of it.

"Anytime I can do the buggers in, it makes my day. Good luck on your plane. He disappeared over the rail. There were two loud blasts from his foghorn that shook the dock area. He was moving out.

It took three weeks to get the plane repaired and assembled. John Rix and I took it up for a test flight and he signed it off.

"You're all set to fly. Lucky we could to the repairs here and didn't have to send out for any parts. As good as new except for the fabric patch. We could have made that invisible if we had matching dope paint."

British Guiana continued to be an enigma; it brought out the worst and best in people. I experienced both ends of the spectrum the first three weeks. John Rix made it his special project to get us flying as soon as possible. He worked every night and brought along his co-workers from B.G. Airways to help. I couldn't thank him enough and had to force him to take extra dollars that he didn't bill me for but more than earned.

Two days later, Caesar came into the hotel to inform me that in no way was he going to let me fly all the way back to the Rupununi by myself.

"We make sure Jan (he pronounced 'yan') gets on the DC-3 tomorrow morning. She'll be met by Nellie who is expecting her. Then you and I take off. I've made the trip hundreds of times and I can point out the check points to look for along the way."

GOOD HOPE RANCH

Caesar, Jan, and I drove the terrible road to B.G. Airways' hangar, an old unpainted, bare wooden building built by Americans during WWII. The airline carried mostly cargo so the passengers were weighed in on the same iron balance scale with freight. I was concerned about Jan flying into the interior by herself, but she assured us everything would be okay. Caesar was amazed. He didn't expect this lady from a genteel background in the States could handle the bush and its primitive ways. He would be *amazed* many more times in the next few years.

While we waited, Caesar brought me to the flight room. "Come, I want you to meet the pilot."

Seeing Caesar, a tall uniformed pilot rose from his chair and broke into a broad smile. "Caesar, good to see you. Missed you at the poker game last night. Was she good?"

He noticed Jan in the background.

"Oh, excuse me ma'am, that was just a joke." He looked back to Caesar. "Do I have the good fortune to have you as a passenger today? Didn't see you on the manifest."

Donald Haack

"No, I'm going with your new competitor. Meet Don and Yan." He turned to Jan. "Julian Pieniazek is your pilot. Yan is flying with you. Don and I are flying to Good Hope in his plane, a Super Cub. I'll show him the ropes and the navigation points. It's his first flight into the interior."

Later, as we saw the DC-3 take off, Caesar assured me that Julian was the best pilot in the world. "Julian flew in the Polish Air Force until Germany invaded. His pilot friend, Vicki Fikes, and he avoided the Gestapo and escaped to England where they flew for the RAF against Germany. After the war they joined a Canadian airline and in their travels met Art Williams, an American from Wisconsin. Williams talked them into joining him to start up a DC-3 airline in British Guiana. Julian flew as chief pilot, and Vicki, copilot. Julian's the only person who can put a fully loaded DC-3 in a spin down a hole in the clouds and land. Done it several times, coming to the Rupununi in bad weather. No one else would even think about it."

With Jan in the capable hands of Julian, Caesar and I took off a few minutes later. Our hour and forty-five minute trip, though uneventful, was picturesque. Caesar pointed out landmarks and the two rivers, Essequiba, and Demerara, which we kept in sight most of the flight. He tapped me on the shoulder and pointed to the right. "There's one landmark you should know, *Tit Mountain*. It's also a reporting point. Want to keep that on your right, particularly in bad weather. If the mountain is dead ahead, you're too close to the escarpment. If it's on your left, you're definitely in trouble."

It was a clear day and I had a vivid picture. The round mountain had what appeared to be a nipple on top and was aptly named. A few miles to the west, the sheer cliffs rose four thousand feet above the jungle and in the rainy season would be hidden in clouds, Caesar explained.

That morning I checked in at the tower and was advised that all interior flights were required to report by radio every fifteen minutes. My first check point was Alcoa, the Canadian bauxite company. The second, Omai Mines, was a shutdown gold mining company easily spotted by its scarred landscape and half-fallen buildings. Caesar indicated it was time and pointed to the picturesque round mountain with the nipple. I looked questioningly at him. He nodded affirmatively.

I picked up the mike. "BG Airways, 29 Bravo."

"29 Bravo, BG Airways. Go ahead"

"29 Bravo passing *Tit Mountain,* 3500 feet, CAVU (Ceiling And Visibility Unlimited)." I expected some sniggering, comment, or reprimand from the operator.

"Roger, 29 Bravo. Check point Tit Mountain."

Most of the trip we were over lush, green jungle, or *bush*, as it was called. The last fifteen minutes we broke into brown, flat savannah extending as far as I could see.

"Rupununi Savannah," Caesar pointed in the general direction. "Good Hope Ranch is just behind that small hill we call Pixie Mountain. You'll see the airstrip in a minute."

I banked and headed in the general direction of the mountain. And then it hit me: Jan, in entirely foreign surroundings survived the first couple of weeks with flying colors. But now, besides being in a more primitive culture, she would be here for a long time. For the first time, I had serious reservations. She was pregnant and would be living on this remote ranch with people she hadn't met. That turned my thoughts to Caesar. After our first meeting and within a few days, he invited Jan and me to live in his home for an indefinite time... and he didn't know Jan. This was an entirely different way of life and these were extraordinarily open, giving people. I hoped I hadn't made a catastrophic mistake. I would soon find out.

Julian's DC-3 arrived a good hour before we did. I learned later Jan was greeted by Nellie, Caesar's wife, and given a heart-warming Rupununi welcome that was the beginning of a close relationship lasting over forty-five years.

Nellie was waiting for us in the jeep along the airstrip as we landed.

"Jan is settled in and is helping me with tea, which should be ready." Nellie exclaimed as she gave me a welcome-back hug. Caesar got his hug next. We threw our bags in the jeep and drove the half-mile to the ranch house, a long, white single-story building with a grass roof. There was a split rail fence around it with a wire mesh at the bottom-for keeping small game out or tame ones in. Several small buildings, a windmill, and a water tank completed the compound. Caesar explained the house was made of mud blocks, adobe plastered and painted on the outside to keep them from eroding during the rainy season. There were several other buildings: the kitchen—not attached to the main house, a workshop and a baracoun, a long building for house staff and vaqueros (cowboys) who worked the cattle. There was a bathroom twenty yards to the rear and a two-story building for drying tobacco that he planned on growing this season. We spent the next fortnight organizing and planning our return to Marquis where we would commence work on the airstrip for our plane, then later for the DC-3 to bring in our mining equipment. Harry would be our foreman, Domingo his assistant. We had decided this on our expedition before we departed. Domingo lived two hours away by boat on the border, the Ireng River.

Domingo had agreed to work at least a year for us. He had his gear and rations of dried beef and farine, all of which had to be transported to Good Hope. We decided to make it an all-day recreational trip. Nellie and Jan accompanied us in our Alumacraft boat we had shipped to Caesar a month earlier. I was anxious to see how it performed with the fifteen horsepower Evinrude from our first expedition. It was the dry season, the Ireng was low and that meant plenty of rocks to avoid. We carried a bag of shear pins as a safety precaution—a wise move; we used most of them on the trip. Our first stop was on the Brazilian side of the river at Gomes' store, a shop that carried everything and anything you could imagine and some things you wouldn't want to. Cats napped in every corner of the store.

"Keep the mice out." Gomes said. Gomes was tall, skinny, and mustached with jet black eyes. He seldom smiled, though he didn't look unhappy. He seldom spoke except to give a price, which I'm sure he made up as he went along. Nothing was tagged and it took a great deal of effort on Caesar's part to evoke any reaction from the proprietor.

We stocked up on machetes, axes, shovels, rum, old bottles of wine discovered beneath some worn sacks of corn, tinned butter, guava cheese, plantains, farine, and some produce I didn't recognize. We loaded it in the boat and again headed south to the Brazilian ranch of Senhor and Dona Galvon.

Whether boat or jeep, the sound of an engine in a remote area precedes the visitor's arrival by fifteen minutes. The Galvons were expecting us. Senior Galvon, short, stocky, very overweight and with what Nellie correctly termed, " a face like a pig," greeted us on the landing. Dona Galvon stood in the doorway in their large but unpretentious house. Like most homes in the region, it was made of adobe blocks, grass roof, and cement floors, but unlike the Gorinskys, was not painted.

Dona Galvon, a pretty woman who was certainly a raging beauty in her youth, looked like she stepped out of a picture. Light skinned with long black hair, she was taller than her husband and wore a colorful black, red, and white embroidered full skirt with a white blouse that emphasized her ample bosom. There was the usual exchange of warm *brazos,* hugs. The Gorinskys introduced us and we were accepted as family. The Golvons prepared a seven-course meal with wine. My first thought was *this is lunch?* It was delicious and too much. Afterwards, hammocks were brought out. I looked questioningly at Nellie. She pointed to the hooks around the house. They were everywhere.

"Pick your place. I'll show you how to hang your hammocks. In minutes she had ours up, securely tied at the right height and held it open to its full double width, revealing a beautiful hand-woven pattern. "When you get in, sit in the middle, or you'll be on the floor. If you lie corner to corner, you'll be flat. We climbed in and experienced our first *siesta.* Even though we were four degrees north of the equator in ninety-five degree temperature, we were cooled by the light breeze passing through the hammock's open weave. In seconds we were sound asleep in spite of Golvon at the far side of the house, snoring up a storm.

After our siesta, Domingo came in with a big smile on his face. It was good to see him again, and I introduced him to Jan. He enthusiastically greeted her with a speech in Portuguese, which neither Jan nor I understood. Nellie translated, "He's happy to see you, anxious to go back to the mines, and oh yes…you have a pretty wife."

Domingo pointed to four burlap bags. Galvon had slaughtered a cow and "jerked" the meat by salting and drying it in the sun. The meat was in two bags and the other two were bulging with dried farine, the rations for the Amerindians.

We returned to Good Hope before dark. In the next few days Harry and Domingo prepared for the trip to the mining area, while Jan and I settled in at Good Hope. The Gorinskys briefed us on: the Rupununi history, the background on the ranchers—all but one who was related—the do's and the taboos of the region, and the *caveat emptors* we needed to know to survive in this country. We listened, wondering how much was fact and how much fiction. We learned as time went on most was factual. This was a beautiful but unforgiving territory. The Gorinskys and their friends were trying to prepare us as best they could.

One afternoon during tea, Nellie motioned for Jan and me to look out of the window.

"Look, There's Dutch. He must have come from Karanambo."

"Walked?" I asked. I saw a faltering, bent over man with a walking stick. "Isn't Karanambo almost forty miles east of here?" I looked at Nellie. "And he walked?"

"Oh, sure. He walks up to the mines, stays a few months 'til he has his *stake* then returns to stay with us or at Karanambo with the McTurks. That's been his routine for years."

He came through the gate and I saw Nellie light up and smile at the prospect of his arrival. "The McTurks, 'C', and I have adopted Dutch. Comes from a good family in Holland but ol' Dutch had a wild hair since the day he was born—the travel itch to see the world. His family's quite well off and he could have traveled with them but he chose to do it alone. The last we saw of him was Christmas last year. We used to worry when he left for the mines, but not anymore. Dutch has his own personal guardian angel. He returns from the mountains looking like a half-starved scarecrow. Now he's coming from the McTurks where Connie McTurk and their cook, Antosh, fattened him up for the last few months. Looks good."

He left his walking stick at the door and slid off his knapsack as he entered.

"Ach, goot. Nellie, here's a note from Connie. Und ve got some guests, I see," as he looked over to Jan and me. Nellie spoke loudly to introduce Dutch to us. He was obviously hard of hearing. He waved his hand at Nellie. "No goot, write it down or I never get der names." He looked at the paper from Nellie and looked up at us "Yan and Don, pleased to meet you. You come to find diamonds or joost tourists? Hah! I can tell you a ting or two about diamonds." He smiled a broad toothless smile. "Nellie, haf you got my teeth? Couldn't find 'em at McTurks and as we haf guests here, I should go formal and put dem in... eh, eh," he chortled in his funny little laugh.

Dutch kept us amused with his good sense of humor, but holding a conversation with him was a chore. Sometimes he could hear a little or he read lips. Most of the time, he was stone deaf.

Nellie told him his family sent another bottle of medicine with instructions to take a teaspoonful twice a week. It was black, syrupy, horrible smelling and tasted worse, according to Dutch, "Anyting dat tastes so bad moost be goot," he grimaced after taking a dose.

A couple of days later while baking on the big cast iron wood stove, Nellie suggested to Jan, "You know, if you're going to live in diamond country, you might consider having Dutch live with you at least for a while...a man around when Don's out flying. Dutchie knows every Indian in the area—he's their good luck charm; they like him. Think about it. He's getting on in years. His walk to the Echilebar River would be five days closer if he still wants to go that far."

I would come to learn that was pure Nellie: looking out for Dutch and at the same time providing extra security for Jan. She never stopped helping people.

CHALLENGING THE IRENG

Harry, Domingo and I, with two Macusi Indians from Karasabai village, made the first trip back to Marquis. Even with our new Evinrude and sixteen foot Alumacraft boat, the trip was a hard five days. Without rapids the first day we made good time and reached the Karasabai valley in five hours. Harry liked our boat, the fastest he had seen.

The river looked all the same to me. Harry pointed north to the right of our boat and shouted, "Karasabai village, two hours walk!" A few minutes later there was a break in the steep bank with steps leading to the top. "Vincent Alenkar landing," he pointed out. "His Brazilian ranch is an hour walk towards the mountains. This is the only crossing in the valley." He pointed to a small dugout perched half way up the steps of the twenty-foot high bank. "There's his boat. Pull over to the right. That's where we pick up our two boys. I hope they're near; it's a hard hour walk to the village if we have to find them."

The outboard announced our arrival. Two Indian boys with their small bag of gear stood at the top of the high bank and came running down the footpath. I guided the boat to the landing; our guides stepped in; I backed up and we were again wending our way upriver between the sheer cliffs.

Introductions were short. "Shaga, Pedro." Harry pointed to them and then to me.

"We're lucky, that doesn't happen often, being on time, Don," Harry shouted over the noisy exhaust of the Evinrude. "In the rainy season the river floods over these banks." I looked up in wonder at the twenty-foot high cliffs and tried to visualize the volume of water necessary to fill these canyons. He saw my disbelief. "That's why everyone stops prospecting in the rainy season—water's too swift and dangerous."

In less than an hour we emerged from the deep canyon into a valley and sunshine bathed us for a few minutes. Lush green vegetation with the sweet, fresh, moist smell associated with rapids and waterfalls provided a stark contrast to the endless brown-gray clay banks of the dusty valley we left behind. Harry pointed to a sand bank, a stopping point. He jumped out and the Indians quickly removed our supplies. After traveling six hours, I was thankful for the respite. It felt good to stretch my legs. It was my job to refill the two Evinrude gas tanks from the barrel.

"We have to waterproof everything, now," he said. "We'll be into rapids and waterfalls for the next three days. We can't afford to lose equipment or get our rations wet if we capsize."

I understood why he bought the Brazilian rubber-lined bags. Everything had to stay dry: hammocks, blankets, clothes, and food were stuffed into the bags, ends twisted, doubled over, and tied. After securing the knots, Harry lowered each bag into the water. Those that floated, he put into the boat. The remainder were repacked until they floated. As they finished the testing Harry must have read my thoughts and explained, "These bags will float, so we can use them for life preservers if we're caught in bad rapids." He tied the floating bags together and secured the line to the stern. "The boat and supplies stay together; we need them both."

The shovels, picks, machetes, axes, saws, and outboard spare parts were tied into bundles, stored underneath the seats and secured with ropes. During that activity, Domingo had a pot hanging on a horizontal stick over a fire. We enjoyed a strong, hot cup of coffee laced with brown sugar and a dollop of tinned Carnation milk. It looked grim. It tasted wonderful. We opened a package of "C" rations, which looked awful and tasted the same. It was quick and kept off hunger pangs.

The gear was stowed back in the boat. We were on our way to a totally different mood of this river, which would challenge us relentlessly with rapids, waterfalls, and portages that required cutting paths through thick bush along precipitous banks. At each portage we untied and removed all supplies and equipment and carried them above the falls. The hardest part was pulling and lifting the boat over rocks and fallen trees on the crudely cut path. Five of us were barely able to lift, push, and pull the four-hundred pound boat sideways, upside down, and end-to-end to move it along the rough path that never seemed wide enough. After the boat was carried up we each made several trips for the engine, gas, and supplies. Exhausted after each portage, we pushed on.

In the bow using hand signals, Domingo pointed out the deepest passages through the rapids. We quickly realized that Domingo wasn't familiar with the channels and in less than an hour we broke four shear pins. We decided to switch—Harry in front, Domingo on the engine. No better. Even though pins sheared, the prop still took a beating from the rocks. I sawed and filed the propeller several times and each time its efficiency declined.

We were approaching an area that separated into several small channels; the two on the outside were narrow. The center channel, though wider, was a long stretch of white, rushing swirling water that cascaded between the rocks like a sluice. It didn't look good. I glanced questioningly at Harry.

"I think we can make it, Don, if we stay in the middle. The engine should push us through." He pointed out the main channel to Domingo. I had bad vibes on this one.

We maneuvered into the main current and our forward speed in relation to the banks dropped to a crawl. Domingo twisted the

Evinrude's throttle to full power. We inched forward between the rocks at an agonizingly slow pace, though we were moving at over fifteen knots *in* the water. It was a constant struggle to keep in the center of the channel. Bedrock, at times only inches away from the boat, threatened us on all sides.

We were almost through when disaster hit: a broken shear pin in the middle of the rapids. Without a load on the prop, the engine revved to a scream. I signaled Domingo to shut it off. His eyes were wide as we surged backwards down the channel. He froze. I jerked his hand off the throttle, turned it to idle, and pushed the stop button. A terrifying impact wrenched the engine sideways, knocking my fingers off the handle.

The boat overturned. I went backwards into the churning water. I kicked up to the surface to see the boat spinning and bobbing like a cork...a four hundred pound cork heading right for me. Before I could duck, I was struck on the forehead by the boat's gunnel. It was a glancing blow that hurt but thankfully not hard enough to knock me out. I grabbed onto the boat to steady myself and catch my breath. The rocks alongside were a blur as we raced by. I glanced over my shoulder. The boat was fast approaching a wall of rocks on the left side of the channel. The surging water swung the boat sideways, placing me between it and the rocks. I dove under, holding on to whatever I could, before I surfaced on the other side of the boat and hoped the boat did not swing 180 degrees again. I felt and heard the crunch as the boat hit the rocks. I hung on to the gunnel and had an image of what could have happened if I had been there seconds earlier. I quickly brushed aside the thought. I had to survive the rest of this event without negative thoughts of *what if.*

The boat swung around in a circle. Shaga suddenly appeared and swam towards me. I wondered what happened to Harry, Domingo and Pedro. I motioned and shouted to Shaga to hurry. There was a second rapids not too far downstream. I didn't want to go through that one hanging on to an upside down boat. I inched forward to the bow, grabbed the trailing line and swam for shore, paddling with one hand and pulling with the other, a slow journey.

Donald Haack

"Shaga, come, help pull the boat," I yelled. He understood what I was trying to do and with the rope between us, we pulled and swam to the bank. The current twisted us in a circle close to an overhanging tree. I grabbed a branch and tied the rope onto it. We pulled hand over hand on the branch until we were on solid footing. Fortunately the boat lodged against rocks that kept it from going downstream. We managed to pull it upside down into quiet waters. The prop stuck up like a stick, one blade bent at right angles, the other had a missing piece as if something had taken a big bite. I hoped it had shut down before we hit, otherwise the shaft could be broken. Or if water surged into the air intake with the engine running the rods could be bent or cylinders cracked, rendering the engine beyond repair. We would know soon enough. We pulled the boat into waist high water.

Shaga looked at me. I grabbed the gunnel and started to lift when he pointed to my head. I put my hand where he pointed— blood! Lots of it, running bright red down my face and shirt. There was a golf ball size lump and I could feel the broken skin. I took out my handkerchief and pressed it on the cut to stop the bleeding. The boat hit my head harder than I realized. The bleeding stopped long enough for me to wrap a bandanna around my head to keep the handkerchief in place. It worked.

I looked back at Shaga and asked, "Harry, Domingo, Pedro?" He shook his head and shrugged his shoulders. "No se," I don't know. Suddenly the price of diamonds took on a whole new meaning. Losing our lives wasn't part of the anticipated cost.

I understood the need for waterproofing our equipment. In my wildest dreams I didn't expect this type of risk. Did Harry, Domingo, and Pedro drown? I didn't know. It all happened too fast and they were gone. There was no way to know whether they were swept downstream and survived. The noise of the rapids made it difficult to be heard. We had to right the boat and salvage what we could. Afterwards we could search the banks for the missing voyageurs.

I couldn't fathom how without warning we could lose three people so quickly. Our situation appeared bleak; we weren't out of danger. If the engine couldn't be repaired, hiking out of this valley would be extremely difficult. It was a major obstacle to cut a path for the small portages. The thought of having to cut a trail all the way back was depressing. No time for that kind of thinking. Survival depended on solving the problems at hand. I took the rope, tied it to the gunnel, swam underwater and wrapped it over the underside of the boat. We pulled, the boat rotated and the rubber bags popped out helping to turn the boat upright. We undid the bags and carried them to shore.

"Don!" I heard my name shouted. It was Harry coming from the jungle upstream. He looked terrible. He managed a smile as he stepped out of the brush. "You made it, are you okay?" He looked around. "Pedro, Domingo not here?" He frowned. "I didn't see them upstream. I was thrown out onto the rocks. The boat shot by. I didn't see any of you, just the boat going down the rapids. I thought you were all gone. What happened to your head?" He pointed to the bandanna soaked in blood.

"It's not as bad as it looks, just bled a lot. Head wounds do that. I'm worried about Pedro and Domingo. I didn't see them. We pulled the boat up. Most of the gear appeared to be intact. Let's go downstream. They may be hurt somewhere along the rocks," I said with more conviction than I felt. I don't see how they could have made it through the rapids below. "Let's go," I repeated.

We untied the machetes from under the seats and started cutting a trail downstream. I thanked Harry several times for the foresight of the rubber bags and securing the tools to the deck of the boat. A few minutes later we heard a shout above the roar of the rapids. I whistled. We listened. We heard a faint shout again, more like a high-pitched hoot. Following the sound we broke into a clearing where Pedro and Domingo were struggling through the bush. Their headway was almost impossible without a machete. I laughed more from the release of tension than anything funny.

"Harry, look, Domingo's holding one of the paddles and look what else...your hat."

Holding up Harry's hat, Domingo was smiling. He looked like hell. We all did. What a relief; we were all right. Pedro took the hat from Domingo and placed it on Harry's head. The hat was dripping, misshapen and askew and made Harry look like a scarecrow. It broke the tension. We sat down and laughed until tears came. We weren't even sure what we were laughing at. Disaster was too close for comfort; we could have been killed. We were lucky to have survived and we even had one paddle, and, of course, Harry's now-famous hat. We were in great spirits. After the elation wore off, we returned to the sobering thought of the work to be done and the fact that we may not have a working engine and would have to abort our trip.

I started on the engine immediately, stripping off the two-piece hood designed to keep spray out. There was water everywhere. The motor wasn't meant to be submerged. I removed the coil to dry in the sun. After the plugs were out Harry pulled the rope starter. Water came out—not good. If water entered with the engine running, it could be disastrous. We'd know in a few minutes. It turned over easily, a good sign—no structural damage. There was hope. The shear pin and prop had to be replaced *if* we could start the engine. I handed the plugs to Harry to dry. We tipped the engine over to drain the remaining water from the plug holes. I poured oil into each cylinder. The rings were wiped clean by the water. Metal to metal without the lubrication of oil can damage an engine in seconds. Harry pulled the starter rope while I placed my thumb over the plug holes. They popped …we had compression. Over another hurdle. I attached the electric leads to the plugs while Harry pulled again—a good spark. We were getting closer. "Okay, lets clean up the gas in this jerry can. Use the chamois to strain out the water." I squeezed it before straining the gas into another jerry can.

Harry followed through while I reassembled the engine. After he finished, Harry said, "Don, we strained the gas. There's still water in it." He looked puzzled.

"Check to see if there's a hole in the chamois and if there is we'll have to sew it."

"No, no hole," he said, closely scrutinizing the cloth, holding it up to the sun to see if he could see even the tiniest of breaks where water could seep through.

Donald Haack

"Harry, that doesn't make sense, there's at least a gallon of water in that jerry can. The chamois should have filtered it out. I don't understand. Wait a minute. I'll finish this and then we'll try it again to see what's wrong." When I was ready I discovered the hot sun dried the chamois stiff as a board. I gently kneaded it into the shape of the funnel, and then tightened the wire around it to keep it from slipping into the funnel. "Okay, let's try it again and see what goes."

We poured and the water stayed on top of the chamois just as it was supposed to while the clean, strained gas went through. We continued until all the gas was strained.

"That beats everything. We did the same thing before and the water didn't get filtered out. I don't see what we did differently this time." Harry shook his head completely baffled at what he saw.

I usually analyze the hell out of things I don't understand, especially when it can be dangerous. I tried to figure out what was different. Nothing made sense. Ordinarily I wouldn't be satisfied until I solved this one but we were pressed for time. The delay put us back a day. We needed to push on. I pumped fuel into the carburetor and let gas run through until I was sure there was no trace of water, which would make it cloudy or settle out to the bottom. I put the mystery out of mind. It would come back to haunt us later in a more critical situation.

"Okay, Harry, give it a pull," I said hesitatingly. I didn't know if we did everything we were supposed to. I couldn't think of anything else. I held my breath in anticipation. Harry pulled once, twice, the engine roared to life. We all shouted. "Okay, let it run on idle for a couple of minutes, then shut it down. I'll put on a new prop and shear pin. We were lucky this time. "Harry, even though we've got lots of spare parts, at the rate we're going through propellers and sheer pins we'll run out. More important, we've only got one set of lives. Unless we make some changes, we're not going to make it. This last incident was too close." He agreed.

I took over the Evinrude with Harry in the bow guiding us through the swift channels, some so turbulent we inched past rocks as the river roared around us. This time it was safer; we traveled only between ten in the morning and three in the afternoon when the sun revealed the rocks below. In the shade, submerged rocks were difficult or impossible to see. We didn't need that risk again. Progress was frustratingly slow. Several rapids proved too swift for our engine at full throttle. Then we eased back to calmer water where we headed to the bank and another frustrating two-hour portage. The fifth day, we successfully completed three portages. On the last as we launched the boat into the water, we spotted the brighter light of the open Marquis valley ahead, less than a mile as the crow flies. We were tired. As the last sun's rays ascended the slopes on the right, the deep shadows from the Brazilian mountains crept across the river, making it too dark to navigate safely. We pulled ashore and made camp.

The next morning we took a leisurely coffee to wait until the sun was high. Shortly before noon, gliding through the last rapids, I spotted the dome-like rock where one year ago Domingo and I discovered our first diamonds. We were returning to make this valley our home. As we rounded the last bend into the valley, my memories of the first expedition came back in a flood of mixed emotions. I wondered how Jan would like living here. Harry cut short my reminiscing.

"Don, we can make our camp here along the river, tie our hammocks in these trees. The boys are clearing the area now. Let's walk the valley to see where to start on the airstrip."

Without paths on the uneven bog we had difficulty walking. This was a huge valley, a sedimentary basin almost totally void of trees made by the river receding over thousands of years.

"Harry, why don't we clear a small area for our plane to land, then bring Jan in and let her pick the house site? It would be more *her* home."

On our expedition last year before leaving the country we filed a homestead lease on the hundred-acre valley and filed mining claims with Lands & Mines, Department of Interior. At the same time an application was submitted requesting permission from the Director of Civil Aviation to build an airstrip in our valley. The leases and claims were issued and we received tentative airstrip approval pending an inspection from the DCA's office. I found out later, those *temporary* approvals went on for years; there was neither a budget nor an airplane available. Most airstrips were abandoned before they were inspected.

Before Pedro and Shaga joined us, they gave out the word that we needed workers and within hours of our arrival at *Marquis* valley we had four more Macusi Indians on our payroll. Harry and I figured it should take two weeks to clear 1,000 feet for our Super Cub. Except for a few scrub trees the area was open. The hummocks and holes had to be leveled. Beyond that point a large outcropping of rocks presented a barrier. Harry assured me that would be no problem.

"We can buy dynamite in Georgetown. Years ago when I worked the *Omai* gold mines, I had a blasting license... needed dynamite to expose gold-bearing quartz. I brought a few sticks back with me. Used them at our family fetes. A half stick in the Pirara River brought up fish to feed everybody."

Surrounded by mountains, the Marquis valley gives the impression of being inaccessible by air. A three-thousand foot mountain on the Brazilian side was in the landing pattern. A twenty-five hundred foot mountain loomed dead ahead on the take off path. My theory, which I hoped was correct, was if I came in low and slow down the Ireng River valley, I could easily turn in front of the mountain. The take off was psychologically more challenging. After lift off it would be necessary to immediately execute a shallow right turn, hold that new heading until over the river, then bank sharply left into an easy, wide sloping valley not visible from the airstrip.

The plan was for our plane to bring in small equipment, tools, rations, dynamite, and house- building tools. The heavy mining equipment was scheduled to be flown in by DC-3 five weeks later. That was the plan. Reality set in. I was about to learn the meaning of *bush timetables* and *South American bureaucracy*. At worst, I expected no delays clearing 1,000 feet of airstrip. It was not to be. Time off was needed to fish and hunt, supplementing the usual Indian diet of farine, the pebble-like cereal made from dried and grated cassava root. Even though they were paid, the Macusis considered working for us an ongoing party and at those *fetes* they expected meat and fish every meal. That meant shutting down while they hunted and fished. Somehow Harry neglected to tell me that had been excluded from our timetable.

Three-and-a-half weeks later, the first 900 feet of the airstrip was completed. Domingo and I made plans to return to Good hope to bring back the plane. We quickly ruled out the option of taking the boat back. Our last trip made that decision easy. Instead we decided to walk out. Harry and the remaining four Macusis would complete the finishing touches to the airstrip and clear the area around the boulders for blasting.

"You should be in Good Hope in five days, Don. You can make Karasabai in two and- a- half, then take the boat across the river into Brazil to Vincent Alenkar's ranch. It's an easy two- day walk if you stay on the Brazilian side and cross the river at Good Hope." It sounded easy.

The next morning it was dark when Harry shook my hammock. "Don, Domingo says it's time to go if you want to reach the Karasabai-Tipuru trail before dark tonight." There was a pot of freshly brewed coffee over the fire. The aroma quickly revived me. Domingo poured a demitasse. I spooned in a heaping tablespoon of brown, sticky Demerara sugar from the burlap bag and stirred slowly until most was dissolved. It was hot, sweet, and strong. We left camp before light, and too early I thought to see where we were going. We traveled lightly carrying three days rations. We could buy more at Karasabai or Vincent Alenkar's.

"Take as little as possible, Don," Harry cautioned. "It's a bit of a difficult walk." Coming from an Indian who walks all day, that was the understatement of the year. Also, there was supposed to be a trail. I saw little if anything that resembled a trail. Domingo instinctively knew where to go but we still backtracked several times. We climbed uphill most of the trip to Karasabai. Even though I was in good shape my muscles ached from trying to keep up the fast pace that Domingo set. He appeared tireless and smiled as if this were great fun. I was dying. He didn't slow down and I had too much pride to lag behind. We crossed what appeared to be the same creek a hundred times: some bigger, some smaller, and a few we had to wade through waist high.

We were constantly wet. We clambered over boulders and pulled ourselves up by vines and tree limbs. Though each time I grabbed the same limb Domingo did, invariably when I pulled back my hand it was riddled with thorns or thistles. At the end of the day both hands were swollen.

In the morning when I tried to extricate some of the thistles, Domingo looked at my hands. "You grab wrong place. No grab branch. Grab close to trunk, no pricks. Grab small trees on trunk above limb, not below, no pricks there." He quickly and deftly pulled out a few of the larger thorns, unwrapped a sticky, sap-like material and spread a thin layer on the damage. It stung. Within minutes the pain miraculously disappeared "Okay now," as he packed up our equipment.

After a ten-minute lunch break, we were back on the trail. Domingo stopped and raised his hand for silence. I didn't hear anything unusual other than the sounds of bush tree frogs, high-pitched beetles, macaw parrots with their distinct cawing, hundreds of varieties of parakeets, and occasionally the unearthly roar of howler monkeys miles away. I listened. There *was* a different background hum, like a timpani roll in an orchestra, gradually increasing in volume. I expected a machine to break through the bush. Then silence blanketed us, followed by a crescendo of unreal crashes.

Domingo was quiet, cocking his head to determine the source of the sound. He pointed to a rocky slope. "Go up tree." The branches were near the ground and would be easy to climb. He went first, I followed. He pointed to a branch below him well above the ground.

"Sit." He said quietly. The rumbling grew louder. I felt vibrations and saw movements far down the trail, as though the path were moving. Something big emerged—a huge bush hog with an ugly short head and two white tusks curving up on either side of his snout. The fur, brown and bristly, was sticking up around his neck like a bad butch haircut. *Mean* and *ugly* came to mind. Hundreds of animals came crashing down the trail. The drumbeat noise turned out to be grunts and snorts, which alternately grew louder and softer as if orchestrated by a conductor. The whole jungle seemed to be moving and I mentally thanked Domingo for sitting quietly in the trees rather than walking on the path. After the last bush hog disappeared, Domingo climbed down and said, "You don't mess with them. Big trouble in pack like that." He smiled and continued, "They real good eating. Not today. No time"

We climbed endless rock faces onto a more discernible trail until darkness closed in. Domingo hung my hammock slightly higher than usual, making it harder to get in. I didn't complain—it felt safer. Earlier we heard guttural grunts of a jaguar. Domingo listened without any indication it was a threat.

"He no bother." I agreed, and too tired to eat, fell immediately into a deep sleep. The next I knew Domingo shook me. It seemed to be the middle of the night. He handed me a cup full of soggy farine. "Dinner! Last night, you no eat. Eat now. We go."

There wasn't an inch of my body that didn't ache. The cereal looked like hard gravel and when I held the cup, a thousand needles shocked my fingers...I hadn't removed the bigger thorns the night before. I was too tired. Using my thumbs on the cup, I gulped down the tasteless *breakfast*. At best it filled the void. Domingo stuffed the hammock into my knapsack, swung it on my back, and was out of sight by the time I hitched up the belt. I struggled after him.

Hiking non-stop for three hours we were soaked with perspiration. We came to a stop at an inviting clear stream. I was about to step in and sit in the cool water when Domingo grabbed my shoulder and pointed to the bank. Three snakes were coiled, heads up, alert to our intrusion.

"Go there," he commanded quietly pointing to the left, upstream. "Bad," was all he said. Later, "Labaria." I knew the snake, one that had a neurotoxin similar to the black, yellow and red coral snake, whose deadly venom affects the para-sympathetic nerves that control the heart and breathing mechanism. Domingo made no attempt to kill the snakes or for that matter any animal dangerous to us. "We all live here, everyone, everything. No one owns land, water, sky. We share together. If me don't hit them, they won't hit me. One day animal hungry, then me their food. I keep eye open." and he pointed finger at his eye. "Another day me hungry then they my food." He smiled. That was a big speech for him.

It was midday when we broke out of the dark bush into blinding sunlight and took a few minutes to accustom our eyes to the intense brightness. The trail was barely visible. As we continued it joined others well worn from centuries of bare feet. The bigger trails headed to Karasabai village. He pointed to the horizon slightly to our left.

"Village there long time. Father, son, father, son." Each time he raised his fingers then lifted his out-stretched hands several times, indicating many generations, a few hundred years. He wasn't from this village and I wonder how he knew. "My father's father from here. He marry Indian girl from Brazil and live with her family." I thought back to the first trip when Caesar and I went by jeep to the Brazilian crossing to meet Domingo's father, Senhor Galvon. His wife, Dona Maria was from Brazil and Domingo was their son. I think I finally had it straightened out.

We headed easterly in the direction of the village. I thought the trail to Good Hope was more southerly. When I questioned Domingo, he shrugged his shoulders, pointing again to the village. "You going to live in Marquis. These people your closest neighbors. You must stop and make friends. Very important."

Harry didn't tell me that. In fact there were a lot of things Harry neglected. When questioned, his answer was, "I thought you knew that. Everyone knows that."

I mentally altered our schedule after we encountered an unexpected delay. I soon realized that in order to be more accurate I would have to double the planned time. Harry simply calculated hours of walking between villages or ranches. The delays, he said, were always unknown so you never figured those in. I had to smile at the logic.

Donald Haack

Domingo told me that if the Tuchow, chief and the Peaymen, we used to call witch doctor, were out hunting or fishing, we could pass on through and leave a message. If they were in the village we must stop and it could be a long delay. It was today. We walked around the village meeting most of the families and by the time we finished visiting the last hut, it was too late to leave. We hung our hammocks outside the Tuchow's shelter for an early start to Vincent Alenkar's landing.

We left before daylight, skipped breakfast and by ten o'clock we were at Alenkar's crossing, climbing down the crude steps to the river. The boat was not tied up or in sight anywhere along the steep banks. I looked at Domingo. He shrugged. "Someone use boat, probably for fishing. Might come back soon"

"How soon?"

"Maybe today… two, three days."

I better understood Nellie's explanation of timetables. "When they say three days, it doesn't really mean *three days*." I didn't understand then. I did now.

"We can't wait two or three days—we're out of rations and our camp will be soon. We have to fly in supplies. Isn't there another trail we could take? What happens in the rainy season when the river is flooded and to dangerous to cross? There must be another trail"

He pointed eastward, shrugged, smiled, and readily agreed. Everything was okay with him. We climbed the bank and headed out along the trail following the Ireng River, not far from the village we left in the morning. I figured we took a *short cut* that added a day and- a- half. I asked Domingo how long to Good Hope on this trail.

"Two, maybe three days, if we walk fast and no trouble." I didn't know what *trouble* meant. I assumed it was like Vincent Alenkar's missing boat.

We had no food the fourth day and drank water at every stream, so much so that I don't think the halogen tablets I put in the canteen had time to de-toxify the water. I had diarrhea, necessitating numerous stops or *trouble,* which added another half- day to our schedule. Tired, dirty, smelly, and hungry, we arrived at Good Hope on the evening of the fifth day. The ranch never looked so good. Nellie greeted us with a cold glass of maracuja, also called *passion fruit* and a towel.

"Take a shower, then we'll have something to eat. C's out looking for one of the newborn calves to bring back and should return shortly. I think you could use a stiff drink." She was right, on all counts. She saw me looking around. "Jan should be back from her pre-natal check up in Georgetown and should be on this week's plane. I see you're missing her already." She smiled. Nellie apparently could also read minds.

BUILDING A BUSH AIRSTRIP

Jan was anxious to hear about our new home. I described the valley, the several house sites and the progress on the airstrip.

Caesar handed us a couple of Dewars scotch with ice and water, a double for me, which went straight to my head. I managed to get through dinner answering their questions as best I could, but not to their satisfaction. The details would have to wait until morning. I thanked them profusely. Jan guided and I followed from the table… into my hammock. The last thing I remembered was the sweet smell of the frangipani outside my window before I passed out.

I heard Caesar calling out in his gruff voice, "Breakfast's on." Sunlight was pouring in; Jan was up and out. I looked at my watch. I had slept eleven hours. Nellie with Jan's help cooked a platter of eggs surrounded by slabs of ham and toast from homemade bread. There was a big pot filled with strong black coffee, the big cup kind. I had more than my fill of Brazilian *coffezina* demitasses. The meal acted like a body battery charger and I felt restored.

After a leisurely couple of hours Domingo and I sorted out rations, checked over and loaded the plane.

The six-day hike from Marquis to Good Hope took a lot out of me. I don't know about Domingo, because he never said much and complained even less, but I noticed that after he hung up his hammock, we didn't see him. We both needed R & R. I didn't recall leaving the table that night or climbing into my hammock.

We flew with a light cargo load and half full gas tanks to provide a safety margin on my first landing. It was Domingo's first flight and was one of pure excitement. He tapped me on the shoulder several times, pointing to one area then another, talking so fast I understood very little. I recognized a few words like *Mahu*, *Vincent Alenkar*, and *Karasabai*. The trip took fifteen minutes by plane compared to the six-and-a-half day walking trip. I understood the earlier comments on how the plane would change the time clock in the interior. The plane was pivotal to our success.

The newly cleared airstrip was visible the minute we entered our valley. We flew over in a low pass for a closer inspection, though I knew I could depend on Harry to do a good job. He had cleared a wide swath at the beginning, marking it with two poles, one with a piece of white cloth for a windsock. There was a slight headwind of five knots, ideal. Two more poles with flags marked the end of the strip at the outcrop of rocks. This had to be a short landing. After a steep bank over the river in front of the Brazilian mountain, we descended with full flaps, low and slow. We touched down at the first flag, braked hard and stopped in less than half the cleared runway. Harry ran over and opened the door.

"If I knew you could land that short, we wouldn't have worked so hard clearing the first thousand feet." He smiled a big grin. "Welcome to Marquis; you're the first plane to land."

With the plane able to guarantee a steady source of supplies, we began in earnest to complete the airstrip and start the house. That night by Tillie kerosene lamp Harry and I went over the priorities for the remaining weeks before rainy season. To bring in the DC-3 with our mining equipment and household appliances we needed the full 3,000 feet of runway and the approval of B.G. Airways. The removal of the rocks became our top priority. Harry assured me that as soon as I brought the dynamite from Georgetown he could blast them out. Having filed an application a month earlier, I felt we would have the permits to bring in dynamite. They still had Harry's blasting license from Omai Mines on file, and had assured me nothing else was needed. That's what they *said.* I would learn otherwise.

We put three Indians to clear the second half of the strip beyond the rocks. And if things went according to schedule, it would be completed in three weeks. In order to expedite the building of the house, we hired more Indians to cut lumber. They found several tall redwoods near by, which they cut with axes into twelve-foot lengths, placing them on a seven-foot high scaffold Harry built. Guided by chalk lines and using a six-foot saw, one Indian on top, the other below, they cut twelve foot boards out of the tree. Harry offered them ten cents a foot. In one day they earned six dollars each, five times more than any other work as a vaquero cowboy or day laborer. No wonder they worked so well unsupervised.

Harry saw me looking at the rough-cut boards. "We need boards for the house and two barges: the dredge and diamond jig. Besides the house needs, there's the store and a warehouse shed for small equipment and rations."

We planned to ship in some lumber on the DC-3 run, but we already had close to a full load. We discussed the possibilities of getting a second flight, but Julian of B. G. Airways cautioned me that he felt we would be lucky to get the one load.

"Plan on one and get the most critical items in on that one. We can sneak the first flight in before they know what's happening, but then they'll want to inspect it. I don't think we'll get an official approval for your airstrip," he advised.

Our whole venture depended on the DC-3. That afternoon I flew to Georgetown to pick up the dynamite. Four days later I was still bogged down in red tape. The police wanted three permits: one for the dynamite, the second for the caps and the third for two cars, because, they explained, caps and dynamite could not be carried in the same vehicle—too dangerous. Another permit was required from the Department of Lands & Mines for a blasting application detailing where, how, dates, and times along with detailed procedures of how the blasting area would be cordoned off. Another application was required from the Security Department of the Home Office to assure the dynamite would not be used for warfare, sedition, treason, or whatever. Any persons involved with the handling or transporting would have to get a clearance.

We would have to hire two police guards to accompany the dynamite and the caps after they left the armory. The Home Office later advised me we also needed a special permit issued by the DCA, Department of Civil Aviation to fly explosives. The police required a monthly report detailing each time we blasted, until all explosives were used. Frustratingly, I was informed of one requirement at a time. After completing it, I was advised of further paperwork…like a treasure hunt, one clue at a time. After five days of filling out paperwork and permits, I still didn't have the dynamite. Our crew would be running out of supplies.

I made a quick flight back to replenish them. Harry was disappointed, but told me everything was on schedule. But without dynamite we couldn't complete the airstrip before rainy season. The next day I noticed a strange structure in the middle of the airstrip. I asked Harry about it. "Oh, that." he shrugged. "Thought I might try an old fashioned method of breaking rocks. Art Williams who started BG Airways had us clear runways in the Rupununi before there were any connections with Georgetown."

I was intrigued. "What exactly are you planning on doing?"

"Well, I'm having the Indians build a scaffold next to the rocks. We're going to put three water barrels on top, build a fire over the rocks, and let it burn for a couple of days 'til it's good and hot, then pull the scaffold down drenching the hot rocks with cold water. If it works, it'll crack them into small pieces." The scaffold took several days.

Harry waited until I returned from Good Hope. The fire burned for two days. All projects were stopped to fill the barrels from the river. Long ropes were attached to the scaffold. I asked why they were so long. "You'll see in a little while," he chuckled.

The attention the Indians were giving this project suggested it would be a special event. Harry double-checked everything. When he was satisfied all was ready, he called me over and motioned to join him in a trench alongside the airstrip about twenty yards from the rocks.

"You'll have to stay here," he cautioned. He stood up, called out to the Indians and pointed to where they should stand. They grabbed the ropes. He raised his hand and shouted something in Macusi. They pulled. The scaffold tottered. Harry yelled. The Indians dropped their ropes and ran for cover in the trenches along the airstrip. The scaffold tipped further and plummeted, crashing and spewing cold water onto the red-hot rocks. Harry was bent over. I was watching the strange proceedings. He looked over and unceremoniously pulled me into the trench.

"Get down," he growled. At the same time there was a loud hissing followed by one loud explosion after another. Rocks, some passing inches above our heads, catapulted in every direction. "Stay down," he said in a big grin. "There'll be more." And there were several more. After a minute, the whooping of the Indians broke the silence. I looked up. Rocks were strewn everywhere. Big ones, little ones, cracked pieces. The airstrip was level except for the broken scaffold lying in a heap. One barrel was totally destroyed, another bent in half. The third was nowhere in sight.

"Harry, you're amazing," I exclaimed. I was awestruck. The huge outcropping of rocks disappeared. There were holes to be filled where the rocks had been. Harry's project had indeed proved to be a success. But it was too late. We missed the rainy season deadline.

The next two weeks were spent closing down: tarps covered lumber and tools, a hut was completed for rations and supplies, and an extension built to keep hammocks dry. Two Indians supervised by Domingo would stay on. I would fly in rations and tools at least once a week. To do that in the rainy season we had to cut one-foot drainage ditches on both sides of the runway. Harry went back to his ranch in the Rupununi. Jan and I were invited to stay at Good Hope for another three months. Caesar and Nellie again made us feel like part of the family, but I know Jan was disappointed in not being in her own house.

THE FLYING BISHOP

The DC-3 arrived amidst a swirl of dust, discharged its passengers and cargo, and headed south to Lethem, the only other outpost on its fortnight schedule. Caesar and I pulled up in his jeep as the DC-3 took off, and greeted Father Quigley standing alongside the cargo. He had an ordinary semi-trimmed beard. With his unpressed khaki shirt and pants, old sun bleached off-white khaki bush hat, cheap brown Bata tennis shoes, and a canvas bag slung over his shoulder, he could be mistaken for anyone but a Catholic priest. The loose-fitting clothes gave him the appearance of being shorter than he actually was. His weather-beaten, suntanned face and hands and his broad smile enhanced by twinkling Irish blue eyes, masked his youth. Though he appeared frail, he was anything but. He stood quietly, hands folded in front, surrounded by his meager, beat-up old baggage.

"Hello, Caesar." He extended his hand. It would be hard not to like this self-effacing young priest. "I hope the Karasabai Tuchow, chief, received my message and sent his Indians to meet me here. If so, I can be on my way within the hour. How is Nellie?"

Donald Haack

"Not on your life, Father. Nellie is fine and has tea waiting for you. We'll catch up on the latest news, and this evening we'll have some Brazilian wine with dinner. We'll have you on your way early in the morning. Your Indian druggers who will carry for you arrived a couple of hours ago and I have them in the baracoun with their hammocks slung for the night. They'll be fed shortly."

Father's smile broadened perceptibly. Though it was evident he had hoped to be invited for tea, dinner, and overnight, he went through the charades of pretending he would leave on his trip immediately. There was an audible sigh of relief after Caesar's invitation, which the priest quickly accepted.

The next morning after a hearty breakfast Father slung his belongings in the jeep behind Caesar and in minutes, skidding and bumping, they disappeared down the poor excuse for a road. Father, one hand holding his hat, the other the rail to keep from being thrown out, hung on for dear life. The forty-mile drive in open savannah took better than two hours to reach the eastern-most bend of the Ireng River. There, the Macusi Indians from Karasabai waited to ferry him in dugouts across the Ireng to where bullock water buffalos would be the next mode of transportation. Father walked. The bullocks carried his personal gear. The bush priests had no physical churches. They said mass, gave communion and taught in the largest Indian huts. If everyone didn't fit in, they would have several meetings until all were included. Father described the trip from Karasabai, Tipuru and back, as *three weeks and 10 pounds*, the weight he lost due to terrible food and hard trails. He looked forward to his return to Good Hope and a feast. Nellie never let him down.

This routine changed with the arrival of our plane. Jan and I were at Good Hope when Father Quigley next arrived. We enjoyed his company and I offered to fly him to Karasabai on my trip to Marquis.

Karasabai airstrip was built ten years earlier for the B.G. Airways' DC-3 airplanes, but no one knew why. With much fanfare, BG Airways made one landing. The Macusi Indians in their misplaced faith in government, kept the airstrip cleared all those years in hopes of another flight. My first flight there was with our foreman, Harry Hart, to get labor for our mining operation. I was familiar with the airstrip and comfortable offering to drop Fr. Quigley there.

In the savannahs, the major event was the fortnight arrival of the DC-3 flight. Consequently, what should have been a ten minute pick-up of Father Quigley turned into an hour-and-a-half social before we managed to get him in our plane. We assured his admirers and well-wishers that he would return to say mass. And I announced loudly, "Please stay the bloody way out of the prop," which nearly decapitated two of the over-eager devotees. A few minutes later, we were on final for Karasabai where I left Fr. Quigley and helped him unload, all in a record fifteen minutes.

Two days later I picked him up for the twelve-minute flight to Marquis, where the Macusis from Tipuru met him for the easy three-hour hike to their village. Four days later he returned to Marquis and I flew him back to Good Hope. With the coming of our plane, Father Quigley's life took a dramatic turn for the better, a fact not lost on Bishop Guilley, the Bishop of the West Indies. After Father Quigley's first flight, the bishop called to thank me and asked if I could continue flying Father Quigley. To my surprise, he went on, "Mr. Haack, in all the years I've been bishop, I've never visited our Amerindian tribes in British Guiana. Do you think you could arrange such a trip for me?" I assured him I could. He insisted it was a business arrangement. I charged him a nominal amount to cover the gas cost.

Six weeks later I was waiting at the airstrip well ahead of the appointed time. I didn't want to keep the Bishop of the West Indies waiting. The DC-3 arrived and Julian taxied back to where we waited. Nellie and Caesar were there to greet the bishop. Nellie informed me that Caesar wanted Bishop Guilley to spend the night at Good Hope.

"You know *C*," she said quietly so Caesar wouldn't hear, "he wouldn't think of the bishop passing through Good Hope without staying overnight. He's persuasive. No matter what Bishop Guilley told you about schedules, you can be assured *C* will convince him to stay for dinner and overnight. You might as well plan on it, too. Jan will be ecstatic. You've been gone a lot, you know." I looked over at her. She was smiling that confident smile. She knew her husband and his persuasive ways. He was the ultimate host.

The DC-3 door swung open and the boarding ramp was attached. The Bishop was the first person to exit. There was no mistaking who he was. Over six-feet tall, big build, squared face, slightly graying hair, and wearing a long white gown accented by a vivid scarlet silk sash, he was an imposing figure. I glanced at his hand for the traditional red ruby; it was there. I stepped forward to greet him.

"Hello, I'm Don Haack. Glad to meet you and welcome to Good Hope." Caesar quickly stepped up and I introduced Nellie and him. Caesar took charge from there. It was a power of wills. Bishop Guilley insisting he wanted to get started on the trip, Caesar, saying, "Nonsense, no one can go through Good Hope without enjoying the Rupununi hospitality." Caesar won by convincing the Bishop it would take time to unload the DC-3 and then re-pack into our plane; and he would get into Karasabai just before dark with no accommodations. Caesar directed his Indian boys to look after Bishop Guilley's personal things and store them in our airstrip house.

"Rather than stand in this 100 degree heat, we can be having an enjoyable tea Nellie prepared. We can relax and freshen up before we have our lamb dinner." Bishop Guilley's eyes lit up at the suggestion. "We'll have you on your way at the crack of dawn. No time lost." Caesar's persuasive argument won the day, aided and abetted by the scorching dry heat and relentless sun. That night, the Gorinskys outdid themselves with their gracious hospitality. Caesar told stories of his earlier days courting Nellie. The Bishop matched tales by recounting humorous escapades in the West Indies. As the wine and brandy flowed on into the night, the stories became funnier. Even the generator gave a stellar, uninterrupted performance. It did not falter once in the five hours.

After breakfast in the Good Hope dining room Fr. Quigley who had come earlier said mass and offered communion. All of us attended. I knew enough about Catholic procedures to refuse communion unless preceded by confession to *cleanse* all sins. To play it safe and not have the roof of the Gorinsky house fall, I passed on the communion.

All Ranchers and several hundred Macusis from the vast northern savannah greeted Bishop Guilley the next morning. Orchestrated by Father Quigley, the event was memorable; the first time a Bishop visited the country. As we prepared for our journey to four villages, he asked if he could bring two hundred pounds of rations to the villagers as a present. I explained it was possible. Our two seater Super Cub had limited space. We could remove the rear seat if he didn't mind sitting on the cargo. He readily agreed and sat on a bag of corn.

I flew Fr. Quigley in first to alert the villagers to the prestigious visit. The arrival of an airplane was a big event, but the Indians were awestruck at the sight of Bishop Guilley disembarking. In contrast to the short, stocky Macusis, the giant Bishop Guilley, in his white flowing gown and puffy red hat, was as foreign a presence to them as a visitor from outer space would be to us. Instead of the roaring welcome planned by Fr. Quigley, the Indians stood statue-still in awe and silence, until Bishop Guilley raised his hand in a Macusi greeting and spoke several words Fr. Quigley had taught him in their language. That scenario was repeated in all four villages. Many Indians never saw a plane before and gave me a nearly identical reception as I followed behind Bishop Guilley.

Later that evening I explained to Jan the phrase *Vaya con Dios* took on a new meaning. "It turned from what could have been just another charter flight into one that I'll never forget. Besides, we did a good deed for the church. Who knows, we may even be rewarded in the hereafter," I said jokingly. The *hereafter* came sooner than anticipated and in a manner never expected.

A few weeks later, Jan, in her ninth month of pregnancy signed into Mercy Hospital, owned and operated by the Catholic

Church. As she finished filling out the forms, she was approached by a middle-aged, kindly looking, round faced nun. "Ma'am, are you Jan Haack?" Jan nodded and replied that she was, surprised that someone in the hospital knew her name. The nun extended her hand. "I'm Sister Generosa, the hospital administrator. I'm from the States, Pennsylvania, and understand you're American." Before Jan could reply, she continued, "Welcome to Mercy Hospital. We're glad to have you here. I received a call from the Bishop of the West Indies, Bishop Guilley, who asked me to make sure your stay here is a pleasant one. We've never had a call from him before. When you're settled in, he's going to make a personal visit. We're all excited. This will be the first time a bishop has been to our hospital." She was genuinely excited. Jan knew immediately that she would have a close relationship with this wonderful nun.

Jan went into labor a few days later. I sat in the waiting room with a view of coconut palm fronds waving in the open air windows and felt the light breeze of the slowly turning overhead fans. A hospital with few walls and unsterile rooms was the antitheses of its American counterpart, I thought.

I heard my name being called. It was Sister Generosa. "It's a girl, your daughter, Diana. Jan is doing fine. Here—" and she started to hand the little bundle to me. I choked up and couldn't say anything. I hugged Sister Generosa. She again thrust the bundle at me. "Here, hold her," she repeated. "Don't you want to count her fingers and toes?"

I looked at her quizzically. "Why?" I stammered.

"Well, to make sure they are all there, but not to worry. I already checked and she's perfect."

I took the bundle gently and quickly felt better about something I didn't know I should even be concerned about. Apparently down here in a less developed country it wasn't taken for granted that most babies are without defects. I gently hugged the little bundle as Sister guided me to Jan where we could share the moment together. It hit me then; we were proud parents.

That night I broke open the special box of Wheating & Richter's finest Royal Jamaican Cuban cigars. Caesar was waiting for the news back at the Woodbine Hotel.

"I'm a father! We have a daughter. Have a cigar," and I handed him a Royal Jamaican.

"Congratulations and thanks. Hmmm, you've got the best, but why the cigar? "

I explained the American custom of giving cigars when you have a baby. He never heard of it. Neither did Anise Khouri, Louis Chung, or Tom Wheating. Tired of explanations about our quaint American custom, I quit giving them out. I tried one. I liked it. It took me one full year to finish off the Royal Jamaicans, by which time I was hooked on cigars.

INDIAN FOLKLORE, GOLD HILL

There were many nights when I didn't make it back to Good Hope during the construction of the airstrip and the building of the house. When I over-nighted at Marquis, Harry, Domingo, the other Indians, and I hung our hammocks in a semicircle under a big tarp. Resting in our hammocks after dinner, we enjoyed watching the coals of the fire produce psychedelic shadows in the grass and shrubs and moving yellow fingers that stretched and painted the underside of the tarp. The chameleon-like color changes and the lulling sound of rapids produced a hypnotic effect of half sleep, half awareness. The river's rapids created an alternating crescendo and softening of background music to the orchestration of crackling fire while the diminished tones of rustling grass teased by the wind made their presence known in very subtle whispers. It was a setting of magical proportions.

In this scenario, Harry enjoyed regaling his fellow travelers with the stories of his ancestors, the myths of the region, and mystical happenings that defied civilized logic. He related several

Indian folk tales, one of which he called *The Forbidden Gold Hill,* the rise across from our house site alongside the airstrip.

"Don, have you noticed that whenever the Indians cross this valley to or from Karasabai village to hunt or fish they always walk as far as possible away from the *hill*? It's bad luck for them to get close or even look at it. It has a curse. The hill is full of gold. Long ago, Indians easily dug up gold and traded it for food, machetes, or shoes. One day two Indians from different villages were working the hill. That evening, one accused the other of stealing his gold. They had a fight and one was killed. The next morning the second died in his hammock from a labaria snakebite. After that, anyone who found gold died within days. Indians believe the Peaymen medicine men from the tribes put a curse on the hill to strike anyone who worked the yellow metal. Now, no one goes near."

I asked him when the last curse was put on. He asked the Karasabai Indian who took a long time to answer. It was a drawn out explanation.

"What did he say, Harry?"

"He doesn't know exactly, but it was a long time ago. His father warned him of it and told him that a few years earlier two boys from their village fished here, then went up to the mountain to see if they could find gold. One of the brothers was afraid and left. When the one left behind didn't return, the brother returned with his father. They found the missing brother in his hammock, sick, unable to walk and vomiting black, smelly liquid. They carried him home, but he died on the way. That story was related to him when he was a little boy learning to hunt."

I noticed that without a calendar, Indians measured time by events: when someone died, when a young girl bled, several moons ago, the dark of the moon. When it came to the time of day, it was easier. They pointed to the sky in reference to where the sun would be. For early morning one would point to the eastern horizon, noon would be directly overhead. It worked for the kind of timetable they used. Harry's gold hill story was, of course, intriguing.

Later when we were working in the house, I asked him half in jest, "Do you think the curse of the gold hill would be on us, too, even though we're not from any of these tribes?"

He looked very thoughtful. He certainly knew I was asking more as a joke than a serious question. He didn't smile. "I don't know, Don. These people believe in the curse. No, I don't think it would affect outsiders. Want to take check on it when we have some time?" he challenged. But now he grinned as he looked for my reaction.

And so the die was cast. Of course we would test it. We chose a time when the Indians stopped work to fish and would be gone most of the day. We took a pick, a couple of shovels, two pails, and my gold prospecting pan. The sun would be hot so we took two flasks of water. We started early at sun-up. Our first two pits were at the base of the hill. We filled two buckets, carrying them to the river to pan. I had two samples, scrapings from six and twelve inches down the hole. I placed them in bags. The last two bags were from the bottom and I took care there were no scrapings from above. I made a note on each bag. Harry was impressed.

"Looks like you've done this before. That's the way the geologists took samples at Omai mines. You didn't tell me. Are you a geologist?"

"No, but I spent a month in Venezuela working with a geologist from Kennicott Copper company. He was the best and taught me accuracy." I carefully emptied the first bag into the metal pan then eased it into the water, letting enough in to mix earth and gravel thoroughly. Then I completely submerged it in the calm water, tilting the pan back and forth and simultaneously swirling it in semicircles, while gently moving it up and down so the material alternately hung in suspension and fell back down.

Each time I scraped out larger stones while the material gradually separated out, the heavier particles falling faster than the lighter ones, gravitated downward and to the center, the lowest spot in the concave pan. After removing the bigger particles, I swirled the pan like a centrifuge and tipped it a bit more allowing the next lighter material to slide out, concentrating more and more of the heavier particles. The specific gravity of gravel, 3.9, diamonds, 4.8 and gold, 19, made gold easy to separate from gravel. Diamonds, close in density to gravel, took more finesse and time. Unless there were heavier Ilminites in the pan, I wouldn't be concerned with diamonds. I emptied all but a few heavier particles in the very center. No trace of the ubiquitous black sand weighing slightly more than the fine brown river sand. No heavy minerals, no gold, and the same for the other three bags and bucket. Nothing.

The next two pits were half way up the hill on the opposite side. Same results. The third batch we dug up from the top of the hill. Midday, the sun with its searing rays bore down on us mercilessly. We stripped down to our trousers, dark brown with sweat. Even our socks were soaked in perspiration. The wind mysteriously died, making the heat even more unbearable.

"Have you noticed even the bloody Kaburi flies won't come up in this infernal heat? It's the first respite we've had from them during the day. I think they're smarter than we are, Harry. God, it's a beautiful view from up here, though. You can see the whole valley. It's worth all this effort for the vista of our valley. With all our work, there are barely any signs of our projects other than a couple of dots and a small line of the airstrip. Kind of puts things in perspective as we try to live in this primitive land. If we don't find any gold in these two buckets, I think the story of the gold curse is just that, a story. Let's go check these last two buckets."

We checked thoroughly and efficiently. Nothing. So much for the curse.

While we were investigating the legend of the gold hill, two of our Indians from camp went fishing and took along their Brazilian suruku diamond sieves, the ones used to separate the diamonds from gravel. While one of the Indians fished, the second dug in the shallow gravel and found a better *catch:* two alluvial bright clear rough diamonds. I examined them with my 10-power diamond loupe, the small pocket magnifying glass used for examining diamonds and carried by all dealers.

"They're small, but gem quality. Where did they find them?" They answered in half Macusi, half Portuguese. "Right down from camp about six arm lengths from shore. River was so deep," pointing to his knee.

"Are they worth much? Harry asked. They want to know if you would buy them.

"Yeah, why not? After all that's what we're here for—diamonds. Tell them they're worth fifteen dollars apiece." They understood numbers and smiled, showing their pointed filed teeth.

"I think you're paying too much, Don," Harry admonished. I assured him that in the long run if word got around that we paid good prices for diamonds, it would pay off and would assure a steady source. We would still have a handsome profit. He frowned but reluctantly agreed.

"Okay, it's done." I counted out six bright green B.G five-dollar bills in exchange for the diamonds. The Indians both grinned and took the bills.

"Obrigado, obrigado," they thanked me over and over as they stuffed the bills into their shorts. Harry frowned even more. I didn't understand his concern.

We were dead tired from digging and dehydration so we slept soundly. Domingo awakened us at dawn. "Misser Harry, boys gone. They take everything. Only few rations left."

Domingo said he heard some noises in the middle of the night, but didn't think much of it because the Indians seldom slept throughout the evening, a habit they acquired by hunting and fishing after dark. They stoked the coals, told stories, or just sat around the fire until they were sleepy again. This time Domingo said they gathered up their gear, our rations, and left before daylight.

"No point in trying to find them. They're long gone by now." Harry added, but didn't seem very surprised. I was furious that they left us stranded. Harry's attitude was definitely more laid back.

"Don, I tried to warn you last night about paying them so much. They only work for what they need. If it takes a month, that's how long they will work. But if they earn the same amount in a few days well…they leave. Eventually they'll come back when they want something from the trade store again, but they won't feel they did anything wrong leaving early this time. That's their way of life, even though it throws off our schedule. We need men and rations, particularly farine, to finish this project. We can hunt and fish and there is some tinned meat, but that'll only last a few days."

I was upset. Another unexpected delay. I couldn't get mad at Harry. He tried to warn me the night before, but I didn't know what I was being warned about. This apparently was part of my education on how to do business in bush country.

LEARNING TO WALK

It was not something I consciously thought about, but rather an underlying feeling that when we came to South America I would be the teacher to the Amerindians. To the contrary, other than my teaching them how to operate our prospecting and mining equipment, I discovered that all the learning was mine.

I took pride in being an athlete and growing up in a hunting family. I considered myself to be a good hunter. My parents delivered me at age ten to our Wisconsin cottage in the middle of winter to spend two weeks hunting with *Rinny*, the local German shepherd. The snow was over three feet deep, the temperatures near zero. The cottage, blocked off to one room in the winter, was heated by an old iron woodstove that served for the cooking source. Wood had to be chopped to fit in the fire bin. I started a new fire every evening and early morning. Our only winter neighbor, Mr. Wallace, checked on me daily to see if there was smoke coming out of the chimney mornings and evenings. The fire burned out by midnight. Any food or drink not in the refrigerator after I left for hunting in the morning froze solid. With that kind of a self-sufficient background, I became competent and independent in the wilderness.

The first trek with Domingo from Marquis to Good Hope proved to be a humbling experience. I felt like a neophyte. A couple weeks after that trip, we were sitting around the fire after dinner and I asked Domingo about traveling in the bush and hunting. I couldn't understand how he moved so quickly without looking where he stepped. He avoided hazards on the path while he pointed out the animals and birds along the way. It was if he had two sets of eyes. He thought for a while then explained as best he could.

"When you walk on trail, you look down with eyes. Feet too slow. You stumble. Better you look down quickly, then look up. Let inside head guide feet. Much faster. When you look down, you no see birds, animals you hunt. You walk through bush on heels, make noise like drumbeat. Insects, animals, birds, feel drumbeat in earth and they hide. Better you walk on toes, then no drumbeat."

He was warming up to the subject now and as he talked he described what was wrong with my clumsy method of walking.

"When you not always look at trail, your head think and become part of bush, trees, animals. You feel where they are and what they do. You no need eyes, better you feel inside. When you think like animal, you hunt good. You feel, you see it here and here, inside." He pointed not to his eyes but to his head and chest.

I tried to keep up with his train of thought, but it wasn't easy. He was discussing abstract thinking with a limited English vocabulary. If it were his first language, he would be referring to deja vu, ESP, or visualizing outside one's body. I smiled because parapsychology was a favorite subject of mine. When I served in the Marine Corps in North Carolina, I visited Duke University to meet Dr. Rhyne, one of the country's foremost authorities on parapsychology. The experience was a bit disappointing. The Russians were years ahead of us. They found individuals with special sending and receiving sensitivities via thought waves or mental telepathy and others who could foresee future events. The

Russians were putting that science to practical use. At Duke they were still experimenting with decks of cards, recording probability against intuitive ability. It was as if they were saying, "See, some of this stuff is really true!"

For hundreds of years, the Macusis and other tribes used their innate talent in everyday life, a fundamental communication they took for granted. ESP and deja vu came naturally to me. I wondered if working with the Macusis might enable me to go to a higher learning level. As if reading my thoughts, Domingo went on, "You can do. Let head relax. Next time on trail, try what I say. Look down quickly at trail, then away. Let head guide feet. Make head go easy, think like bush."

I translated that to mean, relax, and let your mind be a part of the surroundings. Be aware of the vibrations that you don't feel now.

He continued, "You shoot good with gun, but you can shoot better."

He was referring to the day we hiked up river to the dredge and came across a capybara. Domingo carried his bow and arrow. In one smooth motion before I could fire a shot, he placed an arrow in his bow, pulled it back and released it, dropping the animal dead in his tracks. The arrow passed through the capybara's shoulder into his chest and must have struck the heart to stop him so effectively.

"How can you shoot quickly and accurately without aiming?"

"Tell you sometime, not now. Must hurry, take meat to camp." That was two weeks ago and he apparently decided now was as good a time as any to explain. I waited.

"When you hunt, no time to aim. Animal gone quick. Bow, arrow or gun be part of arm, body, head—all one. When you see animal, you point. Arrow or bullet go there. No look whole animal, look at small part…ear, hair in front of leg. Bullet go there. Tomorrow you try, you see."

I knew he was describing the subconscious mind doing the work. The subconscious, if utilized correctly, is much more efficient than the conscious. Every day for the next week I practiced shooting in this new manner. The improvement was uncanny. The latest shooting methods in Marine boot camp were primitive compared to what I was doing here. Each time hiking on trails, I practiced what Domingo taught me: not to stare at the trail, and not to walk on my heels. After a while it became easier and felt natural.

The first indication of progress came weeks later when Domingo and I went up the Ireng to the Tipuru River. Domingo set the pace, which after a while turned into a light jog. We stopped for water. Domingo looked at me.

"You good. You no walk like white man, you like Macusi now."

I don't remember ever receiving a compliment that meant so much to me as those few simple words. I had another accolade when Domingo, Pedro, and I hiked to Karona Falls to check progress on the airstrip. We moved at a good pace. Domingo let me lead, something he had not done before. An hour out, I stopped and held up my hand. There was a premonition, an inner feeling, of game in the tree. I looked at Domingo. He smiled, waiting to see what I would do. I motioned to continue cautiously. Thirty yards ahead in a small opening in the trees I looked up. At the top of one of the dead branches, looking like an ornament on a Christmas tree was a tall, fat, bush turkey. I figured it would be a reasonable shot for a telescopic rifle but I didn't hesitate. I slipped out my pistol, a Remington .22 semi-automatic Targetmaster, slid a round into the chamber, pointed at the bird's neck and shot. Nothing happened. It didn't fly off. Seconds later it dropped like a stone. We walked over to where it fell. There was a hole in the neck just below the head.

I looked at Domingo as he picked up the bird to clean. His eyes met mine. He nodded and knew exactly that I used the *inner self*. I felt like shouting to the world, *Look what I just did, the most impossible shot in the history of mankind!* Yet, I knew this wasn't the kind of prowess you celebrated. You used your inner powers when needed, but not for *show and tell*. Though he didn't utter a word, I knew Domingo was proud of his student. He just smiled. We both knew.

THE DC-3 FLIGHT TO MARQUIS

At the beginning of the fall dry season, I flew in Julian's co-pilot, Vicky Fikes, to inspect our airstrip and give Julian a full report while he lunched with Nellie and Caesar at Good Hope. We followed the route the DC-3 would take. We came down our valley four hundred feet above the water, made the gradual turn in front of the mountain, and landed.

"This isn't exactly an international airport, is it?" he gasped as we got out of our plane. "So now we're here." He looked around. "Do you expect us to get out or is this a one-way flight?" he asked, half mockingly.

I brought out the map and sketch of the airport layout again and went over it with him. We paced out the runway.

"Well, you're right. It is 3,000 feet. And we'll probably need all of that for landing with a near full load." He looked around again. "Tell me once more how we get out? There are mountains on four sides. We can't possibly climb out fast enough to clear the one in front." He looked puzzled when he glanced over to me.

Donald Haack

"Julian's waiting. Let's go," I said. "I'll show you how we get out now," and invited him back in the plane. I taxied back to the beginning of the runway. On take off I explained to Vicky what we had to do if this were the DC-3. We were off the ground in a few hundred feet, but I simulated the larger cargo plane's takeoff by staying a few feet off the runway until the halfway mark, which is where his plane would become airborne. I kept low and built up speed before the end of the runway, made a shallow right turn behind the small hill on the right. We followed that valley to the river. I pointed to the broad valley on our left that paralleled our airstrip but was out of sight from the ground. I eased the plane into a left turn as we continued our gradual climb. Vicky's eyebrows were up and he nodded.

"It'll probably work. But for a while you sure had me fooled." He smiled and gave a deep sigh of relief. "Now I have to sell it to Julian."

"Yeah, good luck," I added, "I'll help you."

After the Marquis check-out flight, Vicki left the details to Julian; and in less than three weeks, safely past the heaviest of rains, Julian scheduled a September flight.

It was a busy time for us. When the rains eased up, Harry brought in the Karasabai Indians to saw more boards. He found four Brazilian builders to make mud blocks for our house. We built four wooden forms 14 x 8 inches, and on Harry's instructions I brought extra shovels, rakes, buckets, a piece of plywood, a wheel barrow, and plenty of tarps. Curious, I stayed on to see how the wooden forms and tools were to be used.

The Indians searched the area and found the right kind of clay halfway between the river and the house site Jan and I picked out. Two of the Indians cleared the site and were in the process of leveling it before we poured the foundation. I brought in twenty bags of cement, enough for the house.

Harry had the work well coordinated. The floor and foundation of the house were completed in a week, during which time the block makers had a production line of blocks lining up in the sun to dry. The men dug a large pit, bucketed in water, cut a special grass into four to six inch pieces and mixed it in the mud for extra strength. When it was the right consistency they shoveled it into the forms on a plastic tarp. After a few minutes, they shook the rectangular block out and filled the next, doing four at a time. The dry air and hot sun stabilized the blocks in minutes and the next day were wheel-barreled to the house. After two thousand blocks, the brick layers started laying the walls while the block making continued. When the walls were half up, Harry had the Brazilian carpenters framing windows and doors, making the dining room table, bed frames, and kitchen counters.

I brought Jan up to the site every few days to supervise and contribute her womanly touch. She never ceased to be amazed at the progress with such basic tools. As the walls were complete, the masons spread on a light coat of sand and cement for durability. Within a day we were able to paint.

"It looks like a Stateside ranch house," Jan remarked, "except for the lack of roof, of course." The frame for the roof went up just before Julian brought in the aluminum corrugated sheeting. The house plan was simple: a combined living room and dining room, three bedrooms, a step down-library with built-in desks and a stand for our Collins short wave radio. The kitchen was on the south side and the bathroom faced west towards the river. It took a bit of designing to get it right; the library and bathroom were both step-downs, contouring the land rather than digging and filling. The septic pit, we discovered, wasn't low enough for gravity feed, so we elevated the toilet onto a three-foot pedestal...very regal looking with a spectacular view of the Ireng River. Unfortunately, the shower was completed before we had an opportunity to explain how the water trap worked. They simply made a hole for the water to drain out, making an irresistible entrance for lizards, mice, rats, and later snakes, which hastened the need to re-construct it correctly.

Our water supply came from the Ireng River. We had a Briggs & Stratton gas pump that brought the water into four cleaned-out gasoline barrels on a twelve-foot high platform. This setup provided storage and a simple but efficient gravity feed system that we filled every few days. We stored two five-gallon drinking water dispensers in the pantry. We let any silt settle before adding halogen pills for purification. By using the tanks alternately there was enough time for the pills to properly sterilize the water. The kerosene stove with oven came in on one of my flights. We assembled it the same day for making big pots of coffee for the workmen and us. The new refrigerator designed to run on kerosene was too large for the Super Cub and was scheduled on Julian's DC-3. Two barges supported by fifty-five gallon gasoline barrels were constructed to float the dredge and the mineral jig that separated diamonds from gravel. They were completed and ready to go. The work was on schedule. We were nervous because the operation now depended on bringing in the DC-3.

On the appointed day, I waited for Julian on the Good Hope airstrip for a last- minute briefing. I was to fly in first and keep radio contact. Apparently, he had a change of mind.

"You leave your plane here and fly in with Vicky and me. We got everything of yours on board and not quite fully loaded, which is good for a first landing on a new strip. You know the strip and the approach. I want you up front with me." Julian left no room for discussion.

The flight in was uneventful. The approach through the mountains and the final approach flying above the river without an airstrip in sight was unnerving for Julian but he handled it with aplomb. On my signal, he lowered the landing gear and cranked down the landing flaps. He looked questioningly at me. I assured him all was well. As we rounded the last turn we had the strip in front of us. He pulled back power and touched down on the first twenty feet of runway, as if he had been doing this every day. We stopped in half the strip's length, turned around and taxied to the river. He hadn't said one word since the final approach.

He got out and panned the vista.

"Cheezus Christ...how are we going to get out of here?" he exclaimed as he looked around at all the mountains. "Vicky, I thought you said there is a valley we can fly out. I don't see anything like a valley."

Our twenty men made quick work of unloading mining equipment, household goods, lumber, bulk rations, and several barrels of gas.

With the unloading finished, I quickly briefed Julian about the takeoff, apparently none too soon—he was pacing back and forth like an expectant father. He climbed back into his plane and we taxied to the beginning of the strip and turned around so that the tail hung on the edge of the touchdown point. Harry had driven a huge stake as an anchor for a rope secured to the tail wheel to hold the plane in place while Julian revved the engines to full RPM. He wanted maximum power *before* he started rolling and using up precious runway. When the gauge showed full revs, I waved to Harry who waved to Domingo who cut the rope. We were on our way, Vicky on the right and me in the middle, kneeling down. We were airborne in seconds and stayed a few feet off the ground. Julian motioned to me to pull the lever to raise the wheels. We heard the reassuring clunk signaling retraction in their sockets. The plane, a few feet off the ground was aerodynamically clean and gaining much-needed air speed. Vicky pointed to the right.

"Now!" we both shouted.

Julian banked the plane in a shallow turn behind the hill. I noticed the right wing tip cutting through the higher grass. Julian knew what he was doing keeping up his airspeed—a shallow turn on take-off makes a dangerous combination. We rounded the hill and in front of us was the steep Ireng valley, not wide enough for the DC-3. Concerned and puzzled, Julian looked to me for an answer. I raised my hand, held it for a moment and then pointed out the window to the broad valley on our left. He smiled, raised his thumbs up and pulled up the flaps. Ten minutes later we settled down at Good Hope.

Caesar, pacing back and forth, stood on the side of the airstrip. When the engines shut down, he was at the door.

"How did it go?" he growled. "Did you get it all in? Any problems? How was the take-off?" he asked without waiting for any answers.

Julian smiled. "I don't think we'll put that landing strip on the report. I'll tell them we landed at Karasabai and leave it at that. No way do I want the company to know I flew into that valley. To tell the truth, I think Vicky shit in his pants on takeoff if he hadn't already on the landing." Vicky didn't say anything, just smiled. Later, his only comment was, "Well, we made it, didn't we?"

MOVING IN

After the DC-3 arrived we gave a huge sigh of relief. We had our heavy mining equipment and household goods, so we had plenty of projects to work on. It was the biggest activity in all the time we were there: a race to get the dredge operating and a push to complete the house so we could move in and stop commuting from Good Hope and living out of suitcases.

Even though many of the built-ins were not ready we moved in and found some unexpected problems beyond our wildest imagination. And put us to a test.

The second day we discovered the mesh in the screens around the house weren't small enough to keep the pesky cabouri fly out. Cabouri, an insects ten times more annoying and irritating than mosquitoes, were intolerable. They flew in and around the eyes, mouth, and ears. When they lighted, they sucked blood and left a tiny red blood spot and an excruciating itch that seemed to never stop. The more you scratched, the more it itched, until the skin became raw and puffy. We had to keep the insects out to keep our sanity. We solved the problem by painting the screens with light motor oil. When the flies landed on the screens, they became oil soaked. Some fell off; others stuck on the screen, which then had to be cleaned off weekly. It was a task that was easy to remember; without clean screens there was no breeze to cool the house

One evening after turning off the Tillie lamps and preparing for bed, we were startled by loud barking and howling, like a hundred dogs running around the house. We went to the door with a flashlight to investigate. What we saw was unreal: a steady line of what looked like gray and white wild dogs circling the house… like Indians surrounding wagon trains in the Old West. Only, these were animals. They continued for hours then one by one left, followed by complete silence. Was it a nightmare or had we actually seen them? The next morning we asked the Indians. They too were surprised and never remembered seeing anything like it. They were as baffled as we were.

With all the activity, we put the incident behind us, but that's not where it stayed. The next evening, there was a repeat performance that lasted for hours, leaving us sleepless and irritable. The third night the event started past midnight. That was too much. I told Jan to get our five-battery flashlight while I checked out my .35 mm lever action Remington rifle. Holding the light, she stood in the doorway behind me while I chose an area safe to shoot.

"Pick out the biggest one, keep the light on him until he's in front of the airstrip." She picked out one, but I lost him in the pack. The second run around, Jan had him in the light; I had him in my sights and squeezed the trigger. The blast shattered the night. He rose up as if he was going to jump, and then crumpled into a heap. The pack continued the chase, circling and howling. We picked out another large animal and dropped him close to the first. That got their attention. The pack slowed down, inspected the two lifeless bodies, then left quickly and never returned. In the morning we had a closer look before we buried the pair. They were much bigger than a fox or a dog. I hadn't heard of wolves in South America. The Indians gave us conflicting stories as to what they thought they were, but they agreed they had never seen an animal or a behavior like they saw here. They spoke as if it were something supernatural. Harry said it was fortunate they didn't consider it a bad omen or they all would've left. Thank goodness for little favors, I thought.

I hadn't discovered the grand entrance our shower drain provided to the lizards, mice, and rats. Jan was beside herself when she discovered mice had gotten into our kitchen food, particularly her freshly baked bread. I inspected every inch of the house including the spacing below each door to ensure neither animal nor insect could get in. Then I discovered the 4 x 4 inch drain, an ideal animal walk-through. Without spare workmen, I temporarily solved the problem by placing a square oil can in front of the drain. After showering, we simply lifted it to drain the water. Not ideal but adequate, or so I thought. Jan made it abundantly clear the *numero uno* house priority was rodent elimination. Every evening they ran around the roof rafters. With flashlight and knife I climbed on top of the eight-foot high open walls to do combat. In less than a week, I eliminated all but one, a large rat that seemed to have a charmed life. Several times I thought I had him, but he would pull some new escape procedure just in time to avoid my butcher knife. He was a little too cocky and the second week I managed to nick his tail into a distinctive right angle.

Whatever I did was not enough. Jan had visions of the rat running around Diana's bedroom. I had to get rid of him. The trouble was, as I came up with novel ways to do him in, he anticipated my moves and changed his pattern. On top of walls with flashlight and knife in hand, my nocturnal ritual of stalking the troublesome rat left me sleepless and bad-tempered. I considered shooting him, an easy solution, except it would have made a hole in the roof.

"It seems you should be able to outsmart that stupid rat. It's been over two weeks and he's still running around the rafters every night, along with you, too, up there," Jan exclaimed in exasperation.

"I know, I know. If you have any better ideas let me know." I tried placing bread in a container surrounded by water, hoping he would go after it and drown. He ate it, and swam out with ease. We brought in Nellie's best rat poison and placed it all over the house. The beast enjoyed snacks of everything else, but studiously avoided touching the bait. I began to have a certain respect for that damned rat and actually gave it a name, which I did not disclose to Jan. She thought I was having "fun" with this game of trying to eliminate the *dirty rat*. I was not having fun and the lack of sleep was getting to me. Unbelievably, this scenario went on over a month. Jan's patience was wearing thin as was my constitution and stamina. The rat problem was eventually solved in a very unorthodox and desperate manner, which I will explain later.

Another morning Harry was assembling the dredge while Domingo and I were showing our new crew how to use the diving equipment. We were interrupted by a piercing scream from the house, a half-mile away. I froze. It wasn't like Jan to get rattled, much less scream. Domingo and I scrambled up the bank and I drew my gun as we approached the house.

"Jan, it's me. What's happening? Where are you?"

"Here, in the shower, come quickly!" She sounded hysterical.

Harry arrived at the same time. I motioned for Domingo and him to wait. Pistol in hand, I hurried into the bathroom. Jan stood on the toilet pedestal, pointing into the shower. I looked over the edge of the stall and there, coiled up, was a three-foot Anaconda snake as thick as my wrist and probably as surprised as Jan. I called Harry who burst in and seeing Jan with only a towel wrapped around, blurted, "Scuse me ma'am. Don't be frightened. It's just a baby camoodie. They look big but Indians keep them in their house to keep rodents out. They make good pets until they're over six feet…then you can't leave them around children."

Jan was having no part of Harry's explanation. "Get that reptile out of my bathroom!" she screamed.

When Harry grabbed the camoodie behind the head it wound three coils around his arm, but otherwise was quite docile. "He's harmless…just scared. Though I don't know who's more scared, him or the missus"

To Jan's relief Harry carried the snake out, but that wasn't the end: Jan wanted out of this jungle home…now! She related the story several times, how she just moved the oil can away from the drain hole to discharge the water, when out popped this monstrous reptile right at her feet. She practically flew to the top of the toilet. She was still shaking as we went to bed, and fully resolved to leave the next day.

Fortunately, a good night's sleep does wonders for the soul. With all the activity and work we had the next day, nothing more was said. But it was evident she hadn't made peace with our house either. We tried to put that event behind us.

A week later, we were relaxing in the library. After several unsuccessful attempts to reach the States, I shut down the Collins transmitter and our generator. With the house lights off our only light was from the Tillie lamp. I was on a bench and Jan was sitting on the top step of the library, her arms wrapped around her knees. It was our quiet time to catch up on the events of the day. Out of the corner of my vision, just left of Jan's bare foot, I caught a movement. I glanced over to see a bright red, black and yellow "S" shape moving towards Jan. Even in the soft light of the kerosene lamp, I knew instinctively what it was—the deadly Coral snake, whose bite can cause quick death. Though small, it injects a poison affecting para-sympathetic nerves, which control the heart and breathing reflexes.

"Jan, " I said forcefully to get her full attention, "don't move. Don't move an inch." I pointed to the snake approaching her feet. Contrary to my request, she jumped back, did a half summersault and landed on the bed ten feet away. I slammed the seat of my bench on the snake and then ground, twisted, and turned the bench until I was sure the serpent was a flattened stain on the floor. I lifted the bench. What was left of the snake wasn't going to trouble anybody. My heart was pounding. I told Jan I would fly her out as quickly as possible.

" A Coral snake in our house!" I repeated. I couldn't believe it. Eventually I settled down.

Jan quietly said, "I really don't understand; it didn't bother you at all when that big fat snake was in my shower. But here this tiny little bright-colored fellow comes along and you're all discombobulated. I just don't understand."

To no avail I tried to explain the difference. There was that *big snake* and here was this *little teeny* one.

There were many settling-in problems and we tackled them one by one. I thought Jan was a brick in her determination to handle all these unusual trials and tribulations, any one of which would have given a lesser woman a full excuse to escape to civilization. Not Jan. She hung in there against all odds..

Amidst everything else, another situation popped up. Seems that the Indians from the Karasabai and Tipuru village were anxious to see what we, their new neighbors, were like. We hadn't anticipated their numbers or enthusiasm. At first we greeted all of them, and through interpreters explained how thankful and happy we were to be their neighbors. They were friendly and curious, but their curiosity became overwhelming. First only one or two, then four, and finally ten of them were standing around the house. We could tell who had been there by the pattern on their noses from the oiled window screen. They hadn't seen a house like this before. Jan had no privacy and eventually felt every move was being watched, like being on the wrong side of a cage.

It finally got to her and I had to do something about it. When the Tuchow arrived, I translated as tactfully as I could about Jan's dilemma. It wasn't an easy concept to explain because Indians live in an open society, sleeping together as a family, watching and cheering each other on in lovemaking and other tasks. The chief couldn't understand, but we came to a compromise: no more coming to the house to stare inside, and in return, once a week we would show off the wonders of running water, flush toilet, kerosene stove that cooked food inside a house without a firewood site, and best of all, the refrigerator. That was a concept they really had difficulty understanding, especially when we showed them an ice cube and told them it was hard water. They laughed, slapped their sides, and discussed it endlessly after each ice cube melted in their hands.

Donald Haack

ANNIE OAKLEY

L ying in the hammock and refreshed after a half hour siesta, so much a part of our bush life, I reflected on how we survived thus far in this hostile environment, where "9-1-1" takes three weeks to respond.

There were three major factors working in our favor: I married an Annie Oakley, we were adopted by the Wapashani Indians on the British Guiana side, and we helped our nearest neighbor, a Brazilian desperado, who instead of being a serious threat became a friend and savior.

Jan was the only woman in the territory to pack a pistol. Her dress of the day was khaki trousers, a white long-sleeved blouse, a pistol on her hip, which she wore like it was there all her life, and tennis shoes—leather shoes, which never dried, caused foot or *jungle* rot. Crossing creeks or stepping in or out of dugouts caused wet feet. Canvas shoes dried in minutes and were ideal

Her pistol of choice was a semi-automatic, long barrel Colt Target-master .22 caliber, with a clip of 8 hollow point long rifle cartridges. On our first expedition, I noticed the locals carried .45,

.38, and .32 caliber pistols, which were heavy and used heavy, scarce and expensive ammunition. I wanted a light but accurate pistol for self-defense and hunting that could be carried all day. The long-barreled .22 Targetmaster filled that requirement.

Harry, our foreman, asked Domingo, who crafted leather, to make our holsters. I had him make them extra wide on top for a quick, smooth draw, tapering down to a small ' V' on the bottom to eliminate dirt. I lathered Vaseline on the inside leather to provide a smooth slide and to keep out moisture, which caused rust. The machined sharp edges of the front sights were filed round to ease sliding on the leather. Domingo sewed on leather thongs for tying around the thigh to eliminate chafing or movement and keep the pistol exactly where it's supposed to be, not an inch or so away if you had to draw quickly. A simple strap secured with a snap button went over the grips to keep the pistol from falling out.

The Brazilian males tried to be very macho. Everyone wore a pistol, the bigger the better. When a *new kid* on the block arrived, they wanted to see how he could shoot, establishing a *pecking* order. Unskilled shooters were the most likely to be robbed, beaten, or killed. On the border few killings were brought to trial. Being able to shoot well quickly became a high priority for me… I was the *new kid* on the block.

Coached by my Wapashani friends, I took the initiative when the first Brazilian came to me with his big chrome plated .38 revolver strapped to his hip, and asked if I knew how to use my *pistola*. And did I know I was wearing it backwards on the wrong leg? "Ha ha," big laugh as he pursed his lips barely showing below his thick, bushy, black, untrimmed mustache with his jaw jutting forward in an obvious challenge. He nodded his head and tipped his big broad brimmed hat in a fashion that was unmistakably *show me*.

I smiled. "You'll have to shoot with my wife first. If you're good enough, I'll take you on. Jan, come here, please." This was a deliberate insult. Brazilian men don't shoot against women. Brazilian women never handle guns. They stay out of sight and keep quiet. Before the insult sunk in, I quickly set up a target.

"Jan, see the bottle on the table? Our friend here wants to see what you can do with it."

Without missing a beat, Jan slipped her .22 Targetmaster out of the holster, released the safety, and in one sweeping motion, seemingly without taking aim, squeezed off one round, shattering the stillness of the jungle. Like an exploding fountain, hundreds of unseen parrots and parakeets, erupted from the trees, and in their terror, cawed in a disharmonious cacophony that competed with the deafening drone of their frantic wing beats. The scene made a dramatic backdrop for the bottle that shattered into oblivion. She slipped her pistol back into the holster like a hand into a glove. The whole sequence appeared as graceful as a ballet movement. In seconds, stillness returned. She smiled, did a pirouette, and walked off.

We had just witnessed poetry in motion. No Brazilian drew his pistol after seeing Jan perform.

When I taught handgun in the Marines, it was rare to find a student with Jan's natural talent: the sensitive feel of knowing the precise trigger pressure. She mastered firing with her arm in a natural arc without a pause, as opposed to holding the pistol steady on target—a slower and less accurate method. With cases of ammunition for practice shooting, she honed her skills to perfection. By contrast, the Brazilians with big guns and expensive bullets didn't have the luxury of practicing.

The locals were impressed that a woman could perform a feat they could not. In their travels Brazilians enjoyed relating and embellishing exploits, kind of like Harry's folklore about Gold Hill. Jan's feats grew bigger and better in the telling. Logically, they thought, "If she shoots that well, what could I do?" They couldn't imagine! It never occurred to them that Jan could out shoot me any day of the week and I wasn't about to tell them. Thus legends are created.

I couldn't always have Jan at my side. On flights to remote Brazilian trading posts, I needed a different scenario. I found one and perfected it. Shopkeepers weren't the problem. It was the few belligerent miners with a few drinks too many who wanted to show off their shooting ability, or in most cases, lack thereof. I tried to avoid them, but when I saw it wasn't possible I deliberately chose to pre-empt their challenge by asking them if *they* knew how to use their *pistolas*.

"Can you hit this bottle cap if I throw it in the air? I would ask, smiling nonchalantly, but never diverting my eyes from theirs. I could see it made them uncomfortable, something they were not used to, but it did command their full attention. I had to be careful not to push it too far.

"No one can do that, not even your wife." was the usual reply. News about Jan's shooting traveled fast in the bush. I ignored the comment, walked a few steps away so I wouldn't hit anyone, flipped the cap in the air and with the same right hand, reached for my pistol on the left leg where I had already unsnapped the leather flap. As I thumbed off the safety, I slipped the pistol out, pointed it in the direction of the bottle cap, just before it was on its way down and blew it away. Without pausing, I pointed at a bottle I previously set on the fence, took a casual but better aim and blew *it* away.

"No bottle cap, no need for the bottle." I slipped the smoking pistol back into the holster. "You're next," as I put another bottle on the fence and fished around for a bottle cap. Never had any takers. No one would attempt an impossible shot like that. They were stunned. The effect, electrifying because what they had seen was impossible, except they had just seen it. What they didn't know was that the first round in my clip held birdshot, the second round a hollow point long rifle, which demolished the beer bottle. Birdshot spreads a pattern over two feet in diameter. They knew of birdshot in shotguns, but never heard of it in a pistol.

My shooting trick along with Jan's legendary fame provided us with much needed life insurance.

TATAHIERA

Survival in this country took constant vigilance and support from friends who sometimes came from unexpected quarters: our closest Brazilian neighbor, Tatahiera.

Harry knocked on our door. Jan was preparing breakfast and I was about to crank up the generator to call B.G. Airways for an update on our overdue cargo. Harry looked worried, but then he often looked worried only this time more so.

"Don, we may have a problem," he said quietly so Jan wouldn't hear. He was concerned about Jan and Diana living here in Indian territory and Brazilian bandit country. He felt this wasn't a place for civilized white women with a young child. He hesitated.

"What is it, Harry?" In usual Indian fashion, Harry seldom discussed what was on his mind without talking around the subject at length. Eventually he would come to it. I didn't have time for that now. "What's the problem, Harry?"

"Well, I think we're getting a Brazilian visitor...Tatahiera. Everyone knows his reputation, and it's bad. He raises cattle, mines diamonds with a diving crew above Karona falls. Very territorial, doesn't like anyone in his area. Killed more men and Indians than anyone can count. Bad hombre. He's on his way here and should arrive at Marquis in less than an hour. He slept over at Tipuru River and the local Macusis from Tipuru came to warn us. They don't like him. He recently killed four Macusis from their village because they hunted *his land*. You know Indians; no one *owns* land." He was frowning as he continued. "I don't know what he's up to, but we shouldn't take any chances. Tell Jan to stay inside and keep her gun handy. I'll put Domingo out of sight near the hangar. He's a good shot and I can trust him. I'll take that .38 revolver you offered me when we first came. I'll talk to him when he arrives, and you can back me up. If it looks okay, I'll call you out to meet him. It could be a social call and he's curious about his new neighbor with the airplane." Harry definitely was nervous about this. "We should brew some strong coffezinia and offer him Jan's biscuits. He's traveling with only one Indian, so that's a good sign. We'll put his man up in the baracoun. It may be all right but we should be careful…especially with his bad reputation."

That was long speech for Harry and I took his concern seriously. Everyone was in place before Tatahiera arrived. Harry met him on the bush trail coming into our valley. Tataheira sat on the back of the largest bullock I've ever seen. Bullocks, strange looking animals, are much larger than steers. With broad shoulders and hips, large head, and long horns, they resemble an overstuffed Texas longhorn. Bred in Asia and brought to British Guiana a hundred years ago to work the sugar cane fields, they were well suited to carrying extraordinary loads in rough fields. Now they populated a good portion of the northeastern continent of South America.

A stranger pair would be hard to imagine: Tataheira, moving in an undulating motion in harmony with his irregular gaited bullock, sat on a colorful blanket half covering the beast. Two saddlebags were strapped on behind him. Huge horns stuck out front like oversized car ornaments. Preceding them and carefully picking his way down the crude trail was a half-clothed Indian, holding a taut rope attached to a large brass ring in the animal's nose. They stopped near the hangar and Tatahiera and the blanket gracefully slipped off the bullock. On the bullock, Tataheira looked formidable. Now he stood a mere five-and-a-half feet high, but his large-brimmed sombrero made him appear taller. He reminded me of a diminutive *Rasputin.* His black, bushy unkempt beard was a stark contrast to his once white linen suit, now stained and rumpled, but still the badge of the Brazilian *jefe* boss. He ambled side to side as if it were a hardship to walk, which it must have been after riding bush trails two days on a bullock.

To our surprise and relief his visit appeared to be a purely social one. He said we were the first neighbors since he moved into his house twenty years earlier. He brought some bloody freshly cut beef, dripping as he extracted it from his saddlebags. Harry quickly took it before Jan could say no to the unappetizing pieces of flesh. He also presented us with blended Brazilian coffee. He couldn't offer sugar—he was short at the moment because he hadn't made his four-day trip to the frontier town of Boa Vista this month.

That was my cue to be neighborly. I sent Dutch to our store to bag up twenty pounds from our hundred-kilo bag of local Demerara dark brown sugar. He was grateful and thanked us several times. He described the difficult trips to get his supplies of sugar, flour, rice, tinned butter, khaki shirts and pants, shoes, gasoline, compressor oil for his diamond prospecting crews, and the exorbitant prices he had to pay and the losses incurred in route.

I calculated our plane could keep our operation financially healthy by supplying the diamond crews with rations, clothes, and equipment. Tataheira would become our first Brazilian customer. We drank demitasses of the strong Brazilian coffee, heavily laced with our brown sugar. Later we switched to tea and biscuits Jan prepared while we discussed the problems of living far from supply sources.

We gave him a tour of our house. He was surprised to see the modern conveniences: solar-heating for the kitchen and shower, kerosene stove, a fridge that made ice, indoor flush toilet, and particularly the Collins transmitter and receiver. He asked many questions about how and who we talked with. Later, we served him a Dewars' scotch on the rocks. It was the first scotch with ice since his trip to Boa Vista two months ago. His eyes rolled in ecstasy as he savored each sip. I gave him a bottle to take back with him and I think that sealed a friendship.

Later in the afternoon after Tataheira left, Harry came up all smiles.

"I think we made a friend. He wants us to come to his house next month. Several years ago he started an airstrip near his ranch, but no planes were in the area. He never finished it. Says he can complete it in three weeks, and when it's ready he'll hang a stocking so you can see the wind. He bought supplies in Dutch's store and couldn't believe the prices. Here's a list to bring when you fly over. I charged him the going rate of 30 cruzieros to the B.G. dollar. It won't be a problem receiving his cruzieros. We can buy Brazilian hammocks and diamond sieves—they're the best. No one uses the ones made in B.G. They're not efficient and they wear out fast." Harry was clearly relieved that we *won over* Tataheira and wouldn't have a war on our hands. "But he 's got a bad reputation, so we better keep our guard up," he repeated for the third time, still not completely convinced about Tataheira's intentions.

Three weeks later Tataheira's Indian brought word the airstrip was ready and would we please come visit. It was an invitation we couldn't politely refuse. Jan stayed; Harry and I went. It was a seven-minute flight. Harry reminded me the same trip was a two-day hard walk.

I flew in low and slow to inspect the runway, and made two passes that scattered dogs and cattle in all directions.

"It looks pretty good Harry. It's lined up directly into the wind. Shouldn't be a problem. Tighten up your belt, we're going in."

If Harry was nervous, he didn't show it. We swung around the little valley surrounded by small hills. I used full flaps, touched down, bounced once, and with runway to spare came to a halt. We opened our door to a welcoming committee of dogs barking, chickens, sheep, and people ranging from babies in their mother's slings to old men barely able to walk. Everyone talked and greeted us at once. My inadequate grasp of Portuguese was only good enough to know they were inviting us to the house and Harry confirmed it.

As we entered, I felt the mood change instantly: no smiles, no brazos. Instead, a sea of sullen faces. The women disappeared to the back room. I could feel the bad vibes. My first thought was this was an ambush and we walked right into it. The adrenaline hit me like a shot in the arm. I looked over to Harry. He looked upset…this was not good. Harry leaned over to me and whispered, "Don, when you enter someone's house it's customary to take off your gun. You're making them nervous."

I scanned the room. None of the men had guns. A pile of pistols and ammunition belts were hanging on wooden hooks near the door. Harry's pistol and belt were on top. I felt foolish, put on the biggest smile I could muster and said, *"Perdonne,* excuse." I loosened my holster belt and placed it on top of Harry's. The change was instantaneous—the men laughed and the women returned. We talked and drank many coffeezinas. The rest of the visit was uneventful. We felt relieved that we filled an obligation and remained on good terms with the notorious Tataheira, a person who could be a serious problem.

Several months later his Indian showed up sweaty and out of breath. He traveled all night on the dark ill-defined trails, across rivers with swirling rapids, and on paths with snakes waiting for unsuspecting game along the river. Nighttime travel was a survival test. His visit must be important. He pulled an envelope from a waterproof pouch and handed it to me.

"Tataheira, Tataheira."

Fortunately, Harry was there to translate the note.

"Don, looks like Tataheira is really sick. They don't know what's wrong. They think he may be dying. He's in bed, severe pain, sweating, fever, can't even walk. They want you to come."

"Jeez, Harry, what can I do? I'm not a doctor. We've got a small medical kit, a few emergency pills, but that's about it. This is a *catch 22.* He looked puzzled. *"Catch 22* means no matter what you do you lose. If I don't go it's a real snub for someone asking for help. If he lives, he'll never forget it. If I go, what are the chances I can help? I've had several first aid courses, but they were mostly for accidents and this doesn't sound like one. They didn't say he hurt himself, so it must be a virus, malaria, food poisoning, or God knows what. He really needs a doctor and there isn't one within a hundred miles."

After much discussion of the pros and cons, Jan quietly said, "You really don't have a choice. You have to go and do the best you can. Let's hope it works out."

She knew the risks of being here by herself. Our plane was the only transportation. Walking out with Diana was hardly an option.

"Take our pills and medicine chest. With three years of pre-med you were about to become a doctor. Here's your chance to practice. Look at it this way—he's got a better chance if you're there."

She was trying to make light of it and I appreciated how hard it was for her to say that. She would be left behind again and would wonder what was happening until she heard the friendly drone of our engine, if and when it came.

I nodded. "Yes, I suppose I have to go."

In less than an hour, I was back at Tataheira's airstrip, walking to his ranch house and accompanied by several of his rough looking vaqueros, all talking at once. They took me to the house and straight to the rear bedroom. Propped up in his bed, Tataheira looked terrible: nightshirt in array, hair tousled, and three women standing alongside holding towels and a bowl. He was sweating profusely. He feebly raised his hand in recognition, his face revealed deep pain.

"Obrigado, thanks, for coming. Can you help me? I have fever," and he touched his forehead." And a bad, bad pain here." He placed his hand on his big belly. I followed his lead and touched his forehead with my palm. It radiated heat, a high fever. My first thought was malaria.

"Do you feel very cold sometimes?" I asked.

He shook his head no. It was an ordeal to talk and whatever he had, it was bad. If no chills, he didn't have malaria. I touched his belly. He said the pain was not outside but deep inside. My hand went from side to side up and down. When I reached the lower right side and probed deeper, he let out an involuntary cry. It was localized in his right lower abdomen. This probably was the only medical problem I could diagnose—appendicitis.

I had it at the University of Wisconsin and it started with a general stomachache. As it progressed, it localized to the right lower abdomen, just as his had. I wasn't about to do a rectal check. He seemed to be in the advanced stage and that meant getting him to a hospital and quick. A burst appendix back here would be fatal. I ordered his men to make a crude stretcher while I ran to the plane and removed the seats. They brought him, eased him onto the floor and in minutes we were airborne. I looked back. Tataheira was stretched out in the back and gave me a weak smile and wave. For such a tough hombre, I thought, he sure looks vulnerable.

I called B.G. Airways' emergency channel explaining the problem and the need to land at the private airstrip of Ogle, Booker's Sugar Estate, and thirty miles closer to Georgetown than Atkinson International Airport. As I approached the small airstrip, I could make out the ambulance waiting at the hangar. I landed and taxied alongside. From my first day in South America, I experienced the worst of government bureaucracy—paragons of inefficiency and indifference. This trip proved to be the opposite. Customs and Immigration were waiting on the airstrip behind the ambulance.

This time the agencies could be proud of how they rose to the occasion. The ambulance crew opened my door before I shut down the engine. In record-breaking time they had Tataheira out of the plane, into the ambulance, and on the way. Customs and Immigration invited me to join them in their car following the ambulance, while I gave them the requested information. I fully expected they would demand passports, visas, or written documentation, ad infinitum, while Tataheira died waiting in the ambulance. None of that. There was not a minute lost. My respect for British Guiana and their government went up many notches.

We went directly to the hospital. Immigration, customs, and the ambulance driver were smiling, proud to be included in this unusual mercy mission. Three hours after being examined by me at his ranch, Tataheira was operated on in the Georgetown hospital. The appendix ruptured as they touched it but since the staff was prepared, they cleaned it, continued the operation, and within minutes had him stitched up.

I waited in his room while he came out of the anesthetic. He didn't know a word of English and the nurses not a word of Portuguese. His biggest concern was how he was going to pay the hospital and doctors. Being a self-made man, he was very uncomfortable in situations where he wasn't in control and was quite relieved when I told him it was all taken care of—I paid the bills. All he had to do was recover so we could be on our way. This big old curmudgeon gunslinger actually had tears in his eyes. He held my hand and didn't let go for quite awhile. His recovery was amazing. But I don't think he fully relaxed until we landed at his airstrip two days later.

I opened the airplane door. He struggled to get out, refusing any help. I knew why. Tataheira did not want to look vulnerable or weak in front of his men and family. He slowly, carefully, and painstakingly walked up to his ranch. They all cheered. In the excitement, I quietly reinstalled my back seats, took off and arrived home minutes later. I told Jan the details. She had no idea what happened in the two-day absence. As John Milton knew, hers was the really hard part: *They also serve, who only stand and wait.*

After that incident, the word was out from Tatahiera: "No one, but no one gives the American and his family any problem or he will have Tataheira to deal with!" And we heard he drew his finger across his neck while he made that declaration. There was no mistaking his intention. For many months he sent notes of deep appreciation, accompanied by quarters of fresh beef, legs of lamb, and eggs.

Life for the Haacks became easier and safer with the addition of one more insurance policy for survival in a hostile environment.

THE END OF 94 BRAVO

O ur second mining year at Marquis was ending and diamond production still proved erratic. Life in the jungle with Indian neighbors became routine, and gave us a false sense of complacency. Nothing was routine in bush life, but after surviving the first year and a half's obstacles, we felt we were over the worst. How wrong we were.

Father Quigley was scheduled to arrive on his semi-annual pilgrimage to the villages. I flew to Good Hope to meet his DC-3. It discharged Father and his strange array of baggage: two well-used inexpensive imitation leather suitcases held together with straps; a flour sack bulging at the seams with everything imaginable in it, except flour; a Brazilian blue and white striped bag—cloth on the outside and rubber lined that everyone who traveled the bush carried to keep personals from getting wet. Dutch, who couldn't swim, tied his bag to his wrists when he crossed rivers. If he stepped into a hole or slipped, the bag saved him from drowning. He called it his Jesus bag…but not in front of Father.

Donald Haack

The previous Monday, Harry came in to tell us that the crews were producing a few more diamonds. With the increased dredging more supplies and gasoline were needed. The pickup of Father Quigley at Karasabai was scheduled for late afternoon, so I decided to make an earlier run to Good Hope for gas and cargo. After the short flight, I came in low over the Good Hope airstrip to clear the cattle off the runway. On the down leg of the landing pattern I noticed the dust of Caesar's jeep coming from the ranch house. Great! He was going to meet me there and I was thankful. Loading up the plane alone was a chore, but refueling from barrels was much more difficult. The gasoline transported by BG Airways came in fifty-five gallon steel drums weighing 390 pounds each. To refuel, I had to lift the barrel into an upright position, break the seal, and unscrew the bung using a special tool. I used a hand pump to fill a jerry can, which I lifted onto a barrel, then climbed on the barrel and heaved the jerry can on top of the wing. Balancing the can at head height, I poured the gas through a chamois-covered funnel into the wing tank. The chamois on the funnel kept water from passing into the tank but it also slowed the filling. Holding a forty-pound jerry can was not much fun. With Caesar on the way, things were looking up.

I landed and taxied to the storage hut as Caesar braked to a halt in a cloud of dust. He had on a bright red tam tilted rakishly, a patterned dark short-sleeved shirt, khaki trousers and white tennis shoes. He could easily be mistaken for a Basque separatist in Spanish mountain country. The effect was complete when he reached into his pocket, extracted a packet of French Galois cigarettes, tapped one out, and clenched it in his teeth.

"Nice short landing. Getting better. Next time you won't make a pass and you will land on top of my cattle." He faced downwind, lit his cigarette, took a deep draw and exhaled it through clenched teeth stained from years of strong tobacco. I didn't know if he was complimenting or complaining. I let it pass.

"Thanks. Don't suppose I could get a hand gassing up, do you?"

"Course, why else would I come out? It's too early for tea; you didn't bring Yan, so you didn't come to socialize. Ya, I'll help. Which barrel do you want?"

None were started so we picked a fresh one, rolled it over to the plane, and heaved it upright. Using a two-foot extension wrench for leverage it took our combined full strength to unscrew the reluctant cap.

"Must have been Moose who screwed on this cap," I said after it was finally loose. Moose was the six foot six inch black man at Shell oil who filled the barrels. I secured the chamois onto the funnel with bailing wire while Caesar inserted the pump and attached a ten-foot hose. I jumped on top of the barrel, opened the wing tank, inserted the funnel, and held the hose above the chamois. Caesar pumped three or four strokes. Out came brown crud and dark liquid.

"Hold up. It's filthy." The chamois had gunk and brown-looking slime on it. I pulled out the funnel and hit it upside down against my other hand. Most of dirt fell out.

"God, looks like they never cleaned those barrels. Good thing you have the chamois or that would be in your tank. Any water or just dirt?" Caesar asked.

"No water sitting on top so I guess it was just dirt and that brown rusty slime." I hit the funnel a few more time and picked out the dirty pieces that clung to the chamois. We tilted the barrel and wedged a rock below allowing any water and dirt to stay on one side. With Caesar pumping, we didn't need jerry cans and were finished in less than twenty minutes. I checked my list for loading: two bags of flour, 220 pound bag of raw brown sugar freshly pressed and dripping sticky sugar syrup, a case of corned beef, six cartons of local Guytan cigarettes, a five gallon tin of cooking oil, a half bag of rock salt for jerking—drying—fish, a tin of ground pepper, a box of number seven canvas shoes for our divers, matches and two cases of beer. The last to go was one barrel of gas for the dredge.

The hot tropical sun was taking its toll, and we were both sweating profusely when we finished. I could feel the drain of energy. Caesar, in good shape but twenty years my senior, felt it even more.

We sat under the wing for a few minutes to cool down. Thankfully the trade winds helped cool us and eased the discomfort of the merciless sun. The countryside was dry as a bone for six months—normal at four degrees above the equator. Caesar looked at me and quietly said, "Only mad dogs and Englishmen stay out in the tropical mid-day sun."

"How true...and a stray American and Russian thrown in for good measure," I added.

I got up, did a quick pre-flight inspection, took out my clear beaker, and drained some fuel from both tanks. No water showed up.

"Thanks for the help. I'm going to drop this cargo at Marquis, then fly to Karasabai and bring Fr. Quigley to our house. Tipuru Indians will take him to their village first thing in the morning. He'll return to our house in three or four days and then we'll come back here. If it's all right, Jan may come along for tea. She needs a change and Nellie's female companionship. She's super-saturated with man talk and mining. Oh, by the way, brought you some avocados." I said the right thing; avocados were worth their weight in gold in this country. I took the burlap bag out of the luggage compartment and handed it to him.

He grinned. "Thanks, we'll enjoy and think of you. Bring Yan."

I climbed into the plane, cranked up the engine, taxied a few yards, and took off. Caesar was shaking his head because I didn't do a check on each magneto. He was a purist. I was in a hurry to get on home for my last flight and call it a day. I cleared the fence by fifty feet, eased back on the throttle and headed north on a compass heading of 350 degrees.

I came in on a final approach to Marquis and settled onto the grass without a bump, *a greaser*. I taxied to a stop in front of the hangar and cut the engine. Fifteen minutes later, with the help of Domingo, I had the plane unloaded and I walked back to the house where Jan was doing laundry, mostly nappies, diapers. With Diney not potty trained, we were knee-deep in nappies.

I told her I was going to Karasabai to pick up Fr. Quigley and should be back in less than an hour. Ramdat, our East Indian boy, could clean up the spare bedroom before Father arrived. We kissed and I left.

The plane was empty and I taxied, this time checking both mags, to the end of the runway. Engine failure here wouldn't provide the luxury of putting the plane down on open savannah as it would at Good Hope. Marquis, surrounded by mountains and dense bush, provided no soft landing spots. I checked the gas tanks. Left was full, right was three-fourths. I switched to the full left tank, ran up the engine, and was airborne in less than half the runway and continued straight ahead until I had altitude, then started my slow turn to the right. The mountain in front was too high to fly over but to the right lay a valley only visible after a right turn behind the foothills that hid that valley from the airstrip. Passengers who flew with me the first time wondered how in the world we were going to climb out of a valley completely surrounded by mountains.

I started the turn at a thousand feet past the end of the runway; all gauges showed A-okay. Then there was a deathly silence. The engine cut off! I couldn't continue my turn. The hill between the strip and me took out that option. Every second counted. This is where pre-planning paid off. I had rehearsed this scenario many times and didn't have to consider my options. I knew what they were…and they were not good.

Instinctively, I threw the plane into a steep left turn and dropped the nose to keep the airspeed up to prevent stalling. Airspeed showed 85. Marginal, but enough. In the steep bank I glanced through the roof window and could see the airstrip, confirming it was too far to return. I also knew I would lose the airplane—that hit with the impact of a punch in the gut. I pushed that thought out of my mind. Priority: get the plane down in one piece and walk away.

Donald Haack

Crashes become fatalities when pilots attempt the impossible: trying to save the plane when it can't be saved and performing hopeless maneuvers resulting in stalls and uncontrolled crashes. I focused on one thing only—get this baby down in a controlled crash. There was never a doubt I was going down, but I needed to increase the odds in my favor by choosing where and how.

From past observations, I knew of one small clearing dead ahead. Seconds later I saw it slightly to my left. Hoping for a re-start, I switched tanks, pulled on half flaps and steered for the hole. I was too high. Over-shooting was as bad as missing altogether. I had to kill airspeed and height, not easy. I gave one more futile try at starting the engine. Nothing. No more options. Going down.

I pulled on full flaps, reduced airspeed to sixty-five, fifty, only ten above stall—still too fast. I crossed controlled aileron and rudder. The plane slipped sideways like a wounded eagle, nose pointing right, and left wing down in one helluva sideslip. I plummeted downward without gaining speed. One high tree loomed ahead. I straightened the sideslip, pulled back on the stick, gained a few yards to clear the tree and then back into a sideslip to a few feet above the ground. If I hit side-slipping I'd have a major crash. Not a good option. I straightened out. Large rocks I hadn't seen from above were coming up fast. At this rate I would slam into them.

I cut the ignition switch to reduce the chance of a fire and unlatched the door so it wouldn't jam shut. I didn't know how bad this was going to be but it wasn't going to be good. *Air speed too high*. I pushed the stick forward. The wheels hit hard. A bad bounce and back in the air. I had to stop before the rocks. *Forward on the stick*. I put on the brakes. I could have saved that effort. The left wheel hit. A bad crunch. I was flung forward against the stick, my left hand bounced hard against the instrument panel and I wondered if it broke my wrist. The plane lurched sideways and forward. The left wheel sheared, the nose dug into the ground. I bounced back and forth inside the cabin, testing the seat belt to its limit. The tail went up and I was looking straight down into grass.

Dirt and dust swirled all around like a miniature tornado. Instead of flipping upside down, the plane hung on end, the tail straight up and teetering as if to go over any moment. I wanted out and fast. I unhooked my seat belt and eased open the door. The airframe above my head was buckled. The wing and landing gear absorbed most of the impact, stopping the plane scant yards before the rocks.

I slid out, grabbing my emergency bag and machete to get clear as quickly as possible. The smell of petrol was overwhelming. One of the tanks or lines must have ruptured and with all these fumes, there wouldn't be a fire, but an explosion. I wanted away. I fell, got up, and fell down again. I wondered if I had broken a leg and the shock kept me from feeling anything. Nothing hurt badly. When I started crawling, I realized how uneven the terrain was. In the high grass, everything looked flat. There were rocks and hard earth hummocks two feet high that sheared the left wheel before the wing hit.

When I reached the end of the clearing, I stopped to look back. Our pretty little dependable Super Cub—friendly, forgiving, our lifeline—all crumpled. Tail in the air, bird-like broken wing no longer fluttering. A dead bird. I tried to be thankful. I was alive and apparently okay. Didn't feel any broken bones. Lots of bruises, sores, and a couple of cuts, but otherwise okay. Looking at the crumpled Cub made me want to weep. What would Jan say and feel? She learned to fly on 94 Bravo, too. It was a special plane, a friend with a spirit of its own. It brought us through so many tight pinches.

Thinking of Jan brought me back to reality and the necessity to move out. She would have heard the engine suddenly stop after takeoff and would have seen the plane go into a steep dive disappearing at the foot of the mountain. I don't think she knew of this clearing and would assume I landed in the trees or worse, a crash and fire. I had to get back to let her know I was okay. That could take hours, though I knew she would direct Domingo and the other Indians to cut a path in the bush towards where the plane was last seen.

Donald Haack

I checked my emergency pack and removed the pistol. I pushed in a clip, pointed in the air and fired off two rounds. That broke the silence with a resounding roar. I hoped the high trees didn't deaden the sound, keeping it from being heard in the valley. I didn't fire three shots, the emergency distress signal. It would indicate I was injured. Two shots would let them know I was alive and well, or at least as well as one could be having lost an airplane in the middle of nowhere.

I fired two more rounds and stuck it back in the bag. I found my leather gloves and put on the right one. I had plenty of chopping to do to get out of here and I didn't want hand blisters to slow me down. I checked the compass to get an accurate heading, and then stumbled across the opening, taking one last look at 94 Bravo. I felt a pang of guilt as if leaving a wounded friend. I turned and started hacking away at the thick vines along the edge of the opening. The physical effort quickly took my mind off the loss.

The thickest brush was where the sun shone on the edge of the clearing, allowing the undergrowth to thrive, something it couldn't do under the canopy of the larger trees. That undergrowth was almost impenetrable, and would have been without a machete. A half hour later with only a few yards of progress, I finally broke through the thickest growth and into the dark canopy of the two hundred foot high tropical trees. It took several minutes adjusting to the darker jungle. Time now became an important factor. I had no conception how long it would take to reach our airstrip. The twelve seconds by air could take several hours by foot depending on the thickness of the bush. The sun would set in less than four. I established the machete cutting rhythm the Venezuelan Arawak Indians taught me: chose the bush you wanted to cut, aim for it, and don't swing randomly. The middle of the blade is the cutting point: too far towards the tip will cause it to bounce, too close in and it will extract a jarring pain to the arm or wrist. A few of those and your hand goes numb, incapable of holding the machete. I started each swing in an arc with an easy rhythm, down to the left, down to the right at knee height. Too low and the sharp stub could impale your foot. Too high, and you risk stabbing your hand or arm on the back swing. The Arawaks taught me to let the weight of the arm and body do the work. The trick was to find a pace that felt comfortable for hours of cutting. Without this finely tuned choreography, fatigue comes quickly and could prove fatal in this unforgiving tropical forest.

I concentrated first on timing and body balance. Soon the rhythm came easily like an old dance step. My mind went into neutral picking out each victim—vine or bush that impeded my progress, a miniature war game. The bush wanted to hold me back. I wanted to get through with the least effort. An hour passed. I mentally set a goal of fifty more steps before a break and drink of water. I was sweating profusely. Heat stroke became a possibility that I couldn't risk. The place I stopped had no heavy vines, offering a bonus of a few clear yards. The water refreshed me and I relaxed for a moment.

I don't know if I heard something, detected movement, or whether an inner instinct alerted me. I froze. The threat was a few paces ahead where I would've stepped if I hadn't stopped for a drink. There were three coils and a big head facing me, slowly rising from the ground cover. It was a dreaded bushmaster, an enormous snake with more venom than any rattler. Unlike rattlers, it grows to lengths up to ten feet. Most snakes strike at the leg, but the large bushmaster when uncoiled can use his length to strike chest or head level, quite often injecting a lethal dose of venom. I shifted my weight backwards to my left foot, grabbed the machete with both hands, like a bat in the bunt position ready for the strike. The black eyes didn't leave mine as the snake continued to rise. My heart, already pounding from strenuous cutting, went into a double-quick beat from the adrenalin kicking in for knife-edge awareness. It was like a batter waiting and looking at a pitcher for a sign. Only this pitcher had no expression. I wondered if there would be any telegraphed signal as a boxer may inadvertently reveal with a weight change or a flexed muscle. I couldn't see any signs in this opponent. Worse, I wasn't sure I had the reflex to stop or slice into a striking snake only a few feet away.

I wondered if he knew how vulnerable I felt. Neither of us took his eyes off the other. I eased back onto my right foot, increasing the distance between us, a slight advantage for me. If he were ten feet long, it was still his game. No longer rising, he remained at a five-foot height, one helluva formidable sight since I was looking only slightly down at him. I had never seen a snake that large or high off the ground in striking position.

I continued inching back. Whatever made him hesitate, gave me the slight advantage of distance, now about six feet, but it was as far as I could go in that little clearing. I pushed back against some heavy brush that didn't give. I eased forward a little for room to swing if he struck, which I expected he would. I poised, raised my machete a little more for a downward slice. Our eyes were locked and our bodies rigid as two statues. I wondered what or if he was thinking. We were frozen in time and remained there for minutes, though they stretched into mental eternity.

His head moved. I tensed to swing. He didn't move to strike; instead he lowered slightly. Or was I imagining it? We were still eye-to-eye. In relation to the bush he was dropping down, but it was impossible to detect muscle motion on his body. He receded like a piece of stage scenery until I could only see two coils. For whatever reason this bushmaster decided not to attack. I was thankful and quietly said so. Maybe he sensed I had enough problems for one day and we both didn't need this confrontation. For whatever reason, I was grateful and gave thanks to whomever or whatever was looking after me, particularly for the water stop that kept me from stepping further into the snake's domain.

When my breathing and heart rate returned to a semblance of normality, I backtracked in a wide detour to the right. I wanted no excuse for a second encounter.

A half-hour of cutting later I heard the first hoot from an Indian. In response, I called, whistled, and hooted. They answered. After a few minutes Domingo broke through, smiling ear to ear. He was talking Macusi and Brazilian so fast I couldn't understand a word. He kept saying "the missus" and pointing. Looking behind him, I saw Jan, machete in hand, dripping wet, hair disheveled. She never looked so good.

"Are you all right?" were her first words, as she looked me over before giving me a big hug. When she was convinced I was in one piece, she pulled back and looked at me questioningly. I knew what she was asking.

I shook my head. "No, 94 Bravo is gone." She bit her lip. "I'm just glad you're okay. I saw you go down after I heard the engine stop. I didn't know what to think, but could only imagine the worst. She hugged me closer and was crying softly.

"It's okay, let's go home." We headed back hand-in-hand toward the house.

THE NEW PLANE

After the loss of 94B, we settled down in our house. The mining stopped. We had to conserve all supplies, especially fuel for the generator. We told the Indians that without a plane we could no longer employ them. The exceptions were the diamond prospecting crew and the family who helped Jan with the laundry and cleaning. We didn't know how long it would be before, or even whether, we would be able to replace our plane.

Ten days after the accident, Fr. Quigley showed up on our doorstep. He was on his return trip from Tipuru, concerned about our safety, and asked what he could do to help. He explained that after he heard about our plane crashing, he walked to Tipuru, spent a couple of days with George, the teacher and then re-routed to our house to see what he could do for us.

My first question to him was how in the world did he know that we crashed? The note I received from him by runner early the next morning was dated and written the same afternoon the plane went down.

It didn't seem strange to him. He explained, "It's the old *bush telegram* communication the Amerindians use, what we call ESP, Extra Sensory Perception. It works perfectly well for them. They communicate over any distance when there's a need, emergency or important event. My theory is that there has to be some intensity of emotions before the system works. The plane crash certainly was a strongly emotional event, particularly since the Indians were expecting you to pick me up at Karasabai."

I told him whenever we flew to Good Hope to visit the Gorinskys, the Indians advised Nellie before we arrived. Same thing when we visited the McTurks at Karanambo. They knew the minute we made the decision and Connie McTurk put on extra desserts and tea for us.

Fr. Quigley thought for a moment and then said, "The plane arriving in this country is a very big event, especially since yours is the first. I suspect after you're here for a while, it will become commonplace and they may or may not communicate your comings and goings as they do now. But then, that's only my theory."

To his question about how he could help us or have food brought in, I assured him we were all right. We would hunt and fish and had a supply of basics. I told him we had received a cable in our Georgetown office from my brother that the insurance has been expedited and they expected to have another plane down here within two weeks. I was realistic enough to know that would be a month to six weeks and we were okay for that period of time.

The priest said a special mass for us in the morning, wished us well and was on his way. He didn't want to impose on our food supply any more than he had to. We were sorry to see him go. He was our last link with civilization for the next several weeks.

Five weeks later, my brother, Bob, and his pilot, Ernie Argentati landed at Marquis. They were the first visitors since Father Quigley. It was a grand sight. We ran out to greet them on the airstrip. The blue and white plane had a tricycle landing gear. I learned to fly with a tail-dragger and the sight of the tricycle gear gave me a momentary tinge of disappointment.

The two stepped out of the plane in front of the hangar and

greeted us. It was an intensely emotional reunion. We were glad to see my brother and he was glad to see that we were alive, uninjured and in good spirits. Ernie, the pilot, was a big guy, Italian descent and a more likable person would be hard to find. He quickly assured me that the Piper Tri-Pacer with the extra horsepower and space was better than our *tail dragger* and—it had four seats. He had already gone over this subject and convinced Bob.

The first two nights in Marquis were spent re-hashing the crash and what we thought caused it. I gave a detailed explanation about removing the damaged plane's engine, which the natives carried to our hangar where I stripped it down to find the cause of engine failure. I didn't have far to search. The carburetor was completely filled with water. I was at a loss as to how it became contaminated. Caesar helped me fuel and we used a chamois, which kept out the rusty dirt when we started pumping. It didn't make sense. I thought about it for days and then one morning I woke up remembering the similar problem we had on our first trip up to Marquis in our boat. After we pulled the engine out of the water, Harry and I filtered the gas through a chamois and still found water in the tank. That didn't make sense but we didn't have time to analyze why not. The following day we filtered the gas through the same chamois and it kept out the water.

With that thought, I returned to the hangar. I first ran gas through the chamois and then poured a mixture of gas and water. The water stayed on top, as it should have. I took a second chamois, wet it with water and repeated the experiment. This time no water on top...it passed right through. I just learned a hard lesson that a dry chamois or one *wet with gas* will strain out water. A chamois cloth that is *first soaked with water* will allow water to pass through. Checking with other pilots, I discovered no one knew that.

The trip Bob and Ernie took down the Windward and Leeward Islands to deliver our plane lasted five days, so we had a blow-by-blow description of all they went through as they left Florida for the two thousand mile trip. Over the years we would fly that trip many times but that was the first one and held the most excitement.

I felt thankful we had Ernie with all his experience and common sense to pave the way for us. Ernie thoroughly checked me out in the Tri-Pacer until he was convinced I felt comfortable with the new plane. He was aghast to learn I was bush flying without an instrument rating or some instrument flight training. He took an extra few days to check me out in "blind" flying—using only instruments in cloud conditions—and some *caveats* on the more serious pitfalls, particularly, the graveyard spin. That training would save my life.

Three months later I was flying above scattered clouds, and due to icing, the engine power cut down dramatically forcing me to slowly descend into thick clouds. Unknowingly, I went into a graveyard spiral, a steep descending turn. The altimeter indicated the plane was plummeting down, the airspeed increased. The natural instinct was to slow down by pulling back on the wheel. But pulling back would tighten the turn and increase the spiral. If the wings didn't tear off from excessive forces, it was usually too late to pull out before hitting the ground. That's why they call it a *graveyard spiral*. I remembered Ernie's advice and training: "Before anything else, get your plane straight and level with the turn-and-bank instrument, then slowly pull back on the wheel." Ernie, with his perseverance and insistence, saved my life.

KARASABAI

One morning Harry came up to the house to tell me we were short of men to work the dredge.

"Is it possible to fly over to Karasabai village to see if we can find any men to work for us? It's only a few minutes flying. I know the *tuchow* and he may help...we're short on divers. Two men left in the middle of the night again. I paid them yesterday. Should've expected it," he said it apologetically.

"You know, maybe Jan would like to fly along. It's an easy flight and the men have mentioned that the women in the village want to meet Diana and her. They can't believe the stories about a white baby with white hair and blue eyes. They say only old ladies have white hair. How can a baby have it? Lot of talk in the whole village. It's Sunday, we're shut down and Jan might enjoy meeting her neighbors," he said it with a twinkle in his eye. He knew I couldn't refuse the idea of visiting the nearby village and it would give Jan a day away from the house and washing nappies. She was getting cabin fever. We didn't get to Good Hope the past weekend. The Gorinskys were visiting friends across the river in

Normandie, Brazil. Harry's idea sounded like fun.

"You're right. She'll welcome the change, any change!"

A half-hour later Diana, Jan, Harry and I buckled up in the plane. It was a typical tropical day: a slight trade wind blowing, clear sky, and a few cumulous to break up the flat blue and give a bit of texture to the beautiful scenery.

Minutes later we were leaving the Ireng River and flying up the valley. Ten miles further east we turned south into the pass where the Karasabai valley opened up. I glanced at the altimeter. We were the same elevation as Marquis. I stored that for future reference if I needed it for instrument flying.

As many times as I flew this route, I never ceased to be amazed by the startling transition from rolling thick lush green jungle to open dry flat brown savannah country. Karasabai was the northernmost savannah of the Rupununi territory that extended a hundred miles south along Brazil. The Ireng River was the border and in that few minutes of flying we had crossed the frontier three times as we descended into the Karasabai valley. The village was located on the east side of the fifteen-mile valley. Lush growth and mountains bordered the valley perimeter. The airstrip, a mile in length, wasn't hard to spot ten miles out.

"Harry, I'm going to make one pass over the airstrip just to make sure nothing is on it and there are no holes, or if there are, I want to make sure I avoid them," I shouted over the roar of the engine. I walked over the strip two weeks ago when I dropped off Father Quigley and told the *tuchow* that if his men filled in some of those holes, I would bring in the family. That was pretty big news for them. They were excited and I'm sure they filled in every hole on the strip. But I'll check it anyway. We can't take any chances. This plane is the lifeline of the business.

The locals heard us coming a long way out and the children had already run the length of the strip chasing off horses, cattle, chickens, dogs, and pigs. I made a low level pass—it looked like one of the best airstrips in the savannah.

We taxied a short distance before we were surrounded by hundreds of curious faces, young and old. Other than my pickups and drop-offs of Father Quigley and the bishop, we were the only plane to land in the past twelve years. This would be the first meeting of the "white man family." What a welcome! Everybody from the village was there to greet us.

The Macusis had never seen blond hair or blue eyes, so our one-year-old Diana was like a goddess to the Amerindian women. They passed her from mother to mother amidst squeals, laughter, and grunts of amazement. I thought Jan showed remarkable restraint. Diana, bless her loving soul, thought it was a great game and smiled. The *tuchow* thought we were special, coming out of the sky in our own airplane; but to bring along a blond, blue-eyed baby really rang his bell. Amidst all the chaos, Harry explained that since this was the first visit, we would have to meet everyone.

"Don, you must do this. It is a big honor for the village. Nothing has ever happened like this before and the *tuchow* is making a big speech to the villagers that this is a good omen for them. To refuse their hospitality would be a big insult to him and his people, particularly because the *tuchow* chief explained we were their new neighbors." Harry translated as the Tuchow rambled on.

"Neighbors? Jeez, Harry, we're at least twenty miles away. That's got to be a two-day walk or more. Neighbors?"

"Good Hope ranch is fifty miles south with a mountain range in between. Tipuru village is forty miles north with two river crossing and lots of bush in between. You're now their closest neighbors," he said.

The enormity of the territory took on a new meaning.

"Twenty miles away and we're their closest neighbors." I shook my head in amazement. Harry pushed back his leather hat and smiled.

"It's a little bit different than the States, isn't it? You'll get used to describing places in days walking, not in miles. Probably going to be different for you. Your plane takes about ten minutes for every day walking on the ground...and that's on *easy* terrain. When you and I flew up to Monkey Mountain and met John Roth that was fifteen minutes flying. No one ever walked that in less than five days. That's *rugged* country with lots of rivers. The plane's going to change a lot of things back here

The *tuchow* was sermonizing. Whatever he was saying and probably taking credit for, he had an attentive audience. He was in a peak of enthusiasm, at least as much as could be expected for someone who ordinarily had a stone face, Fu Manchu mustache, and hardly ever cracked a smile. He must be very unhappy, I was thinking.

He stopped abruptly, came over to us, said something to Harry and then led the way expecting us to follow. We did, in single line, Indian fashion. We spent a half-day going to every house in the village. This valley partially screened the trade winds and we could tell the difference. It was hot and dusty. The houses weren't particularly clean. Some of the women wore cheap print cloth dresses badly in need of washing. The men wore khaki pants in various states of disarray.

We were ushered into the gloom of the first hut. There was little light and coming in from the bright tropical sun, our eyes took a few moments to adjust. Gradually, figures came into view. This was a particularly big house with several older women sitting around a large bowl.

The *tuchow* said something to Harry.

"He wants to make sure you aren't a missionary or would talk to Fr. Quigley. He wants to offer us some *cashas*. The missionaries frown on it. We'll have to accept."

One of the women dipped a clay cup the size of a bowl into the brown liquid and handed it to me. I looked at Harry.

"Sure, Don. It's okay. You can drink some but not too much. We've got a lot of houses to visit and they're all going to make this offering. It's alcoholic and we have to fly back."

I tentatively lifted it up to my lips. It had a strange smell, like malt beer and something else like sour dough. I'm a beer drinker, but this was something I could easily do without. I quickly passed it on to Jan who feigned a sip and handed it to Harry.

"I don't see any artifacts, except cassava squeezers and boards for grating roots. Why not?"

Harry hesitated a moment. " The Macusis had more pride years ago," he answered, and then was briefly quiet, lost in thought.

"Don, a lot has changed since the missionaries came. They do some good but a lot of harm, too. Maybe more harm than good." He was looking up at the Pakaraima Mountains as if he were looking into a picture of the past. Harry was one-quarter Wapashani but with a four-year education in the States, he had the advantage of two totally different cultures spanning one- hundred years.

"Not too many years ago all these villages were much cleaner. The women wore bright beaded aprons and the men wore only a cloth. Some still do in Tipuru village, which is more remote and nearer to your house, so you'll see them for yourself soon. They'll come. They're curious and they're friendly, but they may be demanding of your time." He was diverting from his original story.

"What was it about the missionaries and the Indian cultures that you started telling me?" I reminded him.

He hesitated, apparently contemplating thoughts of past times that caused a deep frown, something I rarely saw in his smiling ruggedly handsome features. He started again, speaking more slowly. This was bringing up some painful memories of a not-so-distant past. Harry's mother was Wapashani, his father, American —mixed emotions, I thought.

"Don, these missionaries were trying to do good, but they just didn't understand the Amerindian ways. We've had a lot of them come through and I guess the best are the Catholic priests but they all make mistakes. After realizing the harm they were doing to the tribal cultures, some changed but in many cases the damage couldn't be undone. When the missionaries first came, they persuaded the Indians it was bad, *a sin*, to go naked. Before long most of them were clothed. They weren't taught hygiene and they didn't have soap to wash their clothes." He was staring into space.

"Indians contracted horrible skin rashes, diseases, and funguses that refused to heal. Everyone was naked in the old days and in and out of water all day and would dry off immediately. They didn't go near water when they wore clothes that stayed wet and uncomfortable."

He looked at me to see if I understood. I nodded. He spoke without rancor, but he was not pleased with the changes that had taken place. I was surprised he wasn't more upset with the missionaries and was waiting to hear about their good services. Harry was a natural raconteur and in due time I would hear the rest of the story. But now he had worked himself up to a state of agitation in remembering the injustices to the Indians, all done in the name of religion

"Even their hunting suffered. An animal could smell a Macusi a mile away when he didn't bathe or change clothes and that affected the amount of game brought back. Many suffered from malnutrition and went to Lethem for medical aid. The District Commissioner investigated the situation and issued a proclamation to the missionaries: Stop clothing the Indians.

"Policing the vast territory proved impossible. Soon the missionaries were clothing them again, justified now, because they taught them about washing and soap. Not quite as bad, but they were better off without clothes." He pulled out his Bowie knife from his belt, slicing slivers from a dry branch, furiously slashing away, which helped vent his anger.

"You know this drink we're having, *cashas*—is made from pressed pulp of the cassava root after it is grated, squeezed and dried. The old ladies of the tribe chew it until it is thoroughly masticated then spit it back in the bowl. They do that all day and let it sit overnight until it ferments into a kind of beer. Well, you can imagine what the missionaries thought of the disgustingly unhygienic, drunken orgies. They were out to save the Indians from their heathen practices. *Cashas* was high on their priorities and stopped them making it."

He looked over at me for some kind of comment. I knew enough not to give opinions until I heard the whole story. This sounded like the missionaries were doing the right thing, but I could tell from Harry's frown that wasn't the answer.

"Well, let me tell you, they damned near wiped out the tribes. The problem occurred so quickly that a high percentage of Indians died and many were in a state of severe debilitation before a team of doctors flew in to find out what caused the catastrophic number of deaths. It turned out to be Beriberi, a severe lack of vitamin B."

He said it again. "Beriberi—simple but deadly. For centuries, the Indians made *cashas* and had their orgies. *Cashas*, that fermented drink, provided the vitamins and minerals that rounded out their nutritionally starved diets." He looked over to me again, only this time he was not smiling. He was waiting for my reaction.

"Harry, back in the States the general public believes the missionaries are doing a fantastic job. It would curl their holy hair if they had any inkling what was really happening in the name of religion. It's a disaster."

"That's not the worst. There were other things just as bad or maybe worse." I looked up at him, almost disbelieving.

"Many men were killed hunting, drowning, or fighting. The women stayed home and were protected. The tribe had a social way to handle that problem. If a man was killed, his widow and family were taken in and provided for by another man—a brother or friend, even though that man already had a wife and family. There simply were not enough men to go around. The wives, welcoming the widows, shared their homes and husbands. It was a society with a conscience. The first missionaries would not tolerate bigamy in any form. They used every trick in the book to ban the custom and for the most part succeeded without giving a thought to what the implications might be…and for the first time in history Amerindian women practiced prostitution—caused by our pious missionaries."

KARONA FALLS

ven though *the curse of gold hill* turned out to be a total bust, Harry's enthusiasm for folklore remained undiminished. He still talked about the ancient burial grounds at Karona Falls, one of two major falls on the Ireng River, and about eight miles west of our house.

"A couple of hundred years ago before white men, and for many generations, the chiefs of Tipuru village dominated other tribes and ruled a large territory. Karona Falls, three hours walking from Tipuru, was where they held their annual *mashramanis*, a meeting of clans to settle inter tribal disputes. The event was accompanied by much feting. Karona falls provided the perfect setting: two thirty-foot falls and numerous small pools. In the dry season when the river receded, fish were trapped in those pools and provided an abundance of food...like the proverbial *catching fish in a fish bowl.*

Part of the ceremony assured a safe journey for the chiefs and peayman who died during the year. In those days Indians adorned themselves with gold. Later when the Indians were exploited or

Donald Haack

killed by white men who came for the yellow metal, the tribes buried the gold and artifacts with the chiefs in the cave behind the waterfall. It was their sacred burial ground. To avoid attracting attention they stopped the ceremonies at the falls, though they still hunt and fish there."

I had to chuckle. "Harry, for God's sake, attract attention? That's one of the most remote areas in this region. Our valley is from nowhere and Karona is even further off the beaten track. I've never seen anyone but Tipuru Indians pass here and certainly no white men. I can't wait to see it but it's a day- long trek there and back from our house."

"I know what you're saying," Harry responded, "but you have to realize that the missionaries came seventy years ago. Some were good, some were bad. Most Indians didn't trust them. They discredited the chiefs and the peaymen, calling them evil witch doctors. That split the tribes; missionaries on one side and elders with traditions on the other. The missionaries caused the tribes to lose most of their skills and heritage."

Jan heard the stories of the Shangri-La Karona falls. When I invited her to come it was a big disappointment to turn the invitation down, but she didn't feel comfortable leaving Diney with natives all day.

"You go with Harry and tell me about it. If it's as pretty as they say it is we'll arrange to go and camp overnight so it wouldn't be a forced march there and back in one day." It sounded sensible, but I knew she really wanted to make the trip.

Harry and I left Marquis at daybreak after Jan fixed us a quick breakfast and handed me a lunch packed the night before. The trail along the Ireng followed the contours of the river, the easiest route since the mountains came right down to the river. By nine o'clock we reached a series of rapids and the Tipuru River, which came through the village twelve miles north. We stopped on the rocks to have our lunch. It was a picture-book setting out of a travelogue. Can Karona be better than this, I wondered?

After an hour and a half of walking, I heard the waterfalls. I didn't expect them to be so loud. We came into the open.

Unbelievable beauty: two sets of thundering falls and rainbows everywhere created from the cool mist that spread in all directions. I was awestruck by the majestic splendor. I understood why the Indians held annual *mashramanis* here. It could very well be their sacred burial grounds. I stopped and stared. Harry understood and didn't say anything. The beauty of these falls untouched by civilization produced an ethereal emotion tinging on the spiritual. As we climbed closer we found it more difficult to talk above the thundering din of water.

"This is about as small as the falls get," Harry shouted. "In rainy season the amount of water is so tremendous the falls extend from bank to bank and become one set of falls instead of the two you see here." It was hard to imagine that much water.

We climbed the banks to the upper falls and looked down. It felt good to be in the sun after four hours of dark bush trails where the only sun fell in bright streaks mid-river. Above the falls, the land opened up into a huge valley. The flat plain extended over twenty miles in three directions.

Harry pointed to the west. "Tatahiera's ranch, the only one in this area, is at the edge of those mountains. Tipuru village is east in that valley. He pointed out an escarpment twenty-five miles on the horizon. Monkey Mountain and John Roth's store lie above that second escarpment. You've been there."

I was mesmerized at the extravagant rough uninhabited beauty. It was as if we were in another world and seeing nature in its purest form.

"See those holes in the rock down there?" He pointed out large circular holes filled with water in the bedrock. "In the turbulent water the big rolling rocks grind out a depression in the bedrock and go deeper and deeper producing those caverns. Look, let's jump down there and I'll show you."

There were twenty or thirty holes above and below the falls, some a few inches deep, others several meters deep. I peered inside a two-foot opening. The small hole revealed a huge carved-out cavern. As my eyes became accustomed to the darkened area I saw something moving in the water.

Donald Haack

"Harry, this hole is loaded with fish!"

He smiled. "Now you know why this is a great place to fish, like the old proverb, shooting fish in a barrel."

We climbed down to the middle of the falls.

"The burial caves are behind those falls."

That was the only mention during our whole trip. I wondered how the Indians discovered caves behind the waterfall and when they did, how they were able to go into them carrying bodies and adornments to the burial sites. I searched for clues as to where the caves were or any breaks in the rock for handholds to get behind the falls. Harry must have been reading my mind.

"I didn't think there were any caves behind there either," he retorted to my unasked question. "But when I passed here a few years ago, I saw birds fly in and out of the falls where the water wasn't so heavy. They come out in the early morning and flew in before dark where they stayed over night. Pretty good protection, but they couldn't fly in and out if there weren't any caves."

I was thinking how and when I could bring Jan and share this with her.

"Harry, there's an area on the flat that might make a small airstrip. Let's take a quick look"

"Okay, Don, but we can't waste too much time. Hiking back will take over four hours and that leaves only one hour before dark."

He was right. Walking a bush trail at any time is not fun, but at night it's hazardous. Without hammocks to sleep in we had to reach Marquis by sundown. Within a few minutes, I discovered a flat section void of rocks or faults. It didn't run true east west, but neither did the wind, which was deflected by a small mountain to the east.

"I think we lucked out here, Harry. This flat area is long enough. A few scrub trees near the end to cut down, a few hummocks leveled off. We only have to fill in that small crevice and we've got a landing strip running into the wind." I was elated. I wanted to show off the falls to Jan and friends. Nellie and Caesar mentioned Karona falls on many occasions. With the airstrip we could invite them to Marquis for a picnic flight to Karona, a unique but small way to repay them for all they did for us. Their daughter, Pixie, would be ecstatic at the thought of picnicking at the legendary *Karona Falls*.

That night Jan listened in rapture to my tales of the falls, the beauty that surrounded them and my plans to construct the airstrip. Four months later, we hiked in with a crew. It took four days of clearing and cleaning to complete the project. A week later I flew in Nellie, Caesar, Pixie, Jan, and Diney, the first to enjoy a Karona picnic. My mother and dad enjoyed the area when they arrived. Its beauty inspired everyone. I was thankful I could give them all that rare present.

Many months later, Harry and I had a free day off the dredge. The Indians were having a major *fete* and asked for two days off. If we had said no, they still would have left. At least they asked and Harry said that was progress.

"Since we have a couple of days off, want to check on the caves behind Karona?" he asked. I had almost forgotten about it but it sounded like a good idea. I agreed and we gathered up the tools we would need: snorkel, mask, and plenty of ropes. Domingo, even though he was part Macusi, felt he was distant enough not to have any curse on him. He wasn't convinced enough, I noticed, to volunteer to go under the falls. Harry had back problems so that left me to investigate the caves. I didn't tell Jan that. I didn't think she would approve even though I would take precautions.

After making the decision, we were on our new airstrip in less than an hour. The river was low and the falls had the least amount of water in years, which should have made our quest easier. Domingo set the ropes across the falls, one on the upper, the second on the lower falls. They would be my guidelines to maneuver from side to side. Meanwhile, Harry and I hung three ropes from the upper falls. The theory was that I could lower myself on one line, work left to right exploring a third of the falls. Then on to the second and third vertical ropes.

I strapped on a face mask and snugged it extra tight so the force of the water wouldn't pull it off my face. I strapped on my razor sharp knife over my swimming suit and put on my oldest, softest Keds to help with toeholds on the cliff. I tied a five-foot reinforcing bar, which I could use to probe for caves, to a rope around my waist. I wasn't sure how much visibility I would have behind the falls...if there were a space back there.

When we were all ready and had thoroughly rehearsed our signals, I slid off the side down to Domingo's transverse rope and gradually worked along the rockface to the center of the falls. The force of the water prevented any fast movement. On my first attempt, I catapulted into the falls where I was battered about like a cork. I couldn't easily get back under and had to maneuver to the side and try again, this time staying inside of and away from the full force. I discovered if I leaned in against the cliff face, the water held me there and I managed to traverse the falls using all three vertical lines. It wasn't as dark as I expected. Where heavy misting reduced visibility, I probed every possible area with my reinforcing rod.

I slid down to the second level falls and came back across. It was easier and quicker. That falls had less concentrated water and in a few areas I was able to use my feet to help guide the way. I exited on the right side and gave the safety line three good tugs. I felt way too tired to attempt climbing back up, and if I didn't get an immediate response from Harry and Domingo, I was prepared to slide all the way down the rope to the pool below the falls and swim to shore. I didn't expect an awful lot of support but much to my surprise, they pulled me up. I came to the edge where I climbed over while they held onto my line. I took off my mask and sat down. They were both looking at me expectantly, waiting to hear what I had to say. After all, we're talking about discovering ancient burial caves of the Macusi tribes.

"It's a red herring," I blurted out. Domingo cocked his head indicating he didn't understand. Harry said, "What's a red herring, Don?"

I had to wait a few moments to catch my breath. I was still exhausted. "A red herring, Harry, is something you throw in a situation when you are attempting to distract someone from finding something you don't want found out." He looked puzzled.

I went on, "When the Macusis buried their chiefs and booty, they didn't want anyone disturbing the site, or for that matter, even looking for it. So they made up the rumor of the caves behind the falls. It sounded logical: the area was very difficult to get to and it diverted the search away from the real sites, wherever they are. So," I paused, "I think we should forget about the fact that there are no caves here and preserve the rumor and thus protect the secret of the real burial sites. I think the Macusis, living and dead, would appreciate it, and it would serve no real purpose to discredit the rumor... besides, it's a great tale; the burial caves behind Karona. Let's leave it at that. Harry, you saw birds fly in and out. There's one area between the upper falls where there is less water. There's a three foot space and its full of bird dung—I guess that's the famous Karona treasure."

Domingo laughed hysterically. When it reached a point that I began to worry about him, he suddenly stopped. Tears were running down his eyes, something I had seldom seen in an Amerindian. He looked at me. "Don't worry, I won't say anything. You right! Red herring, one good story. We leave it like that."

FLYING WITH JIMMY ANGEL

There were many books written about gold or diamond mining in South America and almost every one included tales of the adventurous promoter and legendary bush pilot, *Jimmy Angel*, first white discoverer of Angel Falls, the world's highest waterfall. The stories described his wild flying exploits, plane crashes—fifteen in all—and his uncanny ability to walk away from each one. More exciting were his tales of gold nuggets and diamonds he found while trekking back to civilization. These were thought-provoking stories for adventure seekers but somehow Angel never found those riches in his effort to retrace the trails back to his plane crashes.

He was a legend. Most of his flying took place in Venezuelan diamond and gold territory south of the Orinoco River. His tales of wealth inspired many a prospector to crisscross the jungle trying to find Angel's trails and treasures. His stories not only flourished but were continually embellished by the prospectors.

I felt a connection to Angel because of my daily flights over those same uncharted territories. Over the years there were fewer stories about him and recently so few that I concluded he had one plane crash too many. To have survived as he did, he must have had a guardian angel...or maybe that's how he got his name. No bush pilot lost a fraction of the planes Angel did and lived to tell about it. He was either very remarkable or exceedingly lucky.

Other than in books, my first encounter with the "Angel legend" was the year after Jan and I moved to British Guiana. Our friend and neighbor, Caesar Gorinsky, needed supplies for the ranch and asked to fly with me to Georgetown. I welcomed his company, particularly since he showed me navigational points along the route and related colorful stories of overland travel before air service. Without navigational aids, bush flying was dead reckoning: compass, airspeed, and time, so I welcomed learning new check points.

This trip Caesar talked about his association with Jimmy Angel and the considerable time spent prospecting with him.

"I'll show you one of his planes. It's not far off our flight path to town."

He gave me a compass heading; I plotted a course on the regional map and set the compass at 15 degrees north, 12 degrees off our Georgetown course. We were going to pass over Monkey Mountain.

"There's a village ahead and to the left," I shouted over the engine noise. "Tipuru?"

"Yes."

I knew Tipuru, the Macusi village, a four-hour walk from our house. Those Indians visited us frequently. Beyond Tipuru we flew over heavy bush, climbing to 3,000 feet to clear the Pakaraima Mountains ahead: no place to have an engine failure. Six minutes later, another ridge of sheer rock rose out of the jungle.

"The Echilibar?" I asked.

He nodded affirmatively and removed the handkerchief he was chewing on, an indication, I was to learn, that he was reminiscing. As we neared Monkey Mountain, Caesar began his story:

"Jimmy left me at the Echilibar camp and returned for more rations. It was late afternoon. A rain shower came through, leaving scattered hanging clouds over the valley. Before he took off, I suggested he wait until morning to return but he felt there might be the usual morning fog following a rain. He said it would be easier to navigate around the few scattered clouds later in the day, so off he went. His destination, Monkey Mountain airstrip, was five degrees uphill on a short approach. It got its name from the mountain overlooking the approach, which was supposed to look like a monkey." Caesar was deep in thought staring out the windscreen and again chewing on his handkerchief. He was silent. I waited.

"Coming up over this ridge is the Monkey Mountain airstrip. It starts over there" and he pointed to the left, "and goes uphill almost to the end of the escarpment.

"Aim for the middle of the airstrip. I'll show you something."

We climbed to an elevation of 3,600 feet where we could see the entire airstrip, a grayish line, like someone had taken a paint brush and put one stroke in a sea of green. A string of mud huts with palm roofs bordered this side of the strip. The sky reflected light off two aluminum-roofed huts that appeared to be blue rectangular pools of water. To my surprise, a small plane was parked north of the runway. I did a double take. I knew of no plane within hundreds of miles except Joe Tezerek's English Austin, based in Orinduik quite a bit further north.

I looked questioningly at Caesar. He anticipated my reaction. There was a hint of a smile, but his eyes were on the parked plane.

"Jimmy Angel's plane."

I could tell from his expression and suppressed smile there was more to come. I waited patiently. How and when did Angel's plane land here? Is he alive? When did he come back? Why did he leave it, or did he? I had a hundred questions, but I waited. It should be a good story.

Planes are so rare that as we passed over the airstrip, people came scurrying out of the huts like ants from a nest. I pulled back power and slipped down for a better look at the plane. With bright white wings and a two-tone gray and red body, it was parked in an area that looked fairly rough even from up here. At two hundred feet elevation, that could have been an illusion. Caesar wasn't offering any explanation. In frustration, I finally shouted, "How long has it been parked there?"

"Twenty years," and looked over at me again.

I stared at him, this time waiting for an explanation. I didn't know whether or not he was pulling my leg. Caesar was a master at playing cat and mouse with people. He enjoyed creating an unexpected event or making an outrageous statement to see the expression on his listener's face. This was no exception, but I didn't feel up to his games at the moment.

I pulled into a tight quarter-circle turn to view the plane head on. The right wing was tilted upward in an unnatural angle; the main frame was too close to the ground to be on wheels. It wasn't parked. It crashed.

"What happened?"

"It was the story I started telling you earlier. When he left our Echilibar strip late in the afternoon to go back to Monkey Mountain for rations, clouds and ground fog surrounded the airstrip. After making one pass, Jimmy saw the row of houses but not the airstrip. After that pass, he came in for a landing, lined up with what he thought was the runway and descended. When he was within a few feet, he anticipated being able to make a visual landing and applied full flaps. Mistake," Caesar commented.

"When he saw the ground, he realized he was far left and attempted a go around. Instead, with full flaps he stalled and pancaked...in what could have been a perfect landing except he wasn't on the airstrip. Both wheels tore off and the main wing spar cracked. Luckily, it didn't flip. Jimmy opened the canopy and stepped out. I think that was plane number twelve or thirteen he crash-landed and walked away from. Nothing except instruments was salvageable, so that's where it stayed."

I powered up and put the plane on course for Georgetown. When I found some spare time, I would have a better look. Another interesting Caesar story. There would be many more, I was sure of that.

Caesar and I had plenty of work in town: repairing parts, picking up mail, ordering rations, and finding special orders from

Nellie and Jan. It wasn't until the second day that we managed to have tea at the Woodbine Hotel. Laden with packages Caesar dumped them on the table while Mac, the owner, set out tea. I poured. Caesar added milk and two heaping teaspoons of brown, coarse, Demerara sugar, true English fashion.

"I could use a beer, instead. It's been a hard day." He looked exhausted. "What are you doing in an hour from now?" he asked. "Having a beer," I answered. "I've had one of those days, too. Will you be in the bar in an hour, about five?"

"No, come back here. I want you to meet someone." He sounded mysterious. But then, Caesar had a strange assortment of friends. He went out of his way to help people who were in distress, particularly good-looking ladies. I wondered what she would be like. Whomever, it would be interesting or he wouldn't sound so mysterious. He enjoyed suspense. I was down at five. Caesar looked at his watch.

"It's about time," he said in his best irritated guttural voice.

"I thought you said five," I said smiling. It was exactly five.

"Humph, let's go." And he was down the steps ahead of me.

"You must be needing that beer pretty badly, in which case I'll buy." I didn't get even a grunt of acknowledgment. He was thinking of something two events ahead as usual.

We walked to the Hotel Tower bar on the ground level. Danny, the East Indian, greeted us. Coming in from the bright tropical light into the dimly lit bar, we couldn't see who spoke but we recognized the voice. Danny, who was black as coal, was invisible in his white starched shirt jac and white pants. The voice said, "Good to see you, Mister Gorinsky. It's been quite a while. Your usual?"

He saw me and pretended to recognize me. I had been in twice before.

"And Mister?" he said with a slight bow, glancing at me. I didn't feel slighted. Caesar had been around for twenty years. Danny knew everyone's name and what they drank. He would make a point of knowing my name and preference soon.

"No, Danny, thank you. Someone is waiting for us in the back. Send someone to take care of us." Caesar motioned for me to follow. There were candles on the tables. We walked to the corner where a man stood up from a table. He recognized Caesar and they shook hands. He wasn't tall, but he had a stout build and the face of a determined and tenacious bulldog, highlighted by a slightly pockmarked bulbous nose. The gravely voice matched the bulldog effect.

"Hi, understand you're a bush pilot. Done a little bush flying myself. Nice to meet you. Name's Angel, Jimmy Angel," and stuck his big fist out to shake.

I had seen pictures of him in books and photographs. This was an older version, but I was completely taken aback to know I was seeing him in the flesh. I assumed he was dead. The transition from ghost to real person took a couple of seconds. We shook hands. He was plenty alive with a powerful handshake to prove it.

"I know more about you than you do about me. Read books written about you over twelve years ago and came across a few of your old buddies in Venezuela last year. No one knew where you were or what happened to you. I didn't expect I'd meet you."

"Thought I was dead, huh? Well you aren't the first, and probably not the last. Don't do much flying, though. Doesn't go to well with this." He held up his double scotch on the rocks.

"What are you flying now? he asked.

"A Piper TriPacer, four passenger. Not too fast but it gets in and out of small airstrips. I can pull it out by myself or with my pocket sized rope pulley if it gets stuck," I added, almost as an apology. I knew he flew bigger and more powerful planes.

We talked airplanes; we talked crashes. He had walked away from sixteen. I had one to my credit, something I would rather forget than talk about.

"Hey, if you can walk away, it's a good landing. Don't knock it," and he slapped me on the back. By this time he had belted down a couple more scotches and I, a light drinker and into my second, had more than enough. Caesar recalled several incidents back at the Echilibar days. There was a constant stream of corrections on events and statistics, but considering they went back fifteen years and three drinks, the recall wasn't all that bad. We talked diamonds, gold, and old friends most of whom were no longer around. The number of Jimmy's friends who were no longer alive reinforced the fact that this country was more hostile than I had given it credit for, a reminder to treat it with more respect in the future.

Sometime late in the drinks but early in the evening, Jimmy got serious. He leaned closer so no one else could hear.

"I've got a gold territory that's richer than Croesus, right here in B.G." He reached into his pocket. "I've saved these for years. They're small compared to what's back there. I'm finally coming back to mine it" He pulled out three huge gold nuggets and threw them down on the table.

"Small compared to what's back there." He repeated and went on, "I'm bringing in a group from California, Johnson & Johnson Dredging Company, one of the bigger operators in the West. They'll be here in a week. Can I count on you to fly us in and take care of us while we're back there prospecting and setting up equipment for testing?"

He took me by surprise. How did we switch so quickly from stories to a request for a flying contract? It had great possibilities. I would have time to talk to him, hear more stories, and our business needed the income. In the mining business it's necessary to have a nest egg for lean periods. I wondered where he was going to operate. I didn't have long to wonder.

"Understand your house is on the Ireng near Karona Falls. Well, we're going to be about forty miles north, practically neighbors, so hopefully it won't be putting you out much with your own mining project. 'Course we'll pay well for it. Make it worth your while. Shouldn't take more than a month or two. What do you think?"

I didn't have time to think about it, but quickly said yes and figured we could work out details along the way. Just being with this legendary bush pilot would be a blast and getting paid for it too? I couldn't say no.

"I'm planning to ship my gear to Monkey Mountain and store it there with someone. When my people from Johnson come, I want you to fly this stuff down to the Echilibar's mouth. There's a small airstrip the missionaries tell me is still kept up. In fact, they want you to fly one of their priests into the village in the next few weeks. Got some business lined up for you. Don't pay me no commission." He smiled.

"Then we'll need Indians to *drug* the equipment from the airstrip to the camp, about a half day walk." I was surprised to hear him use the colloquial word *drug* for carrying or hauling. Most people didn't understand the meaning and as far as I knew, it was a local bush expression. "Know anyone who's good with Macusis and can speak their language?" he asked.

There were plenty of people around, but finding someone who could be depended upon, wouldn't steal, and whom you could put up with in the bush wasn't easy. Most bushman were loners; many were outcasts. I could think of only one person. "There's a guy living at Orinduik airstrip who's raising tomatoes. Has a small grant from the government, but he's losing his shirt and lives hand to mouth. Would be glad to get employment. Name's Chaves, Johnny Chaves. He's part Portuguese, part East Indian and part God-knows-what else, maybe Irish 'cause he'll talk your head off, given a chance." I hadn't seen Chaves in weeks but I didn't think he would have left.

"Sounds good to me," Angel said. "Can he arrange all the details with the Indians who do the *drugging*? Make sure they do the job, feed 'em, and pay 'em? I don't want those hassles." He made a face to reinforce his dislike dealing with laid-back Amerindians.

Chaves was good at it and I was sure he would work a bit extra for himself in the payout, but that was part of the way of life here.

"Yeah, he's good and can handle the whole thing if I can talk him into coming. I'll fly to Orinduik in the next couple of days to make the arrangements. Any idea what day your people are coming?"

We worked out most of the details in spite of our scotch consumption. With a working outline, we would keep in touch by radio on B.G. Airways frequency, which I could access with my Collins transmitter back home in Marquis.

I met with Jimmy twice more before we left. We went over his list of rations. I added what I knew would be needed and eliminated most of the goodies he selected for the Amerindians and wondered where Jimmy came up with some of his ideas. It occurred to me that even though he flew around South America all those years, he probably didn't have a close association with the native people. I told him I would arrange separate rations from the interior for the Indians: farine, cassava bread and dried fish from Karasabai village. Jimmy's list included an ample supply of rum and two cases of Dewars scotch from Wheating & Richter's Import Company. It wasn't going to be a dry safari.

Two days later I landed in Orinduik. Chaves was there, determined but destitute and full of reasons why the tomato project wasn't working. Nothing new. He broke into a big smile when I placed a tin of corned beef, some crackers, and a bottle of Demerara rum on the table. He hadn't had decent food for a long time and rum would be a luxury. I outlined the job while he peeled an onion.

"They're strong, too strong," I said. "Did you grow them here?"

"The soil is acidic, needs more lime. I'll have to ship some lime in from town. That'll give me a better crop of tomatoes, too," he explained.

"Johnny, you're beating a dead horse. If you airfreight in lime by B.G. Airways at forty cents a pound, there's no way you can sell tomatoes profitably air freighting them back to Georgetown."

I didn't mean to bust his bubble but watching his project was a study in futility, unworkable, like so many of the agricultural schemes tried before. Earlier surveys stated it couldn't be done, but then along comes sweet-tongued Johnny Chaves who could talk a raccoon out of his coat. Someone in the British Guiana government bought his scheme hook, line, and sinker, and probably a few dollars were passed on the side. Another government boondoggle was born.

It wasn't hard to convince Johnny to take on the Jimmy Angel project. Besides being paid more money than he made in years, he would have good food, good company, and rum— an irresistible combination. I calculated his salary below what Angel offered, but

I knew the inevitable over-runs, and *extra pocket money* would make it come out just about right. Everyone would be happy. I knew Johnny well enough to know he would feel he missed an opportunity if he couldn't finagle a few extra dollars from paying off Indians, extra rations, and extra rum. It was a way of life and Chaves would be happy, even ecstatic and Angel, who didn't know or want to handle details, would be happy because it would be within budget.

I made two more flights to Orinduik to check on Chaves. Though he was ready to go the following week, I came to realize Johnny was not the man to organize Indians for the drugging of goods from Uan Paru airstrip to Angel's camp. He was too laid back to keep on the necessary schedule.

I discussed this with Dutch who spent over twenty years prospecting and knew every tribe, their *Tuchow*, chief, and *Peayman*, medicine man in the area. He agreed that Chaves would be a good camp manager watching over supplies, supervising the cook tent, and running the camp, but not for hiring and supervising Indians to drug equipment and supplies.

"I'll get Indians from Uan Paru village. It's only one hour from dat airstrip ver you going. Ve'll need ten, twelve for goot drugging. I'll get," he said as he struggled with the cigarette he was making. While he spoke, he shaved off small slivers from the end of the hard dry Brazilian tobacco plug, almost the size of a baseball bat, three inches in diameter and two feet long. Heavy, black, and bound with flat vine, it looked more like a lethal club. Wherever Dutch went, he carried his plug and cigarette papers. They were inseparable.

He carefully laid out a small white paper on the table and evenly distributed the plug shavings on it. He double-checked to make sure he didn't leave the slightest particle behind. Nellie said he was more careful with his tobacco than his diamonds, which used to fall out of his top shirt pocket when he bent over to wash his face in the streams. He rearranged the tobacco shavings into a neat line two or three times before he rolled the paper, which he licked, patted and squeezed ever so gently. When he was lucky, the moisture held the *cigarette* together.

Donald Haack

Most men in the bush rolled their own. Caesar did it to perfection. In twenty years of practice, Dutch's cigarettes still looked like a snake that had just swallowed several small animals. Dutch was proud of his creation. He pulled a box of the local Demerara matches out of his shirt pocket. Several tries later one lit, but Dutch was patient and within minutes he was puffing away, eyes half closed with enjoyment. He pulled the strong smoke deep into his lungs.

"Yah, dat's goot, dat's goot." He exhaled to let the smoke drift out in a long stream disappearing upwards. "Ven do dey come?" he asked between puffs.

"The last message said he would be at Monkey Mountain next Friday," I repeated.

"Yah, goot, den you take me up in two, tree days from now und I'll haf dem druggers on the airstrip Friday. You come, too? It vud be intersting ting for you, you nefer see before. Yah, you shute come. Intersting, vatching dem drug." He thought a while. "Yah, und den bring me Karasabi farine, cassava brot, und dried fish. Dey von't vork von day mitout rations."

"Yeah, I might come." I wasn't interested in watching the druggers, but the only way I was going to hear more of Jimmy Angel's tales would be in his camp where there would be nothing to do at night but sit around the campfire, drink coffee, and talk. Though there was always a short wave radio in camp, other than the seven o'clock news on the BBC, bush people, intimate with nature and the harmony of jungle sounds, were content to be away from the cacophony of civilizations' noises. Radios, for the most part, stayed turned off.

Jan knew I wanted to spend time with Jimmy Angel and encouraged me to join the druggers to Angel's camp for the night. The Tuesday before the shuttle, I dropped Dutch at Uan Paru strip.

Thursday I cranked up the generator early to be first on B. G. Airways before the other bush stations signed on with their more social communications. It was tough on those of us who had to keep schedules.

Our Collins transmitter had four slide-in bands. I inserted the five-kilocycle band and then attached the 200 foot long wire antenna. Positioned at 90 degrees to Georgetown, it produced and received a strong clear signal 225 miles away. For international Ham traffic, I used PY4DL call sign on my ten-meter antenna. Today's business had to do with meeting B. G. Airways. I used my airplane call.

"Piper 36 Delta calling B.G. Airways, do you read?"

This early in the morning reception was at its best but deteriorated throughout the day. I seldom called in after 10 a.m. We hoped emergencies would be early or could wait until the next morning. A few seconds later I repeated the call.

The response was immediate and clear: "36 Delta, B. G. Airways, you're loud and clear. Traffic for you."

"Roger, reading you, B. G. Airways, go ahead with traffic."

"To Captain Haack from Captain Jimmy Angel. Flight to Echilibar confirmed for tomorrow, Friday 10 a.m. Please meet us as scheduled. Let me know if any change of plans. Otherwise will proceed with your schedule to transport seven tons and three souls from Monkey Mountain to Uan Paru Friday and Saturday. Best regards, Thumbs up. J Angel."

The operator continued, "Captain Haack, that was Captain Angel's message. Our office wants to reconfirm with you our scheduled flight tomorrow and that there will be two drums of 80-octane gas on board for your shuttling. Captain Pieniazek will pilot the flight and sends his regards. If you are at the airstrip earlier he would appreciate if you could radio weather information from Monkey Mountain. Did you copy all?"

"Roger, B.G. Airways, copied message and confirmation one hundred percent. I will be there earlier and will call in any weather information at that time. Over, 36 Delta."

"Roger, Roger, 36 Delta, thank you. Will pass on your acknowledgment to Captains Angel and Pieniazek. B. G. Airways over and out."

I double clicked the transmitter in acknowledgement and shut down. Our East Indian houseboy was in the kitchen helping Jan prepare breakfast.

"Ramdat, switch off the generator." He stopped what he was doing and ran to the shop. The generator chugged to a stop. The valley was quiet and only the wind could be heard. I walked into the kitchen. Jan was setting out breakfast. Diana was in the little seat on the counter taking in the activity of the kitchen.

"Well, it's all set with Jimmy Angel tomorrow at Monkey Mountain."

"The flying income will help out and I know you're anxious to spend some time with Jimmy Angel. I'm anxious, too, to hear some of his stories first hand. Wish I could join you, but that's impossible. Harry sent a note that he needs more *tasso*, dried beef, so I'll send some with Domingo in the morning. All the rations from Karasabai are in the storeroom. You might have one of the boys load the plane tonight so you can get an early start."

I don't know what I would have done without Jan and her organizational skills.

"Anything you have to do to the plane before you go, or is it okay?"

She knew I kept it in first class condition, but this would be two days of shuttling seven tons in our plane. At seven to eight hundred pounds per trip, along with an elevation difference of 3,000 feet between airstrips, it would prove to be a couple of hard days.

Besides my usual rations, semi-automatic pistol with three hundred rounds, and my emergency kit, I added two spare spark plugs, two quarts of oil, a funnel with a clean chamois, tool kit, tire repair kit, and a special tool I had Demerara foundry make for me to open gasoline drums. A gasoline pump, hose, and Jerry cans completed the list. I left out my scale because all Airways cargo is weighed and prominently marked in big purple numbers. I couldn't think of anything I might have missed and neither could Jan.

The next morning we were up and had a five-thirty breakfast before it was light. Jan handed me a bag. "Made you some lunch. If I know Dutch and the other guys they won't think of the pilot. You'll need sustenance. There's tea and goodies. Take a tea break and don't overdo it." She kissed me. "Going to miss you. Do already. Hurry back to Diney and me."

She didn't have to remind me. Ramdat and I pulled 36 Delta out of the hangar, I did a run up at 3,000 RPM, checked both magnetos. The 150 horses sounded beautiful, almost a purr, and I took off.

With no load and a cool morning I was airborne in seconds. I pulled the throttle to 2300 RPM, raised the flaps and did a 180 degree turn over the house. I dipped a wing. Jan was standing in the doorway holding Diney and waving. I felt a lump in my throat. It was always hard leaving them alone. There aren't many wives who would give up the luxuries of U. S. living to go 250 miles from civilization, with two primitive Macusi villages as nearest neighbors. Jan had reserves of strength I was only beginning to discover.

Two days earlier, I had picked up Chaves at Orinduik and dropped him off at Uan Paru airstrip, which gave him two days to set up camp for our arrival. Dutch would supervise the cargo I flew in and load up the druggers. In camp, Chaves could check Dutch's list to make sure goods weren't lost along the way. Dutch had to ration food to the Indians so they wouldn't eat everything the first day and then leave because there was no food. In their villages, the Indians rationed their food, but when they worked for someone they gorged themselves because they weren't paying for it. I had been there before and knew in some ways Macusis were like children. In other ways, I would soon learn, they had a mature stoicism that defied logic.

I chose an indirect heading of 300 degrees north to Uan Paru and stayed at 800 feet elevation rather than climb to 3,000 feet, clear the mountains and then descend steeply to Uan Paru. This more picturesque route followed the river above Karona Falls and provided a constantly changing landscape painting. The moist ravines nourished the bordering gullies into lush green jungle, a stark contrast to the patches of open ground where wild grass withered to shades of brown from lack of rain. Hundreds of beautiful macaw parrots and brilliantly colored parakeets rose in clouds of color as 36 Delta shattered the silence. On my left, the Ireng with its myriad of rapids and small waterfalls appeared to carry millions of strands of speckled tinsel that reflected off the sky.

This territory with its raw beauty, bare of any signs of civilization, gave me the eerie feeling of traveling back in time.

I crossed the last hill. Uan Paru strip was less than a mile ahead. I flew over in a low pass. Hanging from a stick was a colorful piece of cloth—Dutch's windsock. I touched down, taxied back and two Indians ran to the plane. The warm breeze hit me when I opened the door. This was going to be a cloudless, hot, hard day.

One of the Indian boys who looked about twelve had a big smile and handed me a piece of paper. "From Dutchie," he said. He stepped back and in typical Indian fashion, put one hand on his hip, the other hung in front of his loincloth while his head tilted to the side, looking at me as if to say, "It's your move now."

I took the paper and unfolded it. Dutch's note said to leave the rations with *Arnos*, the bearer of this letter. He was trustworthy. There would be more druggers at the airstrip by ten o'clock. I smiled. Dutch wouldn't know ten o'clock if his life depended on it. He hadn't worn a watch in twenty years. Dutch was European, but he judged time like everyone else in the bush. When the sun was halfway between sunrise and directly above, it was ten o'clock. The Indians simply pointed to the sky where the sun either was or was going to be—that was their clock. After thirty years in the bush, Dutch still called it ten o'clock. He also mentioned, with a not so subtle hint of disapproval, that Chaves was not out of his hammock particularly early the day before yesterday. Dutch finally rousted him out, but he didn't leave until noon. Good old Dutch, he was a maverick, but I could always depend on him one hundred percent.

After the boys unloaded the rations, I motioned for them to stand back while I started the engine. The airplane held a fascination, which made the Indians want to stand as close as possible. In less than a minute I cleared the treetops. Monkey Mountain, only eleven minutes away, was a climb to 3,000 feet where the plateau was partially hidden in a white mist I hoped was scattered. As I came over the edge, I felt the usual thermal bump. With the bright sun and a light wind that ground fog would dissipate quickly.

Donald Haack

The airstrip was almost clear of fog. As usual, I flew over to chase away pigs, chickens, or dogs and then landed. I taxied to John Roth's shop, the biggest building in the area and shut down. John was there in his usual attire: short khaki pants three sizes too large with his Stan Kowalski underwear top. He stood five-foot ten, his black hair slicked back with hair tonic. It gave him a gaunt, starved look. His nose, sharply pointed like a beak, projected out from under sunken jet black eyes framed above by pencil thin eyebrows. John's dark deep-set eyes were difficult to see even in bright sunlight. Arms were a skin and bones extension between shoulder and wrist to thin hands with long spindly fingers; the left middle and forefinger had one-inch nails used to sort rough diamonds. He was a classic caricature of a Portuguese trader one reads about in African novels. I didn't know him well enough to pass judgment on his character, but he exuded an aura of evil. John Roth was a throwback from a different era.

"Couldn't have long nails on my right hand. Couldn't shoot fast if I did," he later explained to me.

He carried a .38 Smith and Wesson silver-plated revolver in a leather holster that hung loosely from a military web belt. Two skinny legs, not much bigger than his arms, extended below his Khaki shorts and disappeared into dirty gray woolen socks. He wore leather sandals that flopped at every step. He reminded me of a wounded crow the first time I met him. That impression was reinforced again today.

"Hi, John, ready for a big day?"

He knew the DC-3 was coming in and I'm sure he had some cargo on board for his shop. He would also receive money or accounting from his wife whom he hadn't seen in ten years. For bushmen whose livelihood was mining and trading, separate living arrangements were not uncommon. What was uncommon, was John, unlike other traders, never traveled to town to visit his wife and family. He often talked about going but never got around to it. She received his diamonds from the pilot, sorted them out and sold them to Clem Krakowski who staked John to whatever he needed. In hard times John owed him. In good times John had a credit, but either way, his wife got a regular stipend from Krakowski. That was the way the system worked between the bushmen, the buyers and traders and their families in town.

John was a chronic complainer, but not today. Diamond production was up and he was in a rare upbeat mood.

"Know what time the plane's due?" was his first question. I hadn't seen him in weeks. John didn't engage in small talk.

"I'll try to call in a weather report now if I can reach Julian on my radio." I clicked on the plane radio, tuned in B.G. Airways. It took several seconds to warm up.

"B. G. Airways, 36 Delta, over."

I was taken by surprise with the immediate response and clear distinctive voice of Julian Pieniazek.

"Hi Don," he said, breaking the rules of proper radio protocol. Julian, the captain and head pilot of the airways, broke the rules regularly.

"We're over *Tit* Mountain and should be there in fifteen minutes. What's the weather like? Are you at Monkey Mountain?" he asked.

"Roger, I'm at Monkey Mountain. Just landed. There's a bit of scud, but it's burning off fast and should be clear by the time you're here. Are my people on board, Jimmy Angel? Do you know who he is?" I asked, and then wished I hadn't. Julian had been around for years and certainly would have met or known about him. Angel's other plane, a radial engine gull wing Cessna 190 had been rotting on Atkinson field for over fifteen years. It was a conversation piece.

"Yeah, he's on board, in fact he's sitting in the right front seat flying this bird. Can't keep a good pilot down. He wants to land it, but he's never flown a DC-3 like this one before. Don't worry; I'll do the landing. Vicki's coming up now." Vicki Fikes, a fellow Polish pilot was Julian's co-pilot. On the nose of their plane, they painted PPP in big letters, which was the same designation of Cheddi Jagan's communist party—the opposition to the existing government. At closer inspection it read, *Poor Polish Pilots* Julian's little joke. The company didn't appreciate his political humor, but they let him keep it.

I waited a few seconds to see if he had anything else to say. Apparently, he didn't. I clicked on: "OK, see you in a few minutes. I'll keep the radio on if you call in. Over."

I heard him click the mike button twice, acknowledging he heard. In a few minutes we heard the plane. He did a short 180 in front of Monkey Mountain, almost sliding down the face, greased the big plane in like a Piper Cub, and came to a stop in front of John Roth's shop.

Ranjan, the big East Indian who did all the bull work for Julian, swung open the doors and the next person I saw was Jimmy. He waved and I noticed that the bulldog face changed, some of the hardened wrinkles relaxed into a broad smile. He came over and was followed by a big man in an oversized red plaid shirt and sporting a Texas-sized ten-gallon hat. He looked rugged, like he'd been around a bit.

"Want you to meet my friend, Johnson, I told you about. Johnson and Johnson Dredging Company from California. He's gonna check out the claims... if you can get us in there. Everything okay?" he asked. The smile was gone and he looked serious, anticipating a positive answer, but not sure until he heard it directly from me.

"Everything's fine. You do have aviation gas on board, right? They told me there were two barrels?"

Now he smiled again, almost grinning from ear to ear. He had an infectious smile and you couldn't help liking him. He slapped a beefy hand on my shoulder. "They're rolling them off now"

I looked over. Ranjan in his dirty khakis had maneuvered the first barrel on its side, eased it over the door jam and let it go, shouting a warning to those standing nearby. The rubber truck tires he laid down absorbed the initial impact after which the barrels bounced away and no one was ever sure in what direction. The first barrel landed near Roth's Amerindian wife who had her baby slung on her hip. She nimbly jumped out of the way. They were used to being bombarded from cargo when Ranjan was unloading. The airstrip could be a dangerous place. The dog behind her almost wasn't as lucky. He was scratching his ear and barely jumped in time to escape being squashed by the rolling 355 pound steel drum.

Fifteen or more Indians and porknockers arrived. Porknockers were miners who lived in the bush existing on salt pork—the only meat that didn't spoil in the hot tropics stored in wooden barrels. Each time a barrel was opened they would have to *knock* off the top. That loud distinctive knocking sound gave them their name.

Everyone helped Ranjan unload. The cargo literally flowed out, handed from one to the next. Jimmy stood alongside, directing where the boxes, bags, and containers went. He obviously planned ahead. He had the cargo into precise piles.

"No, no, that last one goes on the pile over there," Jimmy said pointing to a second reasonably well stacked pile of goods. I watched in fascination wondering what he was doing so methodically and then it struck me. This legendary, experienced, efficient bush pilot weighed out piles for each load on my plane. That would reduce loading time by half. I was impressed and told him so.

"I've got loads starting at 550 pounds, maybe a bit light, but if you're heavy on fuel and you've got a downwind takeoff you might want to go lighter until you're comfortable with that weight. As you burn off gas, you can add more poundage on each flight." I was impressed with his thoroughness. No wonder he survived as long as he did.

The shuttling went on all day and into the next without any serious hitches. It was hard work under hot conditions. No one complained. On the second to last load, I flew in Angel and Johnson who took off with three of the Indian druggers. At noon I flew in our last load.

"That's it, Dutch, everything and everyone. I'll tie the plane down. Ready to pack in to their camp?" I asked.

"Yah, let's have some vater to vash down dis farine und vee go." That was Dutch's idea of lunch; the gravel-like hard, dry farine that would break your teeth if you bit into it. If soaked for hours it had the texture of oatmeal, but Dutch never planned ahead for luxuries and just washed it down with water. I silently blessed Jan for providing lunch.

There were eight Indian druggers, six women and two men. The men were almost useless. They used the excuse that they had to carry their bows and arrows to shoot quickly in case they encounter game. They carried light loads, letting the women carry the heaviest share.

This last plane load wasn't full, so no one was overloaded. The warashis, backpacks made of vines and palms woven into a contoured pack with a head strap, allowed the carrier to push forward with the head strap easing the strain on the shoulders.
I wasn't used to backpacking, so I took a light load but had a sore neck the first hour. "Dutch, one of the women is pregnant and pretty far along. Can she continue drugging?"

"Oh yah, dat don't make no difference. She strong und can go all day. Chust you see."

After an hour on the trail, I shifted my pack several times and stopped once to tighten the thong on my holster to keep it from chafing my leg. I had a new respect for these Indians. I was carrying less than half of their load, yet they didn't tire. The real eye-opener was yet to come.

After two hours, the leading Indians stopped. The women took off their packs, gathered in a huddle and were doing a lot of talking. For people who exhibit little or no emotion, their manner indicated something out of the ordinary was going on. I was grateful for the respite and quickly took off my pack.

"This is the first time they took a break, Dutch. Don't they ever get tired?" I managed to say between heavy breaths. I was soaking wet from perspiration, breathing hard, and aching. I decided to catch a quick nap. I used my pack as a pillow. I was asleep before I hit the ground. I woke up to excited shouting and yelling. It took a moment to realize where I was. Dutch was having a smoke. The noise came from the Indian women still in a group.

"What's going on, Dutch? They're excited about something."

"Yah, vee got vun more den vee start wid. Dat pregnant vun, vell she not pregnant now. Joost had her baby. Vee haf to wait a bit more to clean tings up und den vee go."

I started getting up. Dutch put his hand on my shoulder. "Stay put. Nutting you can do. Dey do better job den vee can. Rest. You'll need it. Vee haf two hours more to go."

I looked at the huddled women and tried to figure out what they were going to do.

"Who's going to stay and take care of her and the baby? And what about the extra load?" I asked.

Dutch just kept puffing his cigarette, totally unconcerned about what I thought was a major problem. I didn't want to let Jimmy Angel down by not delivering his goods on time. Besides, this was serious, a drugger having a baby.

Dutch was gathering his things together. "Everting okay now. Vee go."

I was dumbfounded. I started to ask a question, but he cut me short.

"Deez people take care of every dam ting. Dey mek a shoulder sving to carry dat baby.".

"She's going to walk… with the baby?"

"Oh yah, wid da baby. But dey lighten her load. She carry vat you carry now. Da utter vimmin dey gonna drug more to lighten her load. Everting fine. Vee go now."

And we went. I thought that because we had the woman who just gave birth on the trail with us, we would move at a snail's pace. I was wrong. It was only slightly slower than before. I was pushed to keep up and I wondered how in the world the new mother could do it. I saw it, but I really couldn't comprehend it. We arrived at camp two hours later than our original estimated time. I was glad to drop my pack and rest. Everyone gathered around to greet us, especially the Indian women who were anxious to see the baby and take care of the mother. Before we arrived, the Amerindians knew of the birthing event. It was the main talk of the camp and yet another example of *bush telegraph* or ESP as we call it.

Most of the creeks were dry so Chaves and the Indians made the campsite along the Ireng River. Less than a half-mile away a 2,000-foot escarpment overlooked the camp, providing a picturesque background that National Geographic would have envied. Chaves was at his best directing the natives here and there to unload their gear. To give him his credit, the camp appeared well organized with everything in place and the grounds immaculately clean. I noticed the cook tent had a few canvas chairs around the table bearing scotch, gin, and rum bottles. The camp had quickly adjusted to going *English*, that is, drinks without ice.

It was too early for me. I took out some clean clothes, walked to the river, stripped, and took a swim. The water was cool, stimulating and refreshing compared to the hot sun. I swam up and down along the bank, which helped loosen up some of the achy muscles unaccustomed to long hikes and packing a knapsack. Dutch, I noticed had the same idea only he found a small pool where the water was only three feet deep. I swam over to him. I was surprised how pale his body was, like he was wearing white underwear in contrast to his deeply tanned face and neck. His hands and wrists were so dark it looked as though he was wearing brown gloves. He was soaping himself and dunking his head when I swam up to him. He smiled.

"Ya, vell I can't drown in dis shallow water. You shvim goot out dere. Me? I go down like a rock if I go dere. Ach, dis feels goot."

We walked carefully on the boulders and air dried almost immediately in the hot dry breeze. We slipped on clean clothes and returned to camp where Chaves declared, "The sun was past the yardarm," and officially opened the bar. Johnny already had a hint of rum on his breath, which was no surprise. He wasn't a true alcoholic, a circumstance not caused by choice but rather because he couldn't afford the expense. With three cases of rum on the list of supplies brought in, I knew he would be nipping constantly. I alerted Jimmy about this beforehand, but he felt much as I did: Chaves could function quite well sober or otherwise. In fact, we agreed he did better when he had a few drinks, that is if you could put up with his non-stop dialog.

Chaves had been cooking when I arrived. When Dutch and I returned from the river we found two tables, Tillie kerosene lamps hung but not lit, and a bar set up on a white tablecloth. The food smelled great, probably because it was heavily laced with onions, garlic, and curry. I silently hoped everyone liked curry because it was Chaves's favorite and his specialty.

The sun, a glowing orange-red ball on the horizon, slipped out of sight. The wind subsided, the cabouris disappeared, a peace settled over the valley. The few cumulous puff clouds were illuminated like lanterns in the sky. It was a magical moment with the illuminated pink, rose, and shades of green clouds drifting west. To the east looking down at us, the rock face became a canvas for the sun as it painted brush strokes of dark and light lines that marked its descent. As the sun descended, the dark shadow rose visibly as if it were an elevator rising on the escarpment. Each foot it ascended produced a magical potpourri of colors and textures in rock. Hemingway had his movable feast. We had our movable art by the Creator himself. No one spoke a word.

Except Chaves. He broke the reverie several times, simply because he talked incessantly, but each time someone put his fingers to his lips. It was a moment too precious—one to be cherished in silence. Finally Chaves actually shut up long enough to appreciate what he had formerly taken for granted. He saw how everyone reacted to God's paintbrush. He put down his glass and got up. At first I thought he couldn't stand the silence. We all watched the shadow racing up the rock face to the top then leaping off into oblivion, stealing the last light to plunge us into darkness. The whole spectacle lasted less than ten minutes. Seconds later Chaves lit the three Tillie lamps that produced the familiar hissing of air, so much a part of bush life at night.

He brought the food in a large iron pot filled with his famous curried beef stew that he ladled out over freshly baked bread. Nothing could have tasted so delicious. Everyone had second helpings, but it hardly made a dent in the enormous portion still left in the pot. There would be enough for several meals. Chaves knew quantity cooking. Afterwards he brought out a huge coffee pot and hung it over a small fire. It had black fire streaks that covered the bottom half. The fire and the Tillie lamp's flickering light bounced off the mottled blue and white enamel coffee top giving the illusion of little brightly shining gems. The matching enamel mugs were filled with steaming black coffee and alongside, a Carnation milk can for those who wanted *coffee leche*. For the next two hours, we sipped coffee with rum on the side.

I prompted Jimmy to tell some of his tales. Chaves was reminded to be silent—not an easy task. We'd heard Chave's stories, most of which were anecdotes on his attempts to grow crops in unlikely places and his frustrations of being as poor as a church mouse. Thankfully we coaxed Angel to talk about his adventures.

I reminded him of the Stetson airplane he landed on top of Angel falls, an area that appeared to be flat but in reality was a wet swamp bog. At 10,000 feet elevation, the thin air didn't provide much lift. He stalled and crash-landed the Stetson. Twenty years later it still looked as if the wrecked plane were ready to take off any minute. He explained it took weeks to get down and how on the way he had found fabulous gold nuggets. He searched for years and spent small fortunes retracing his trek down the escarpment, but never found the *mother lode*. I heard these stories from several sources years ago, but it took on a new meaning hearing it from Angel, the old master himself.

I told him about the second airplane alongside of his. Ten years after he crash-landed his plane, an American flying over the falls spotted it. Figured if someone landed there, he could too. He crash-landed right along side. The Venezuelan government had to send in a helicopter to bring him down. He knew about that one, but he let me finish the story for the benefit of the others. Five years later another American pilot saw the two planes sitting there and added his to make a third, which now made the area look like an airport. After that incident and rescue, the government put severe restrictions on flying near or around Angel falls. Jimmy hadn't heard about the third plane and the story provided him with a good laugh.

We talked long into the night. I'd pay a price for that: an early morning departure and a four-hour walk to the plane. To meet the Good Hope mail plane at two o'clock, I had to first refuel at Marquis and complete a scheduled charter flight.

Donald Haack

I didn't know when I would get another chance to sit with Jimmy Angel and as it turned out that was the longest session we had together. I was thankful I didn't get practical and cut short that visit.

That night I recalled a few of the books I had read about his flying exploits in Venezuela and the stories that Caesar related working with him and three others twenty years ago. It was on a makeshift dredge at Echilibar mouth a few miles south of where we sat. Angel provided the ending to that story. They struck a good pocket of diamonds. When prospecting he always used his gold pan underneath the diamond sieves. He found a few tiny gold nuggets and went to trace the gold upstream to this area. He returned to camp with several nuggets and was met by a very disturbed Caesar who explained that their two divers had trouble with the lines across the river. They were in swift water along the bank struggling with the ropes when they slipped, were swept downstream and drowned. Without rations and boys to help, Caesar and Jimmy had to break camp.

Caesar returned to the Rupununi and bought Good Hope ranch with his share of the diamonds. Angel bought another plane and returned to bush flying and prospecting in the Caroni River in Venezuela, but vowed to "one day" return. That was twenty-five years ago and this trip was the *one day*.

Suddenly it seemed I could see the whole picture: the books I read years ago, the vivid accounts by Caesar and the belief by many that Angel had died in one of his many crashes. But here he was, the legend himself and I was sharing the moment and stories with him.

KARAKARANA

We were checking the plane before leaving Good Hope when Nellie came over and whispered to Jan, "Be sure to come next Wednesday. 'C' and I have a surprise. Oh, and bring your swimming suits." No explanations, nothing. It sounded intriguing so I rescheduled my flying dates to free Wednesday, the mystery day. In the Rupununi, time took on another dimension. We weren't sure whether the surprise was going to be all day or several days, so I made sure the diving crews had ample supplies for the week. Dutch assured me the store and trading business were fine. We packed for an overnight, strapped Diney in the back seat and winged our way over Karasabai Valley. Crossing Pixie Mountain and with Good Hope in sight, we spotted a wisp of dust along the road: Caesar's jeep coming from the house to the airstrip. We arrived at the same time.

I made my usual low pass to ensure a clear strip, landed, and taxied to the tie-downs alongside our storage shed. I cut the engine and heard Nellie's, not Caesar's, voice. It was usually Caesar who met us while Nellie waited at the house preparing tea or lunch.

Donald Haack

Caesar and Chris, their three-year-old son, were in the jeep with her.

"Don't bother getting out. We're coming on board to join you—flying to Brazil. Did you bring your swimming suits? I hope the plane isn't loaded with too much gas, we have a full load. Can you take all of us in one flight?" she asked, without taking a breath or waiting for an answer.

I did a quick calculation, checked the fuel gauge and answered, "Yeah, just. We're a little over but not as much as usual when I'm carrying cargo. Caesar, sit in front and hold Chris. Nellie, Jan, and Diney sit in the back. That'll keep the weight and CG, center of gravity, in limits. Where are we going exactly?"

"Karakarana, Tenient's place. We haven't been there in years. Long, hard ride by jeep and horse. A day and a half. It's been almost ten years since our last visit. Last month Tenient sent a message he'd finished his airstrip. A plane from Boa Vista landed there twice and he asked if you would bring us. We'll have a picnic at the lake."

Caesar and Nellie had fondly talked about Karakarana, the *Shangri-La* oasis in the middle of Brazilian ranch country. The feature was a one-mile long spring-fed lake, surrounded by palms along one shore and cashew trees on the other. The water was clear, with sugar-white sand beaches and superb fishing. It sounded too good to be true and we were on our way to see it ourselves. Tenient Cicero built his ranch along the lake thirty years ago when he was discharged from the Brazilian army with the rank of Lieutenant, *Tenient*, which was the title he kept. Caesar said no one knew if he had a first name.

Technically, flying into Brazil was illegal, but in the back country planes were rare…army and police more rare. A problem was not expected. After a thorough pre-flight, I checked everyone's seatbelts and we were on our way. Caesar gave an approximate heading and assurance he could find Tenient's, even though this was would be the first time by air. We stayed south of Normandie, the Brazilian outpost of a hundred people and two policemen. I felt there was no point in advertising an American plane was flying into Brazil. We headed southwest for five minutes.

"Head northerly now!" Caesar shouted over the roar of the engine. I made a shallow turn heading fifteen degrees to the north. "See that long dark line?" he pointed out the right window. "That should be the creek leading directly to Karakarana…if I remember correctly."

I made the turn and followed the creek.

"Right in front," he pointed. "See those trees? Look a little to the right." And there it was—from ten miles out the reflected light from the sky produced in an otherwise dry, brown, savannah, a brilliant blue mark. A veritable idyllic oasis. Tall trees surrounded the ranch house and a long straight line sketched in the landscape revealed the airstrip.

I made two passes to check for holes or ruts and clear off any animals. A landing accident in Brazilian territory was to be avoided at all costs. Everything checked out, and with a stiff head wind we used only a portion of the airstrip. Tenient, his wife, four children, and many vaqueros came to see the plane land on their new airstrip. We taxied down the road to the house and shut down the engine. We opened the doors to a blast of hot air and a group of shouting, laughing, happy Brazilians. They had not seen Caesar and Nellie for years and this was a grand reunion with plenty of hugs for the women and brazos for the men.

In his white linen shirt and pants, Tenient stood out from the khaki and denim dressed crowd. He was thin and wiry, almost gaunt looking, with smiling eyes and a shock of white, thinning hair pulled straight back into a pony tail that accentuated his long nose. His face was weathered and tan with ample wrinkles. His wife, Anna, was short and darker skinned, indicating Amerindian blood. Smiling broadly she stepped forward with outstretched arms and hugged Nellie. It was a warm welcome. They were glad to see the Gorinskys and extended the same warm reception to Jan and me. As Caesar and Nellie's house guests and friends, we were again accepted as family, a warm, touching and wonderful custom. I particularly appreciated it because of my original concern as to how Jan would react to this primitive life, light years away from the one she left. I gave another silent thanks to Caesar and Nellie for accepting us so unqualifiedly into their home, family, friends and lives.

"Come, we will have a bite to eat, catch up on old times, take a nap. Then you must go to the lake and enjoy yourselves. I am sure that is one of the reasons you have come. It is still the same."

We walked to the house where they had prepared a feast of pork, lamb, home-baked bread, yams, and copious amounts of red wine. A lunch that left us limp. We managed to walk the short distance to the lake in spite of the suggestion that we put up our hammocks on their veranda for a siesta.

Caesar had something in mind and wouldn't be deterred. He led us to the lake where we slung our hammocks in the cashew trees. Chris and Diney had their own mini-hammocks. After tying the last knot and just before falling asleep, I leaned over the edge of the hammock to appreciate our view. The six of us we were stretched out in hammocks, shaded by cashew trees decorated with beautiful bright red fruit, each with a cashew nut attached. I felt like a giant Camoodie, anaconda snake that doesn't move for days after swallowing a meal. The waves were gently lapping on the white sand beach while a gentle tropical breeze made swirls on the water and across the lake it moved the huge palm leaves in slow undulating movements as if to wave their welcome to Lake Karakarana. With that peaceful picture, I fell asleep.

Siestas were usually half an hour. Not this time. An hour and a half later we left of our hammocks, put on swimming suits, walked along the beach and snorkeled in the clear blue water. Chris and Diney had their first experience snorkeling and it was hard to get them out of the water. Later we unpacked our afternoon tea. We swam again and took a leisurely walk, kicking the white sand and sifting it between our toes as the sun settled near the horizon... picture perfect.

Reluctantly, we packed our gear, said our thanks and good-byes to the Cicero family, climbed into our plane, and headed back to Good Hope. During the fifteen-minute return flight, we were quiet in the reverie of one of the most satisfying, leisurely afternoons we could recall.

Donald Haack

"You and Nellie certainly picked a winner on this one," I commented as we landed.

Caesar smiled. "I thought you and Yan would enjoy. Nellie and I were there years ago. It was even better than I remembered, but maybe that was because we didn't have the hard three days enroute on horseback. Tenient insisted we come often now that we have the plane. They enjoyed the company. I've invited them to Good Hope next month and hope you can join us when they arrive. He specifically asked if you and Yan would be there."

I said it would be a great idea and would work my schedule to fit, not an easy task now with the pressure of charter flying and keeping our dredge and men supplied. In the following weeks we reminisced about our ideal vacation, never realizing our next trip to Karakarana would be so different and traumatic.

The Cicero family came to Good Hope a month later and it was a grand reunion, a two-day affair with plane rides for Tenient, his wife, and two children. I circled Good Hope, showed them Normandie across the river, and then did a slow pass along Pixie Mountain. We flew down the river below the banks, a sensation akin to being in a boat but ten times faster. It was the first time any of them had been in a plane and they later said it was the most exciting thing they had ever done. I thought it successful—no one wet his pants.

We returned to Karakarana in April as the clouds built up announcing the onset of rainy season. When the rains start, the savannahs gradually flood, making it impossible to land on many of the airstrips. We took the opportunity on that sunny dry April day to return with our fishing tackle to Tenient's ranch. He and his wife were at their outstation and wouldn't be back for a couple of hours. Happy and clueless, we went directly to the lake.

"There were quite a number of fish in the lake when we snorkeled last time," Caesar commented. "Let's look for that little dugout down the beach. We can cross the lake and try our new spinning rods along those weeds in front of the palm trees. We might find bigger fish there. Tenient told me the fishing is better on the far side," Caesar went on, "but he doesn't fish much anymore. His boys do. They caught some nice Lukananis." My mouth watered at the thought. Lukananis, about fifteen inches long, weighing five pounds were the best tasting fish I had ever experienced. "With a little luck we may catch a few," he added. Little did we know how much good luck we would need that afternoon.

We swam to cool down. Nellie spread a sheet on the sand and we ate our picnic lunch. Caesar and I had a few beers and the ladies drank pre-made tea. We enjoyed our usual twenty-minute siesta. I was first up and went to Jan's hammock. She was awake. I whispered, "Caesar and I are going out in the dugout to try our luck fishing on the other side. Be back in an hour or so, depending on how the fish cooperate."

"Umm, okay," she responded, sleepily.

Caesar was up, the dugout ready to go. I knew he was anxious to try the new spinning rods. He heard about them, but no one in the Rupununi had seen or used one. He was skeptical that so light a rod and line could actually pull in a large fish, but he was eager to put it to the test.

The narrow, tippy dugout—obviously constructed for smaller-boned Amerindians—was barely wide enough for our hips. We weren't deterred. Caesar picked up the paddles and handed me one. It was crude, but would suffice to move us around the lake. The dugout was more unstable than anticipated and to remain upright we alternated: one paddled while the other used his paddle as a stabilizing keel. With cautious practice, we arrived on the edge of the reeds on the far shore.

Caesar picked up his spinning rod. "Steady with your paddle while I cast. Then I'll do it while you try. Otherwise we'll wind up in the water."

"Okay," I agreed. My paddle steadied the boat. His second cast got a response.

"Think I've got one, but it must be small or it gave up quickly. Too easy to pull in," he grunted as his plug popped out of the water. "Must have lost it."

Several casts produced the same results, a strike, a short struggle, but no fish. I tried. On my third cast my rod bent over in a 'U' shape, the line *singing* from the strain as I tried to reel in. The brake drag, set for five pounds to keep from breaking the light line, clicked away. Whatever I had was more than five pounds. The clicking on the brake stopped, the pull on the rod lessened and I reeled in quickly.

"Can't believe he's giving up so quickly," I said. "He's coming up too easy or he somehow threw the hook."

The water boiled around my line. The plug popped out of the water with the end hook firmly imbedded in the lower jaw of what appeared to be a big Lukanani, but turned out to be the head only— no body. Several small fish were viciously biting on what was left of the head. Hundreds of others were churning the water below.

"Pirhani," Caesar shouted. These were the deadly man-eating fish we heard so much about before we came down.

"Don't move!" he spit out in his heavily accented guttural voice that became pronounced when triggered by emotion or anger. "Put your oar in to steady the boat...I'll paddle. We get out of here quickly. They cleaned that Lukanani in seconds. Must be thousands of them. Let's go."

Hardly breathing, barely moving, I stuck my paddle firmly in as a stabilizer and I could feel the vibrations of pirhani biting it. In their eating frenzy, they were attacking each other, churning the water twenty feet in all directions around our vulnerable dugout. I, too, wanted out...fast. Tipping would be fatal. Our movements were slow and deliberate. I shivered at the image of the lukinani head popping out of the water with the carnivorous fish clinging and biting. We could still hear the clicking of their sharp, serrated teeth, like a hundred metronomes out of control. We glided ten or twelve lengths before the worst of the churning disappeared. A few fish still broke the surface. Caesar picked up the pace. I continued to stabilize the boat. It took forever to reach the beach in front of the hammocks. Jan and Nellie were coming to take a swim.

"Don't go in the water." Caesar shouted. "It's loaded with pirhani."

Donald Haack

Nellie and Jan stopped in their tracks holding fast to Chris and Diney. Not wanting to step into the water, I balanced on the front end and stepped onto the sand.

"Keep sitting!" I told Caesar. "I'll pull it up and you can step onto the beach." In his haste, he ignored me and stepped into the shallow water, but jumped quickly onto the sand.

"That was too close," Caesar whispered. "I should have known that at this time of the year pirhani could be a problem." He went on to explain, "In the rainy season, the Amazon and its tributaries, the Rio Negro, Rio Branco, and the Mahu (Ireng) flood over their banks onto the savannahs creating one big lake. As the rains subside, the rivers retreat into their banks leaving small lakes scattered throughout the savannahs. As the dry season progresses the evaporating ponds become smaller and hold less food, starving the trapped fish. They attack anything including each other. That's when they're most savage. You've heard or read some of those horror stories that we just witnessed. If we had tipped back there, we'd be history—a couple of clean skeletons," he added for visual effect.

We picked up our gear and walked to Tenient's to tell him about his *idyllic* lake.

"Oh, yes, the boys should have told you. This late in the dry season, it's not a good idea to go in the lake. A year ago a horse was drinking water from the shallow edge when the pirhani attacked his feet, cutting the tendons and stripping the skin off his front legs. Never had a chance…fell into the water. In less than an hour the front half under water was totally stripped of flesh, just bones left. Another time my vaquero saw a seven-meter anaconda partially submerged in mud. When the water receded, the mud dried and he slid into deeper water to re-bury himself. Never made it. The pirhani got him first. In that mad churning bloody water the snake was stripped clean in less than a half hour and in the feeding frenzy they attacked and ate each other. Terrible sight."

We just looked at each other. They forgot to mention it to us, we thought?

For months, that incident remained the topic of conversation for the Haacks and the Gorinskys. Caesar thought he found a solution to the problem

"We could throw some chicken innards in the water from the shore near where we fished. We would feed the pirhani until there was a strong concentration of them and then we toss in a stick of dynamite and blow 'em up... kill everything within ten meters, certainly most of the pirhani. We'd repeat it until we rid the lake of *all* pirhani." We were confident of our *perfect* solution until Nellie popped up with her own observation.

"That's fine for a few weeks. Then the rains will come, flood the area, and the cycle will begin over again."

Of course, she was right. We didn't go back to Karakarana after that.

MERCY MISSION: BIRTHING BABIES

Word quickly spread that the *Americano* with the airplane was available for mercy missions. With no scheduled flights and a need for supplies, I flew to Good Hope. The jeep pulled up and instead of the expected Caesar, Nellie was behind the wheel. I taxied to our storage shed and shut down the engine. She opened the passenger door. "C's not here so I thought you might want some help. Can't lift your diesel barrels, though. "C" tells me you load and unload them yourself. They weigh almost four hundred pounds. Don't know how in the world you do it. Can I help refueling?" she asked.

I told her it would be great if she pumped gas from the barrel while I stood on top. As we were refueling I asked how she was doing and if there were any emergencies lately. Nellie was half Wapashani, educated in Guiana's primary and secondary schools through the British "A" levels and continued on to earn a nursing degree. With that background she was frequently called upon for medical emergencies, not only with the ranchers in the Rupununi, but lately and more frequently by the Macusi Indians. Travel was slow and with only one doctor in the vast territory, he couldn't be depended on for a quick response. "9-1-1" type emergencies took three weeks. My question to Nellie gave her the opening to ask for help.

"Funny you should ask," she added quickly. "Nadya, our house girl, just received notice that her aunt who lives near Karasabai is starting labor, but is having big trouble. From the description it sounded like a breach, and they don't know how to handle that problem. Trouble is, it would take me a day to get there and that would be too late. Don't suppose you would like to do a mercy mission and drop me at Karasabai? I could find my way back myself." She looked over at me to see if I was upset with her request.

Nellie did so much for Jan and me: giving us a home in her house for six months, accepting us as part of the family, and being there for Jan during her pregnancy. Nellie was like a surrogate mother and sister. I don't know how Jan would have survived without her ever-ready help. This was the first time Nellie had asked for anything, and typically, not for herself. I could hardly refuse.

"Are you ready to go soon?" I asked.

"Actually, I have my medical bag in the jeep. I could go now," she added a bit sheepishly. I smiled. She knew I would say yes.

"Okay, let's go." We rolled back the barrel, checked the fuel for water by drawing from the drain tube. All clear.

I thought for a moment before starting up the engine. "How long do you think it will take? Because it might be easier for me to wait for you and then fly you back again. My day is free, so it wouldn't be a problem."

"It shouldn't be more than a couple of hours at most. Have you any experience in birthing babies? I could use help," she added. I shook my head, no.

"Well, we'll change that fast. On the job experience. Nothing like it," she laughed heartily. "You should see your expression," she added. "I should have a picture of it. Okay, let's go. We have work to do."

Donald Haack

In twelve minutes we touched down at Karasabai. I marveled at the air travel time difference. It would have taken Nellie the better part of a day, possibly two, walking or riding a horse, in contrast to our short trip. Nadya came along to guide us to her aunt's house. It was near the river, a half hour walk. She pointed to a well-kept, small, mud-walled hut with a thatched palm roof. There were two more huts alongside. The only other sign of civilization was a narrow footpath to the river.

Beads hung over the door entrance. The darkness inside discouraged the Kabouri flies. To the right of the door was a lean-to area covered by palm leaves. That was the kitchen. There was a small fire below an old black iron pot that boiled furiously.

Before we entered the hut, Nellie had her bag out and handed me some torn up pieces of white sheet.

"Here, take two of these smaller cloths and drop them in the pot, but make sure it's water and not their dinner stew," she directed.

The woman in a hammock, drenched in sweat and appearing very weak, looked up at Nellie and extended her hand in a feeble greeting, saying something in Macusi I couldn't understand. Nellie went right to work.

"She's pretty far along and tuckered out. We have to work fast." She placed some palm leaves on the floor and laid a sheet on top. "I have to have her flat. Give me a hand getting her on this sheet."

We lifted her from the hammock and laid her down gently. She weighed less than a hundred pounds. The smell was a bit hard for me to take. There was liquid and coagulated blood in the hammock. Her water had broken, but fortunately just minutes before we arrived.

"We have work to do, and fast, to save the baby… if she's still alive." She bent down and put her ear to the woman's abdomen. A few seconds passed. "Strong heart beat, we're lucky. And she's lucky, so far."

She diagnosed the situation as a breach. She washed her hands with one of the boiled clothes and put some salve on her left hand.

"Left hand is smaller than my right and I have to go inside and turn the baby around. She stuck her hand in between the woman's legs. It disappeared. I stood by feeling more than a bit useless and uncomfortable. The contractions came every few minutes. I heard some distinct moans coming from the next hut. That wasn't unusual but there were no sounds of pain from the woman. Every time she had a contraction, her face contorted, but she remained silent. The sound that should have come from her came from the wailing next door, in perfect synchronization with the contractions. I was puzzled and wanted to ask Nellie about it, but she was too busy at the moment.

"Okay, I've finally repositioned it. Let's hope the umbilical cord isn't wrapped around—it's a fifty-fifty chance of that happening. If the delivery isn't fast the cord can be pinched. That's a problem for the baby. Serious damage without oxygen, if it goes on for more than a few minutes." She spoke quietly in a voice that would dispel any sense of alarm to the patient. The girl smiled. She didn't understand English and Nellie's soothing voice gave her added confidence and raised her spirits.

"We need her full cooperation at this point," Nellie exclaimed to me, as if to answer my anticipated question.

"Look, hold her hand. She thinks you're almost a god because you flew the airplane that brought me in. You know, of course, that men aren't allowed during birthing. You are the exception. You should feel flattered. Father Quigley is the only other man they allow to be present. Hold her hand, smile, and when she has a contraction you say, *ohai, ohai*. That means push in Macusi, and keep smiling. It'll help."

I did my *ohai* during the next contraction. I didn't squeeze her hand; she squeezed mine. She pushed and pushed. I heard the yells coming from outside, still coordinated with her contractions.

I looked up at Nellie. She shook her head. "Never mind, I'll tell you about it later. Keep your mind on your work. You're doing well," she smiled. "I've got the head." Contractions were coming one after another.

"Ohai, ohai," we both said. Seconds later Nellie raised up a bundle of blood, mucus, and a baby. She turned it upside down, slapped it, and we heard a loud cry.

"A girl," Nellie exclaimed, "And a healthy one, if her voice is any indication. Now hand me those other cloths." Nellie tied and neatly cut the umbilical, cleaned up the baby, and handed her to the proud, but tired mother.

She looked at Nellie and said something, then at me and uttered a few more words, the first I heard since she greeted Nellie. I expected loud and anguished yells or screams that I always associated with labor pains and birthing. But she never uttered a sound and now she was talking.

"She's thanking us," Nellie translated for me. I nodded and smiled, not knowing what else to do. We walked outside.

"Nellie," explain something to me. That girl never uttered a sound during labor. But I heard yelling and shouting outside when she had contractions. What gives?"

She stopped outside the second hut and was about to pull me inside. As she reached up to grasp my arm she noticed her hands. "Oh, excuse me. I have to clean up, but poke your head inside and take a look. I'll explain in a minute."

It took a minute for my eyes to adjust to the hut's dark interior. I could see a hammock with someone in it: a man drenched in sweat wearing a loincloth. A woman was alongside wiping his forehead. He was still groaning, but more in relief than the anguished sounds we heard earlier. My first thought was he might be wounded or very sick and in need of Nellie's ministrations also. Before I could make the suggestion to Nellie, she was at my side pulling me along the path.

"It's okay to leave now. They don't need us anymore. We're finished here. Let's go."

I started to tell Nellie about the man in the hammock who obviously needed help. Nellie threw her head back and laughed. "You have much to learn of bush ways. *He* was in labor, sympathetic labor for his wife. That's the way it works down here. The girl quietly has the baby while her man has sympathetic labor pains and screams. That way they share the burden and joy of labor and birth of their children. Seems a good way to me," she added and waited to see my reaction.

"You're serious. You're not kidding?"

"This tradition goes back thousands of years. You looked at me when she was having contractions and he was expressing the pain. Modern scientists have witnessed this but are at a loss to explain how it works. But it does. He's not in the room but he experiences real pain during her contractions. There are accounts where, during severe labor complications, the husband died and the woman barely survived. There are many cases where the man remained bedridden for days. After birthing, the woman gets up immediately and has both the baby and the husband to take care of. A bit different, eh?"

I certainly did have a lot to learn, I thought, as Nellie and I walked back to the plane.

MERCY MISSION—CANDIRU

L ess than ten days after our last medical emergency, we had
another. Nellie met me at the airstrip. Caesar had not yet
returned from Georgetown.

"Would you like to fly a mercy mission, this time just a couple
of minutes over there?" She pointed to the east. "Our outstation. I
could probably make it through by jeep, but "C" told me that the
road washed out with the first heavy rain two weeks ago and, as
far as I know, no one has fixed it yet. The airstrip is supposed to be
in good shape and only a couple of minutes flying from here. Can
you spare the time?"

"Sure." I answered. "Another delivery problem?"
"No, this is something you haven't seen. Might not be a pretty
sight. You've heard about the little candiru fish, haven't you?" She
raised her hand and measured about an inch between her finger
and thumb to indicate the small size. "But first I have to go back
to the house to get some special supplies for my medical kit. Did
you ever heat glass in chemistry class?"

"No, but I used to play with glass in our basement, heating

and pulling it into all kinds of designs. It was fun."

"Good, because that's exactly what I need. I have test tubes in my bag. I'll score them with a file and you break off the bottoms. Can you smooth out and flare the broken ends?"

"Yeah, I think so." I was about to ask why when she interrupted me.

"You have to twirl it in the flame so it won't crack when it gets red hot."

"Yup, I do remember that; broke too many when I first started. Do you have tongs to hold it with? And what do you use for a Bunsen burner?"

"I have one with two small butane tanks I use for sterilizing instruments."

We went into the dining room. She brought in her small black medical bag and took out two glass test tubes, while I hooked up the Bunsen burner. I turned the knob and the gas hissed out. It took a couple of tries to get a pointed blue flame. Nellie used a small three-sided file and with a few deft stokes, scored the tube all around near the closed bottom. She wrapped the end in a cloth, and tapped it lightly on the edge of the wooden table, cleanly separating the bottom of the tube. She handed it to me.

Holding it over the blue tip of flame and constantly twirling it so as not to apply too much heat in one spot, I warmed the tube until it turned a glowing red. I took the little stick Nellie handed me and slowly rotated it around the broken edge, both smoothing it and flaring out the edge. I was surprised how easily working the glass came back after all these years.

"Good, excellent, couldn't have done better myself. That's enough of a flare."

I started to ask her what she was going to use a test tube for when it didn't have a bottom, but she brushed me aside.

"I'll explain later on the way; let's go. You're in a hurry and so is my patient."

We picked up her bags, climbed into the airplane and were airborne in minutes. I recalled stories about the tiny tropical candiru discovered in the Amazon near Manaus, at Fordlandia, the rubber plantation. The Amazon and its tributaries: Rio Negro, Rio Branco, and Ireng overflow their banks during rainy season and flood thousands of square miles. All species of fish including the candiru are distributed throughout the area.

The candiru might have gone unnoticed except for its unpleasant habit of going into the rectum, open wounds, or genitals of humans. The fish sucks its way in and extends small barbs from behind its head The barbs stick in the flesh making it almost impossible to remove the fish without surgery.

Nellie explained that an Indian girl squatting in the water, legs apart, was washing laundry in the creek. "A skirt doesn't prevent candirus from entering the private parts. In spite of all my preaching about not sitting on your heels in the water without panties, some girls still persist…but not if they or one of their friends has the misfortune of a candiru going up her genitals. That just happened a few days ago and the girl tried unsuccessfully to remove it with a knife. Could be messy. How are you with blood? Don't faint, do you? On this one, I do need help. Just don't faint or get sick. 'C' won't do any of these operations with me. He absolutely refuses to help except as a driver. I hope you're better," she added and looked at me.

"I guess so," I said, without too much conviction because I was beginning to expect the unexpected and never knew what would turn up next. She wasn't convinced, so I added, "I took pre-med in Wisconsin working on cadavers and later first aid courses, which I used on some bloody Marine Corps emergencies. I'll be all right," I hoped.

Nellie was right—the outstation was close, five minutes by air. I barely raised the flaps after take off when she pointed out the airstrip and the little house in front of us.

"That's the outstation we built just over a year ago that 'C' was hoping you would move into. You did the right thing building your house at Marquis and having Jan with you. At first I didn't think any American girl straight out of college would survive a month down here. But Jan is as solid as a brick. She'll handle anything that comes along. You've got quite a girl there. She's obviously a lady with a good background and education, but she's tough in a way no one here expected. Hang onto her. I love her," she added.

It was the first time Nellie ever spoke about Jan. I knew there was a special bond between them though their backgrounds couldn't be further apart.

"Jan couldn't have made it without your help, Nellie. You've been like a mother and sister."

"Oh, posh."

We landed and Juan, the husband, waited for us to shut off the engine before opening Nellie's door. He spoke hurriedly in Macusi. Nellie questioned him in Macusi, Wapashani, and a bit of English thrown in. He understood and answered Nellie's questions to her satisfaction.

"His wife's inside; let's take a look. Bring my bag," she ordered as she struggled to get her long legs out of the plane and onto the small step. "Women should design airplanes. They could do a much better job," she said as she finally half slid, half jumped onto the tire and then the ground. She patted down her skirt, straightened out to her full height, and picked up her bag.

"Come on, El Doctor, we've got a patient awaiting," she said to me and smiled. The husband grinned from ear to ear, a complete change from when he had approached the plane looking like death warmed over. In a medical emergency Nellie was in high demand. She had the confidence of the Rupununi ranching community and the surrounding Macusi and Wapashani villages. What a woman! I looked at her admiringly. In her fifties and not a wrinkle in her face. Wavy black hair framed her attractive face: high cheekbones, beautiful deep brown eyes under large eyelashes, which probably came from her Scottish father, John Melville. He had two wives, Nellie's mother, Coco Janet and Janet's sister, Coco Mary.

Nellie was beautiful, inside and out. She walked with a regal air, but was never condescending. There was always a warm and personal greeting for everyone, yet she could take charge in any situation when needed. She exuded confidence and sincerity and I felt proud being with her.

She broke me out of my daydreaming. "Are you coming?" she raised her eyebrows in question.

"Sorry, thoughts were miles away. I'm ready." I followed her into the house.

There was a gentle breeze blowing through the bedroom. The girl lying on the bed and glistening with sweat looked feverish. Her hair, splattered flat on her forehead and cheeks, was caked with sweat and dust. Obviously in pain, she tried to smile as she looked up at Nellie.

"Don't worry, girl, we'll have you well in no time." In response to the girl's questioning look towards me, Nellie added, "It's all right," as she pointed to me. "He's both a pilot and a doctor's assistant with lots of medical experience."

I had just been promoted, I noticed, and tried to look professional as the girl nodded confidently. I discovered that sometimes it was more important in how you did something than what you did; a page out of the Shaman's book, I thought.

The girl closed her eyes, maybe out of modesty, but that was out of character when I thought of them making love in a community hut with the other inhabitants cheering them on. Perhaps that didn't extend to outsiders like me. Nellie eased back the light sheet covering her patient. She had no clothes on; her thighs were covered with dark black caked blood and bright red blood not yet coagulated. It spread out over the small cot and left a big spot in the dirt below where it had dripped through the thin matting of the bed.

Nellie quickly examined her. The girl's face grimaced at every move, but not a sound came out. Her eyes remained closed. I noticed small tears trailing down her cheeks. Another stoic woman.

"It's not real good, but not as bad as it first looked. I thought she cut herself badly, but with this candiru problem, she's also having her period. Makes it look much worse. Hand me my bag. I need a sponge, the flashlight, the diamond tweezers with the lock on them and the test tubes you worked on. See if we can get some boiled water. Ask the young girl. The husband's useless."

I handed everything to Nellie like a nurse's aid in an operating room, though this was far from a sterile room. I tried to concentrate on doing what Nellie was asking.

"Hold this up," she said to the girl raising her arms to hold up the sheet, shielding her from us. Nellie had spread her legs and beckoned me closer. Rather than feel embarrassed, I felt sympathy and quietly hoped the girl didn't feel uncomfortable by my presence. Apparently Nellie's assurance removed that possibility. Nellie spread her open. "Put the light right here." She pointed with her forefinger and cautiously dabbed with the sponge. "See that little white spot there? That's it. We're lucky it hasn't gone in very deep. Take the test tube with your left hand and put the end right up to it."

I slipped it in around the little spot, which now took on the more definite form of a broad tiny flat tail.

"Okay, just hold it there for a second." She used her finger and thumb of her right hand to hold the test tube in place. "Hand me the flashlight." She took it in her left hand. "Now, here comes the tricky part." she spoke quietly. "Take the tweezers, slide them inside the test tube and bend down here so you can look where to grab. I want you to turn the tweezers to the side, parallel to the tail. Close them gently on the sides of the candiru's tail. Try not to bump it. It could push in further and we don't want that. It's about 3/4 of an inch long. Right behind its head are two side fins with barbs. They're about 1/4 of an inch long and they spread out at right angles and are anchored in her flesh. Try to secure the tweezers around the tail, then hold firm. I'm then going to push the test tube to the left while you hold the tweezers steady. Don't move because if you do, you might push the right barb in deeper and she's going to feel that. We don't want her moving around too much and have to start all over. I'll tell her not to move."

She spoke in Macusi. The girl responded. Nellie said, "Good."

"When I say now, move the tweezers slightly to the right. I'm going to move the tube to the left at the same time. Now!" Nothing happened. "Just a little more to the right."

Donald Haack

I moved it to the right. She moved the tube to the left and in slightly.

"Okay, good. The left barb is inside the tube. I can see it. Ease the tweezers back to the left. That will compress the left barb and pull out the one right one at the same time. There, good, you've got it. Now very slowly draw it back inside the tube."

In unison we slowly drew back until the candiru was free of the vaginal opening.

"Success. You were very efficient."

I grunted. I was sweating, my hands and arms drenched in perspiration. I didn't think I did anything at all except follow instructions from Nellie, and I said so.

" I needed the extra hands. You can see now why I couldn't do this by myself," she assured me.

I looked down at the little fish. It looked innocuous enough. Both barbs were retracted and it didn't look much different than a minnow, except its mouth was round, sucker-like. It wiggled. I opened my 10-power diamond loupe to examine it, particularly the lateral barbed fins. They were flat until I squeezed. They came up and forward until they stuck out at right angles. I had seen enough. I squeezed harder and did the little bugger in. Meanwhile, Nellie wiped the blood off her hands, opened her black bag, selected two items, and squeezed ointment onto her finger.

"One is Bacitricin, an antibiotic, the other's, a topical anesthetic. Should give her immediate relief. Her husband said she hadn't slept in two days." Nellie applied the ointment on the affected area, eased the girl's legs down, and covered her with a fresh sheet. She was asleep before Nellie finished tucking her in. We went to the back room and washed up.

"Nellie, you did a fantastic job back there. I see why they depend on you so much. You do more than most doctors, and probably a better job, to boot." I added.

She scoffed. "Nonsense. Just doing the best I can. You were a big help." She was always giving someone else the credit instead of herself. Nellie was one in a million.

A fortnight later we had another emergency call from Karasabai. A woman, suffering for four days, was in worse shape and her candiru was almost twice the size of the first one. We used the same procedure, securing the fish on the top and bottom, moving it to the right as Nellie slipped the test tube to catch the left barb. But when we moved it back to the left, folding in the left barb, the right appendage was too long to ease inside the test tube. It was still sticking in her flesh. The candiru was almost bigger than the test tube.

"Hmm, now what?" Nellie pondered. We were head-to head between the woman's legs, both hands full, and the patient was bleeding. We couldn't sponge off the blood fast enough to see what we were doing. But, from the size of the fish, I knew the usual procedure wasn't going to work.

Nellie asked me, the assistant and neophyte, for a suggestion. We had to do something and my mind raced for an alternative procedure. Then I remembered looking at the last candiru with my 10-power loupe. The fins came up and forward. *Up and forward*, I thought again. So If I twist counter-clockwise, the right fin should fold in and down.

"Look," I said, sounding slightly desperate, "I think if I rotate it counter- clockwise while you push in ever so slightly, I can fold the right fin in enough to fit inside of the tube."

"Okay, it's worth a try. We sure aren't getting anywhere here and I don't know how much longer she can hold still with everything but our feet inside her. Let me know when you start twisting."

I did, and Nellie moved the test tube forward. There was so much blood we couldn't see. This was going to be strictly by feel. I eased the tweezers counter-clockwise. There was no resistance and the woman didn't jump.

"It must be loose, Nellie. We have the right barb in." We reversed the procedure. "I think we have both barbs in—slide the test tube back out and I'll pull back slightly." Our patient didn't jump. It worked. We let out a whistle of surprise, the little beast was over an inch and a half in length. No wonder we had difficulty getting it in the test tube. I said a quiet prayer that I took the time to examine the first candiru with my loupe or we would still be trying to extract this one. We breathed a sigh of relief.

"That's enough for one day. Next time we'll get a bigger test tube, but at least we know an alternative solution if there's a big one."

As we were leaving, Nellie took the time to explain to the women in the village about the hazards of squatting legs apart while doing laundry in the creeks. This time, however, she had a very attentive audience. She told the women that I would have ladies' panties in our trade store and they should wear them when they went down to the river to do laundry or swim.

I made a mental note to order panties for the store and wondered what Dutch would say when they arrived. I smiled at the thought. The next day I called Anis Khouri, the dry goods merchant in Georgetown, and ordered four dozen small and medium-size panties.

"What colors," he asked.

"Colors? I questioned back. "I don't know. Any color, it doesn't make any difference, just send the panties." I wasn't about to explain to him over the short wave radio the reasons why we wanted them. That story would come later. Two boxes came by DC-3 the next Friday. Dutch unpacked them and looked at me questioningly.

"Panties?" he asked. "Vat for, a vind sock? Moost be a mistake. Shood I pack dem back up for return? No one ever asked about panties," he winced as he said it, "since we opened der store."

I put a price on them and said, "No, keep em, there's a good reason." I wasn't going to explain to Dutch with his hard-of-hearing problem. It would take all day. I just walked out the store and knew without looking that Dutch was shaking his head and grumbling. So be it.

A few days later, Dutch came up for dinner and the first thing he said was, "We sold every one of dos dam tings, dos panties. Vat goes?" He looked puzzled. I made our drinks for the evening:

Jan's Bourbon and water, my Dewars Scotch and soda, and Dutch's Demerara rum with water. We sat down at the table and in the next half hour with much shouting, drawing in the air and finally drawing on paper, Dutch looked up at me.

"Ouch," is all he said, as he wiggled in his chair uncomfortably.

In the next few weeks our store sold over two hundred panties. We simply couldn't stock enough. But there was one persistent problem for Dutch. He kept excellent records. Over two dozen panties disappeared mysteriously. He knew they weren't taken while he was in the store and the store did not seem to have been broken into. It bothered him for days. I had enough problems with the dredge, maintenance, and scheduling of the airplane. I didn't intend to keep track of the trade store goods, and I told Dutch that.

I left the panty problem to him. That was all he talked about. Two weeks later we solved that mystery when we discovered a strange, totally unexpected problem.

WAI WAI COUNTRY

As we left the breakfast table and our last cup of coffee, I touched Dutch on the arm to get his attention. Being almost deaf, he could barely hear me even when I shouted. He looked up.

"Start the generator," and turned my hand in a circle, as if cranking.

"Yah, yah. I get one of da Indian boys to shtart oop. Yah."

The noise of the generator shattered the tranquility of this isolated and peaceful valley. I stepped into our library and turned on our Collins radio that had two local radio crystals: one tuned to British Guiana Airways for flight information, and the second to Georgetown Telecom, the local telephone service.

With fourteen stations operating in the interior a clear line to Central Telecom in Georgetown was a constant problem. A few remote stations were the worst offenders because they wanted to converse with someone, anyone from the outside world while others had business to conduct.

To eliminate delays, I called Guiana Airways early, 0700, and would get right through. This was mutually beneficial since their three DC-3's delivered cargo and passengers to eight airstrips in the interior. Because my plane was capable of landing on the numerous small airstrips, it quickly became the new mode of transportation. B.G.Airways and I coordinated schedules so as not to leave passengers or cargo stranded in the middle of the interior.

At 0700: "B.G. Air, B.G. Air, This is Marquis calling, do you read, over?"

They acknowledged my call immediately. "Traffic for you...Urgent, from the Director of Civil Aviation. He is here and wishes to speak directly to Don Haack, are you ready?"

Alex Phillips, the director came on and after many *repeats*, *overs* and *confirms*, the message came through: an American registered plane crash-landed in the extreme southern tip of British Guiana in Wai Wai Indian territory. The Wai Wais were a primitive tribe in an almost impenetrable rain forest 150 miles from the nearest and seldom-used airstrip, Lumid Pau, 300 miles north of the equator and 200 miles south of my familiar territory.

The pilot of a Helio Courier, a STOL Short Take-Off and Landing aircraft, reported it crash-landed with three passengers on board near the Wai Wai village. It was not known who they were or what they were doing in that remote territory. They had a B.G. Airways' crystal and were able to call in their emergency landing and approximate location. The plane was damaged beyond repair. No injuries reported, but they advised it would be impossible to walk out and were requesting assistance. They were near an abandoned airstrip, which the Wai Wai were clearing. To conserve their battery they would call in two weeks when the strip should be safe for a rescue plane to land.

Alex asked if I would do it. I agreed. It would have been difficult to turn him down, since I had the only small plane in the territory. The two-week time frame would be enough to get my plane ready and learn all I could about this new territory.

With Jan's efficient help, I organized a list of maps, equipment, and flying schedules. The emergency equipment I carried on board would have to be different for this mission. I eliminated most of the heavier airplane tools, which I replaced with rations, picks, shovels, axes, and machetes for clearing trees and improving an airstrip.

My feelings were ambivalent about this rescue. I could sense the nervousness Jan felt about the risky venture. I was placing our plane, the lifeline of our mining operation, at risk. On the other hand, in this territory where everyone depended on every one else, a mercy mission couldn't be ignored. On the positive side, the excitement of exploring a new frontier and meeting the primitive and isolated Wai Wai Indians was a heady experience for a young bush pilot straight out of college. It would be a once-in-a-lifetime experience if I succeeded. It might be the end of one if I didn't. I didn't want to consider that alternative.

I had flown mercy missions before but never in so remote an area. This territory was uncharted even on the latest maps. The ranchers claimed that the Wai Wai bush region between the south savanna and the Amazon was the most remote, hostile region in South America. If our plane went down, walking out would not be a realistic option, a fact already known by the people from the downed plane.

I had good maps, but nothing in detail of the area in question, so the next few days were spent talking to the old pilots of World War II in B.G. Airways. Colonel Williams from Wisconsin, the founder of the airways, Harry Wendt, his engineer, and my friend Julian Pieniazek, the chief pilot, were the only three people known to have flown into that territory… seventeen years earlier. A World War II DC-3 went down and the three of them spent months doing repairs and flew it back.

Phillips, the director, arranged for Julian and Harry Wendt to meet me at Good Hope the following Friday. They would bring World War II maps and their best recollections of the rescue.

Jan, Diney, and I flew into Good Hope early that Friday to meet them and surprised Nellie and Caesar who didn't expect us until noon. We sat in their dining room with a cup of coffee and explained about the downed airplane and the DCA's request for help.

With a hint of a smile, Nellie gave Caesar a meaningful glance. Jan and I looked at each other wondering what was going on. Caesar, in his inimitable way, took out his handkerchief, held the end in his mouth while he silently paced the room, his way of mulling over a subject before he came to a decision.

"Did you know that Nellie and I used to live at the edge of the south savanna, a place called Para Bara?" he said quietly.

I looked surprised. "No, I didn't know. When was that?"

"Just after we were married. There were rumors about gold in the small clearing below Ishalton and Lumid Pau. The Indians called it Para Bara, but none of them lived there. The hunting was excellent. Some of Nellie's relatives brought back gold. We decided to move there, raise cattle and prospect for gold. Remotest place in B.G. We encountered a few Wai Wai Indians, mostly from Brazil, who were being driven out by Amazonion miners and the Brazilian government. None came from the British Guiana side. There were no trails back then. The trip to their village, where you're planning to go, took over a month. Many Wai Wai didn't survive the hardship on the trail.

With the exception of Para Bara, the savannas had less game than the bountiful bush, so there was no reason for the B.G. Wai Wais to come out except every few years when they needed tools: machetes, axes, and sharpening files. The jaguars killed most of our sheep and some of our cattle. Conrad was born the third year. There was no doctor or medical facility within 150 miles. A year later we left and made Good Hope our home."

He was still chewing on his handkerchief. "The Para Bara savannah and particularly the adjoining bush is the most desolate country on the face of this earth," he repeated and looked up at me. "You've already decided to try the rescue, I assume?"

I nodded. He cleared off the dining room table and brought out some old sketches half eaten by ants and partially dry-rotted. We could distinguish a few areas and trails, which he had copied on fresh paper. Nellie coached him on some of the finer details of creeks, bush, the size of the savanna, the distances and heading to the only DC-3 airstrip in the area, Lumid Pau near Ishalton, the southernmost Wapashani village. Lumid Pau would be my jumping off point into Wai Wai country.

When the DC-3 arrived Caesar and I were waiting on the airstrip. Julian let Vicky, his co-pilot, park the plane on the runway take-off area. That would be unthinkable at a civil airport, but not at Good Hope since the only two B.G. Airways planes were on the ground, one in Lethem and one here.

The three of us climbed into the jeep and after a bumpy, hair-raising few minutes we arrived in a cloud of dust at the ranch house. Nellie had a big spread laid out for lunch but Caesar pre-empted her.

"Nellie, we need the dining room to lay out our maps and make plans. Hold the lunch for an hour. This is the only opportunity we have." I felt sorry for Nellie having done all that work, but knowing the urgency, she quickly cleared the table.

We poured over the maps, sketches, and notes scattered over the table. The somber faces revealed the seriousness of our mission. The atmosphere turned Nellie's dining room into a war room. Caesar did not have a handkerchief clenched in his teeth, but he still paced the floor

Julian spoke first. He described the Wai Wai villages located on the headwaters of the Essequibo River approximately fifteen miles north of the mountain range dividing British Guiana and Surinam. He recalled the main village was situated on the left bank of the Essequibo headwaters, about a mile or two east of the only open savannah in the flat hundred-square mile area. That clearing, a mile long and half mile wide, was part grass, part swamp, and had patches of white sand easy to spot in an all-green jungle.

"That must be the small savannah where the plane went down, the one you call Gunn strip. Did you actually get a DC-3 out of there?" I asked Julian.

"Yeah, but it wasn't easy. Took two months of repairs on the plane and clearing for an airstrip. The only reason we were able to fly it out was because it was the driest season the Wai Wais could remember. The place is usually a swamp."

We agreed that it would be necessary to strip my plane to bare essentials. Seats, carpets, matting, and unnecessary radio equipment would be removed. Julian and Vicky would fly in two barrels of 80-octane gas to Lumid Pau.

We checked and re-checked the maps and finally concluded that a magnetic compass heading of 115 degrees from Lumid Pau would get me a few miles north of the village. Julian emphasized how imperative it was that I locate the Essequibo River. If I missed the river, I would have to abort. There were no other landmarks in the area.

He taught me a critical lesson about bush flying in new territory. "You never fly an exact heading to your destination, in this case, the village. The chance of arriving precisely on target after 150 miles of dead reckoning? Less than fifty percent," he said with emphasis. "Because, when you reach the river and the village isn't in sight, you don't know whether to turn left or right. Your chance of success just dropped fifty percent. If you plot a course north of the destination, you know you have to turn south when you locate the river— eliminating that big error." As he talked he drew a sketch of the route. "Look for smoke. In the rain forest Indians keep fires for warmth at night and for cooking and tempering their arrows in the daytime. Carry extra gas in jerry cans. Keep in mind they're only good if you can land to refuel. You're going to be on a marginal airstrip at best. You'll need every advantage. If you land with extra fuel on board, dump most of it for the return trip."

I looked at him in surprise.

"Yeah, I know. That's hard for a bush pilot, throwing out good petrol. Better that than hanging up in the trees because you were a hundred pounds too heavy. Take every margin you can. You'll understand when you're down there...and hopefully back." He smiled. "You'll make it all right. Just don't push the margins. Good luck."

Plans were made to the last detail even the best way to pancake onto the trees in case of an engine failure.

Donald Haack

The next two weeks were spent doing checks and maintenance of the airplane and consolidating what little maps and information we could find. Julian and Harry Wendt were the only people I could find who had actually been in Wai Wai territory. Caesar and Nellie had lived in the southernmost savanna near the jump off point, but that was over twenty years ago. I hoped their recollections were good.

The day before I left, I removed the unusable VHF radio and navigation equipment. There were no navigational aids or receivers in that territory. I double-checked my high frequency radio with its 150 foot retractable trailing antennae tuned to B.G. Airways. It was effective over 300 miles, well within my range.

Ten days after our Good Hope meeting, Guiana Airways advised me that they received a weak signal from the Helio that the airstrip was ready. There would be no further communication. Their battery was too low. The airways confirmed delivery of two barrels of 80-octane aviation fuel at Lumid Pau.

After a heart-rending goodbye to Jan and Diney with promises not to take unnecessary chances, I took off.

In less than an hour, I passed the government outpost, Lethem a few miles north of the Kanaku Mountains, the furthest point south I had flown. The next hour would be in new territory. The 5,000 foot Kanakus were bathed in cumulus clouds. Rather than going around, I opted to take a short cut through the valley Julian had pointed out on his map. Twenty minutes later and through the valley, I was in the flatlands of the 1500 square mile Southern Rupununi Savanna, occupied by two ranches and three Wapashani tribes. One of those ranches, the Rupununi Development Company, was an important checkpoint along my flight path for adjustments on the continuing flight to Lumid Pau.

The local ranchers had been very helpful, giving minute details on the south savanna, but their information, learned on horseback or walking, was definitely not the same as flying at 1,000 foot elevation at 135 mph. Foot tracks, trails, and water holes were frustratingly elusive. Caesar and Nellie's information proved to be the best on the area. Nellie's mother was Wapashani and her

Scot father, John Melville, founded the Rupununi Development Company, the ranch I hoped to see at any moment.

Moments later, I spotted the ranch dead ahead and a good omen, less than three degrees off course and within two minutes of my Estimated Time of Arrival. So far so good. I made a minor adjustment on the course heading for the next leg to Lumid Pau. On my left in the distant east, I saw the beginnings of the dark unbroken bush that extended to Wai Wai country and the Amazon. That sighting gave me a foreboding sense of *darkness* that I couldn't understand, but quickly shook it off as I continued navigating.

The next hour was critical. I checked and re-checked headings for possible wind drift. Ten minutes before my Lumid Pau ETA , I started a visual left and right, front and below sweep for the bush airstrip.

The terrain looked all the same: flat, semi-grassy land accentuated by darker green wet areas and palms, but no distinguishing land marks. Thirty-five minutes after passing the Rupununi ranch, the bush a couple of miles to my left curved in an arc close to my flight path. Once again there was that dark ominous feeling.

I continued my search pattern and caught a glimpse of closely clumped trees bordering a slender white line heading east-west that appeared to be manmade; hopefully, Lumid Pau. I flew directly over thinking how easy to miss.

There were the two drums of fuel below the palm trees. Coming into the wind, I landed in the first few hundred feet. The strip was in good shape. After taxiing to the trees I turned off the engine and looked in all directions...nothing! It was a totally remote and isolated area.

I tied the plane down with two screw-in stakes and gave a silent thanks that I found Lumid Pau on course and within four minutes of my estimated time of arrival. Another good omen.

I refueled, checked the oil, secured the tie downs, and found two trees to hang my hammock. From the bruises on the bark, it was evident I wasn't the first to sleep here. Dinner consisted of a can of *bully beef,* canned beef with generous slices of onions on crackers, and washed down with a warm beer. Later, when the temperature dropped, I built a fire and sat with a cup of strong hot tea.

Before I slept I reviewed my plans for the next leg—the critical one. I thought of the Gorinskys' first home a few miles south in Para Bara. They were adventurous and brave to live so far from a civilized area. Their knowledge was a help to me. Para Bara would be my only checkpoint between Lumid Pau and Wai Wai country.

My feelings were mixed. The excitement of discovery was tempered by the magnitude and hostility of this new unexplored territory. I had lived in the bush long enough to understand its unforgiving nature. You could depend on surprises but seldom were they good. I was prepared for a rough trip. I wouldn't be disappointed.

I awakened at daybreak. The sun's rays were a warm welcome after a cool night. I leisurely started a fire and brewed a strong coffee adding a good dollop of Carnation tinned milk. Jan had packed a breakfast for me: two eggs and two pieces of bread. I fried the eggs and put the bread in the pan for toast. It would be the last *elegant* breakfast for some time.

I didn't want to reach my destination too early so there was no rush to take off. In the humid jungle, morning fog clings to the ground for hours until the sun burns it off. The last thing I needed would be poor visibility at the headwaters of the Essequibo River. Close to its source, the river would be a small stream, difficult to spot under ideal conditions and virtually impossible below scattered fog.

The savannah in the morning was beautiful. The bush with low intermittent patches of fog a few miles east gave a *fence, keep out* illusion. A brisk walk down the runway to inspect for holes or obstacles was followed by stretching exercises and ending a slow jog of three lengths to juice up the body and pour oxygen-laden blood into the gray cells.

It was 0930 when most of the ground fog dissipated. This next leg would be the ultimate test of precision and dead reckoning navigation: no physical or electronic aids, just time, direction, and distance.

I completed one last check, more for ritual than need. I had gone over everything several times. There was nothing else. I settled into the left seat, took off. At a thousand feet I leveled off and set the engine at 2250 RPM, the best fuel flow for distance. There was a very light breeze at ten o'clock on the "clock" compass, requiring a one-degree course correction. After eight minutes I passed the demarcation between savanna and bush, light to dark…symbolic, I thought. Unknown territory, no outside help. Once again the dark mood raised its ugly head.

A few scattered clouds persisted after fifteen minutes, but weren't thick enough to hide the Gorinskys' Para Bara Savannah. I could almost feel the isolation that ultimately drove them out; no sign of life or civilization in any direction. Para Bara was my second checkpoint. Leaving the savannah was the first. I marked the two points and drew a line. It coincided with my heading, a small but welcome satisfaction.

The endless flat green carpet remained the same for forty-five minutes but then, upon closer scrutiny, I noticed a few rounded hills—the first change in terrain. Not being able to afford the slightest error, I constantly checked wind drift and compass heading, which is relatively easy in a no-wind condition. I hoped it was correct and would find out soon enough.

At 1,000 feet elevation changes were visible and the height should be sufficient to spot the Essequibo River. The 200 foot trees formed a seamless umbrella that made it extremely difficult to detect water below. I looked for a slight dip or shallow to pinpoint my search pattern. I would only have mini-seconds to see a reflection of sky from the water directly below. From this height I wondered if it were even possible to distinguish between the Essequibo and the streams leading into it. This close to its headwaters, the Essequibo River would be narrow and I didn't have a clue as to its size in relation to the other streams.

Seventy-five minutes out, I felt the first of several bumps indicating a breeze and irregular terrain. Now at the Essequibo River headwaters, I gradually climbed above the scattered small clouds to locate the 3,000 foot mountains twenty miles south on the Surinam border. According to the map, I should see them in minutes.

To go into *slow flight* I reduced RPM from 2200 to 1900 with enough flaps to hold an altitude of 1500 feet. Still on my original compass heading, I calculated my position to be seven minutes from the Essequibo plus one minute added to my ETA to compensate for the slower speed. I started my visual quadrant search pattern: forward, straight down, and left. I scanned the right quadrant in the same pattern. On every line sweep, I glanced directly down so as not to miss water reflected below. Unfortunately, the rising sun shining into my eyes made the search more difficult.

I was wet with perspiration from the intense concentration. The sun streaming in produced tiny rainbows on the round balls of water on my hand. I was hoping maybe the rainbows would bring luck. I searched the horizon for telltale signs of Wai Wai village smoke, which according to calculations should be on my right this side of the Essequibo.

Still nothing. Three minutes before ETA, I spotted a reflection directly below and to my right. I banked for a better view. It turned out to be small creek or swamp. Too small. I turned back onto my original heading.

Five minutes later, beyond my ETA by two minutes, I saw a larger reflection directly below and turned 180 degrees for another look. This stream was bigger and moving faster and appeared to be going in the right south to north direction. Hopefully this was the Essequibo. I turned on a southern heading to follow the river…not easy. It meandered erratically east and west along its southerly route. There were seconds of panic each time it turned more than 30 degrees and went out of sight, until I found it again. I flew shallow "S" turns to keep it reasonably in sight and couldn't help thinking, if this isn't the Essequibo, I just used up precious minutes.

In between navigating and flying, I continued my visual sweeps for a fire, hut, or village. On the horizon between cumulous clouds approximately fifteen miles ahead I saw the steeply rising land: the watershed mountains on the Surinam border. According to Harry Wendt, the Wai Wai village lay ten or fifteen miles north of those mountains. If I were on the Essequibo and my calculations were correct, I should be over the village within minutes. No sign of smoke. The wrong river? Nine precious minutes gone, leaving twelve more to find the airstrip or abort.

Two more minutes elapsed and at the two o'clock direction, I noticed a definite lighter color in the jungle. I headed in that direction to what appeared to be the only open area in the last ninety minutes of flying. It had to be *Gunn* strip that Julian and Harry Wendt used in WWII. On closer inspection I saw white sand, grass, and a creek bordering the west side. It was *Gunn* strip. Relief washed over me like a cool shower. I wouldn't have felt quite so elated had I known what awaited me in the next few minutes.

Midway on the opposite side of the creek and on the grass, a small plane was tilted at an unnatural angle. I checked my time, ninety- four minutes in route.

No one was near the plane. I made a low level pass and saw a crude "X", the international sign for *closed airport* or *runway unusable* next to the plane. Flying near the ground, I saw water everywhere with the exception of one or two isolated very rough areas.

I was confused. The survivors' last transmission was not ambiguous. They clearly stated they had an adequate airstrip for a small plane, but this wasn't it. Yet their Helio Courier crash-landed here. I climbed 200 feet above tree level to scan the surrounding countryside. A mile to the east and near the Essequibo, I spotted a wisp of smoke. I expected the pilot would have built a roaring fire as a beacon visible for miles, but this little trail of smoke barely made it above the rain forest where it quickly dispersed. I banked sharply heading directly toward the smoke. As I came closer there several oval clearings, which had round grass huts—the Wai Wai village.

Donald Haack

Thick smoke hung above the trees, especially from the back of a large clearing. An airstrip? I dropped lower to check it out. Apparently it was supposed to be. One end of the long clearing perched on the edge of a ridge, which then sloped downhill and ended in a field of fallen trees. A sheer wall of tall trees formed the far boundary. My stomach tightened up.

I was good at short field landings, but this would be minimal at best. I might land and take off on the cleared section, but it seemed impossible to climb fast enough to clear the trees. They were much too close and too high. I tried to think logically: there was a pilot down there and he should know what he is about. Should, that is.

Naked red-skinned Indians ran into the cleared area. Among them were two white people who waved and pointed to where the so-called runway started. I made one pass simulating a landing and spotted a stick with a limp hanging cloth—the air sock. No wind. I came around and made a second pass, which made me even more uncomfortable with what I saw. The first problem was landing. I had to be low and slow and touch down at the very beginning. The high trees before the ridge on the approach required a steep descent, which in turn builds up airspeed. High airspeed requires a long runway, which this wasn't. Worse, it was downhill making it difficult to stop.

There was a bigger problem evident on the first pass. When I came in steep and fast, then applied full throttle and take-off flaps, I barely cleared the trees on the far side. That reinforced my feeling it would be impossible to climb over those trees from a start-up speed of a ground take off. I understood their belief I could land, but I was at a loss as to how they figured I could take off.

For a simulated touchdown in the first thirty feet, I made a third pass, cross-controlled aileron and rudder to create a severe side slip that lost altitude and speed. It worked and the approach was as slow as a simulated landing. When I powered back up for the go-around, I barely cleared the trees—a clear warning to abort and head back to Lumid Pau.

Donald Haack

Checking my clock, I had three minutes left before the point of no-return, not enough fuel to make it back. I hadn't calculated on so many simulated landings using full throttle, which could easily leave me with less than my twenty-minute reserve for the return flight.

Sometimes I'm not too smart. My gut feeling and calculations on the last go-around told me not to land. I ignored those signals. I came around once more, this time for the landing. Once committed to touching down, I couldn't turn back.

I skimmed over the trees in a severe sideslip with the stall horn beeping, full flaps and half power. I dropped slightly below the ridge, and then just above stall speed I applied full power to rise up to the lip. For a few seconds I literally hung on the prop at full power. Thirty feet before the edge, I cut the power, stalled, the wheels touched down in the first ten feet. I stood on the brakes and bumped to a halt on the rough surface in three hundred feet, less than half the strip.

It took a few seconds to realize it was a safe landing and the plane undamaged. I was drenched in sweat and exhausted. Before I collapsed I had the presence of mind to immediately shut down the engine. Seconds later I was surrounded by hordes of painted naked Indians. I vaguely recall being thankful that the engine was stopped, avoiding the catastrophe of Indians walking into a lethal spinning prop.

It took minutes to wind down mentally and for my heart rate to return from 150 beats to my normal 76. I swung open the door to be greeted by the Wai Wais who seemed genuinely thrilled to see me. I would have shared their elation and smiles if I hadn't the overwhelming conviction that it was impossible to fly out of this God-forsaken mistake of an airstrip. A quick glance around confirmed those fears.

My immediate attention went back to the impressive Wai Wais. Their deep red ochre skin color was the first I had ever seen in South American Indians. Besides the patterns of red, black, and white paint that covered their bodies and faces, they wore elaborate decorations with colored feathers from parakeets, toucans, and macaws. Their painted faces projected a hostile facade, which their broad, guileless smiles totally negated. The stocky, well fed, good-looking men wore skimpy loincloths, barely covering the essentials.

The women, only slightly smaller, were also painted but not as elaborately. They were naked except for a beaded apron in front that hung from a waist string. Their jet black hair was pulled back, the same as the men's. Both men and women tied their hair into a tight ponytail stuffed in a piece of bamboo and decorated with beads. Many of the women had miniature hammocks slung over their shoulder holding tiny newborn babies. Others, while walking were breastfeeding older children who held on to the mother's teat. They women stopped feeding long enough to approach, smile, and touch me, satisfying their curiosity of the visitor from the sky then went back to nursing.

They pointed, laughed, and watched every move I made. I was their source of amusement; however for me, it was like being on the wrong side of a cage at the zoo.

The Wai Wais, unlike other Indians I encountered, were friendly, loved to touch, and laughed a lot. As fascinated as I was with them, I was more curious about our survivors and their state of health. A thousand questions raced through my mind, but were delayed by the raucous welcome I was receiving. I finally spotted a disheveled, unshaven, smiling white man pushing his way through the closely packed Indians surrounding the plane.

Tall, thin in an expensive safari outfit, he could have passed for the actor, William Holden, except for the unkempt beard and on closer inspection, the need of a clothes change. As he approached, the look and smell confirmed that washing or changing clothes these past three weeks had not been a high priority.

He extended his hand and sported a big smile that revealed picture perfect white teeth.

"Tom Slick. Are we glad to see you!"

I shook his hand. His grasp felt firm but not strong. He had long, thin fingers, soft skin, small hands that obviously were not familiar with manual labor. His gaunt look was understandable—they hadn't been eating gourmet food for three weeks.

"Hi, Don Haack," I answered. "How you ever got in this remote place, I don't know. Two World War II pilots were the only ones in Guiana who knew anything about this area. They said I had a fifty-fifty chance of finding you and less getting you out." I looked around at the towering trees surrounding the makeshift airstrip. I would come to that problem later.

"First off, are all four of you okay? Anyone injured?"

"We're fine, just a bit shook up from the crash landing but nothing serious. Our Helio came in real slow, and it would have been an easy landing except the wet bog stopped us in a semi-crash. The plane won't fly again. Understand walking out isn't an option. They say two months at best… if you survive. Even Wai Wais lose a few men on that trek to the savanna.

"We checked out the reason for our engine failure—dirt in the fuel. When our pilot, Jack Barber, switched tanks over that open area, contaminated fuel shut down the engine completely and he dead-sticked the plane into the sand where it nosed-over."

Tom appeared to be the leader of the group and the owner of the plane. After the rest of his disheveled party arrived, he introduced Jack Barber, a Canadian bush pilot, Dick Macklin of the California Macklin Engineering Company, and lastly, Leonard Clark who wasn't much taller than Tom, but his big frame carried at least fifty pounds more. In contrast to Tom, Leonard Clark seemed to thrive on bush rations. He looked robust and appeared to be enjoying this whole episode. Strange guy, I thought.

Leonard grabbed my hand in his *big* hand. "Leonard Clark," he said, "Really glad to see you."

I looked at him closer. The name Leonard Clark rang a bell. "Are you the writer, by any chance?" I asked.

He nodded affirmatively, "Yeah, I've written a few books."

"If there are only a few, I've read most of them. Glad to meet you in person," I added. "I read *A Wanderer 'til I Die*, *The Rivers Ran East*, and *Life in The Himalayas.*" I hesitated a bit before I continued. I didn't know what kind of reaction I would get from my next remark. "The last chapters of *Rivers Ran East* were set in the area where we now live. After living there a couple of years, I wondered if you didn't stretch the poetic license a bit describing some shocking adventure stories in that area."

If I expected my remark to evoke a response or explanation, I was disappointed. He shrugged, smiled, and said it would be enjoyable to talk about it some night. I thought he handled that diplomatically. I explained the reason I was in this country was from my reading interest in stories about Jimmy Angel, the bush pilot, but more coincidentally, Leonard's *River Ran East*.

Tom Slick immediately picked up on that, pointing out the strange twist of fate: that I read Leonard's books, which in turn prompted me to come to this country and then rescue him from a plane crash. Too much of a coincidence to be a mere chance happening, he said.

I smiled and quickly reminded him that we hadn't accomplished the rescue yet. That depended on our ability to fly out of here, something I wasn't yet convinced we could do.

We moved the plane, secured it with tie-downs, walked the length of the airstrip, and afterwards hiked to their makeshift camp where we discussed what needed to be done. Jack Barber and I were the only two who understood the enormity of our problem. The other three offered plenty of ideas, few of which were practical.

We talked long into the evening about everything except the reason they were in this area, a subject they avoided like the plague. This was a strange group: a wealthy playboy, a Canadian bush pilot, an author, and a manufacturer, all with seemingly nothing in common.

Tom Slick, I later learned from Jack Barber, was the son of Tom Slick Sr., who founded the Slick Oil Company in Dallas that young Tom recently inherited. After the war Tom Jr. organized and operated *Slick Airline* the competitor to the famous Flying Tiger Cargo Airline. In his spare time, which he had plenty, Tom dabbled in Extra Sensory Perception, a two year pursuit of the alleged *abominable snowman*, and clairvoyant people. He met and sponsored the famous Dutchman, Peter Hirkus, who read people's background by holding a personal object of theirs. I related that I met the *Father of Parapsychology*, Dr. Rhine from Duke University. Sitting around the fire at night, Tom and I had much in common to discuss.

Most of the conversations concerned the airstrip. The group felt that the cooperative Wai Wai Indians could surmount all our problems. We started on a plan.

That night the hospitable Wai Wais were omnipresent. They brought an unappetizing pot of something smelly and vile looking. I brought some cassava bread with me, and to show our appreciation we dunked it in the stew and pretended to eat some of the indescribables floating around. We went to bed hungry.

The next morning before breakfast we were on the airstrip to implement our plan. We paced off the runway and though the area was cleared of trees, it still had stumps. The wall of two-hundred foot trees lined the far side of the stump area. The measurements confirmed my worst fears—no way could I take off, even empty, and clear those trees.

We began the project immediately by directing the largest group of Wai Wai men to cut trees at the end of the open area. Upon closer scrutiny I noticed slightly left of the take-off path the trees were considerably lower and the logical place for Indians to start. A mere ten degree turn on take-off would not be a serious compromise, but the height of trees straight ahead presented a major project and more than we could handle.

I gave the Indian work crew four new broad head axes with sharpening files. They honed the axes to razor sharpness and before noon trees started falling in all directions. At minimum, I figured we needed to extend the clearing another 200 feet. Quite an undertaking, but with the willing Wai Wai manpower, it began to look feasible.

Jack Barber explained that the area known as Gunn strip where their Helio crashed was low and wet. They first thought they could firm up five hundred feet, but that had proved to be impossible. Too much water. The WaiWais showed them this clearing near the village, a partially completed airstrip started years ago by some missionaries. It was condemned as unsafe by the Jungle Aircraft Rescue Service, JARS. Looking at it now, I easily understood that decision. Sited precariously atop a small cliff with a poor approach, the airstrip itself was marginally short for landing and much too short to take off. Worse, the space to clear the high trees on the take-off path was inadequate. Any one of those factors warranted condemnation, but together made JARS' decision easy. Now it was my problem.

There were bumps, holes, and soft spots in the runway. In order to bring it up to minimal operating standards, I needed plenty of willing hands. At best, I anticipated one-and-a-half to two weeks of hard work. My primary concern was the tall trees on the take-off path. Having chosen the lower flight path on the left, we would save weeks of work. Seeing the good start by the Wai Wai in cutting those trees, I felt we might solve our problems.

In broken Spanish, Portuguese, and sign language, our team of five conveyed the plans to the Wai Wai. Within hours we had more Indians than we knew what to do with, but by afternoon all were working. As we directed the work, we consulted every hour to ensure coordination.

All the Wai Wai including women and children knew bush work and pitched in. Trees continued to fall and it seemed a miracle no one was killed or injured.

The women and children took on the task of improving the runway. They filled the soft spots with dirt, tamping the fill with tree stumps until they were hard. Shovels I brought with me and their flattened pieces of wood made for clearing in and around their huts were used to scrape down bumps. Twice a day I stretched a hundred foot string to check the level. The third day, the women surprised me when they had the string stretched out to show me how much and how well they had leveled the adjacent area. I was impressed and told them so. They understood, laughed, and slapped their thighs in appreciation.

The next few days, instead of showing them how to do the work, I only inspected it by stomping across the airstrip to detect soft spots. In anticipation, the women stood in a line awaiting my comments. T*humbs up*, a smile, and verbal A-okay was given when they did a good job. That brought on equally big smiles and a cause to celebrate with a kind of shuffle dance and plenty of laughter.

To them it was a game. They quickly learned to do their own inspections in the morning before I did mine and watched to see my reactions. They did a great job and before I could acknowledge it, they did a *thumbs up*, shouted *A-Okay,* jumped, hugged, and slapped their thighs, laughing uproariously. They were a happy people and it was infectious. I enjoyed working with them. Every day yielded another pleasant surprise.

We marked off each area as it was completed. The progress amazed me. I never thought they could accomplish so much in so short a time. On the fifth day, most of the trees were cleared and the runway was reasonably flat, free of bumps and holes.

We reviewed our progress. The first 200 feet were smooth and compacted to bear the full weight of the plane and minimize drag for maximum acceleration. The next 300 feet still had to be smooth, but not as well compacted because the lift from the wings reduced the load on the tires. Once airborne, the climb-out was critical to rise above the trees. The remainder of the runway would only be used in emergency, in case we had to abort. We left piles of deep soft ground to slow the plane quickly and prevent it from running into the stumps. We angled the last part of the runway slightly to the left avoiding a huge stump in the middle. That saved us the extra work of trying to dig it out and gave us another fifty yard safety factor if we had to abort.

On one of the early morning inspections of the plane, I discovered a six-foot arrow dangling from the tail. While two Indians held the tail down, I carefully extracted the arrow, stitched the canvas fabric, and smoothed it over with a tape patch. We never found who shot it, or why. It seemed to be a singular unexplained incident.

On the sixth day I felt satisfied I could make it if all the margins were in my favor, though I kept the crew cutting down trees. I drained all the fuel into the extra jerry cans I'd brought. Then I refueled with a carefully measured twenty-five gallons, all double strained through a chamois to eliminate any chance of contamination. It was particularly important here where we were experiencing hot and humid days and cold nights, optimum conditions for water condensing in the tanks. Twenty five gallons would take me to Lumid Pau with thirty minutes reserve. Ordinarily I would carry more reserves, but with take-off weight so critical, I didn't have that luxury. I would take only one passenger at a time. Dick Macklin volunteered. Since he was the lightest, he was also the best candidate.

The weather had to be perfect: clear sky, no rain, and hopefully a breeze on our nose. There could be no compromise anywhere. I knew my plane's limits and in this situation there were no margins for error. I planted a flag on the 400 foot mark, where I would either be airborne or abort. Because the Indians compacted the earth into a smooth hard surface, I over-inflated the tires, further reducing drag. Procedures were rehearsed until I was satisfied we had every aspect perfect. We left nothing to chance.

Day seven, our first attempt was canceled because of ground fog. Later, when the fog burned off, a light breeze came from the west, the wrong direction. The next morning thirty minutes before daylight, we were back on the airstrip. I preflighted the plane then did a double check. The plane was hauled as far back as possible with the tail hanging out over the open space of the cliff. Dick and I climbed in and tightened our seat belts.

After all the engine checks, I shoved in the throttle to full power and locked the brakes. It took several seconds for the Lycoming engine to rev up to full RPMs, eliminating those precious seconds on the runway at less than one hundred percent power. At 3500 RPMs, I gave the hand signal. Jack and three Indians pushed on the strut while running as fast as they could to the thirty foot marker, then dove to the side to avoid being hit by the tail. We practiced that maneuver until we had it down do perfection. It paid off.

Excellent! Maximum horsepower with a perfect push start. The first hundred feet felt good. To lessen drag, I used no flaps until I reached thirty knots, and then gradually applied flaps for lift, which reduced weight and drag on the tires and in turn increased our speed. It was a fine balance between leaving the plane on the ground too long or pulling off too soon and mushing with an inefficient climb rate. At the 300 foot marker, we indicated fifty-five knots. It felt right. I gently pulled back on the control wheel. We were airborne...and committed!

I resisted the normal temptation to gain altitude quickly. Instead, by increasing airspeed and remaining inches off the airstrip, we accelerated to ninety-five mph, the best rate of climb in the shortest distance according to the Tri Pacer performance book. I hoped it was accurate.

Five seconds passed. Dick and I held our breaths. We cleared the trees by a margin of twenty feet, more than I anticipated. The rehearsals and planning paid off. There were a few scattered clouds but not enough to obstruct visibility. I set the compass 180 degrees from the track in, correcting only for wind drift. I tried to relax for the next hour and a half, but it didn't come easy after all the tension-laden moments.

The trip to Lumid Pau was uneventful, a welcome let down from the previous days of frenetic planning. I dropped Dick Macklin off at Lumid Pau, tied up a hammock, and pointed to the rations tied in the tree. I told him BG Airways was aware he was here, in the event I did not return. I didn't even like the thought of that. He helped me refuel and in less than five minutes I was airborne again. With the more accurate compass settings, I shaved fifteen minutes off the flight.

They were waiting on the airstrip when I landed. With a brisk breeze out of the east, the approach and landing were considerably easier. Taking advantage of the stronger wind condition, I decided to fly out the heaviest person, Leonard Clark, next. Leonard was the only one who balked at leaving gear behind. He reluctantly agreed when I said I could return in three weeks to make the extra trips: one for him and one for his *toys*.

Donald Haack

Just before boarding I asked whether he took a pee to empty his bladder to save another pound or two.

"You've got to be kidding, right?" He wasn't sure if I was joking.

I kept a straight face and said, "Hurry up, you can go over there in the bushes. We don't have all day. Every pound counts and you're the heaviest. If this breeze stops, I can't take you out today...and who knows when?"

He hurried to the bushes, leaned against a tree, and took a couple of minutes to relieve himself.

"Jeez, for the time it took, that was probably five pounds we won't have to worry about. Let's go."

We took off. From the look on his face, he wasn't sure if I was pulling his leg or not. I made no comment and concentrated on flying. Even with the helping wind, the extra seventy pounds cut our margins. We cleared the trees by a scant few feet, way too close for comfort. The next day it was noon before the clouds lifted for the third trip. Tom Slick, also a lightweight, was an easy lift-off. I returned to Wai Wai country a little after five o'clock, nearly exhausted. Jack was waiting on the strip to help tie down the plane.

"Hey, mate, you've had a hard two days. Come and join me for a drink. I'm moving to the tree house where Tom bunked. Said it's great sleeping. You get a breeze way up there but sounds a bit scary climbing up. At least nothing can bother us that high up." Little did we know what we were getting ourselves into. I wondered how high was *high*?

"We could both use a good sleep tonight," he added.

He was right about that. I was totally exhausted.

"A good sleep," I recalled him saying. Famous last words. There would be no such thing.

Slick's group came with an assortment of the latest prepared camping food, which they used sparingly since they didn't know how long they would be here. Now there was an ample amount left. We opened several packages, added water and heat. We sat around the campfire and shared our bounty with the Wai Wais who thought the instant food was magic. We gave the balance of the packaged food to them with instructions on how to use it, and kept out two packages in case we were delayed another day.

They were grateful for such an intriguing gift. We gave them our knives, machetes, axes, and files along with all the personal belongings of the group. It was a fair amount and since I was adamant about not taking anything other than passengers, I felt it was a means of partially compensating the Wai Wais for all their work. They had so much fun, they would have done it for free, which is what they thought they were doing.

We ate our fill. I was dead tired and all I wanted was sleep. The tree house turned out to be quite a structure. The base was formed by four trees 200 feet tall that disappeared into the overhead jungle. It was awesome.

Jack explained, "The house in the treetop is constructed of bamboo and grass. According to Tom, it's put together well." I wasn't convinced. Not too happy about the idea, I questioned Jack about the security.

"I know it appears fragile but the Wai Wais built it and they know what they're doing," he added.

At this point I could have slept standing up. "Let's go. It's early and still light. I don't think we should climb in the dark."

He agreed. We climbed and we climbed. "This reminds me of the Beanstalk," I said to Jack, a few rungs below. If he heard, he didn't respond. We went up and up, hand over hand. I looked down. I shouldn't have. The Indians on the ground looked damned small.

The whole contraption was swaying. It would prove to be an interesting night if we lived through it. This was a major climb. The thought of climbing back down these rickety-looking rungs tied together with vines felt even less appealing. I climbed faster to get it over with until I reached the hole in the bamboo structure. I crawled through, and then helped Jack onto the floor of our house. He stood up on the far side while I placed the woven panel of sticks securely over the ladder hole. I wondered if we accidentally stepped on it, would it keep us from falling through? I didn't voice that question.

Donald Haack

It was still light, but the sun was going down fast. Jack and I both carried flashlights. I looked around our makeshift nightstand. On one side, there were two wooden boat-shaped Wai Wai stools to sit on. Several blankets, which we could give to the Wai Wais, were folded on top of a large locker. I asked Jack how in the world they got the locker up there.

He just shrugged. "The Wai Wais can do just about anything."

I believed it. I was also thinking that at three degrees above the equator, the daytime temperatures could be unbearably hot, but the nights were cool. I was thankful for the blankets.

The sun went down, the temperature dropped. We sat on the stools with the blankets wrapped around us.

"We really look silly, you know. Here we are swaying back and forth high in the jungle tree tops, sitting on wooden Wai Wai stools, wrapped in blankets. What a picture this would make." I had to chuckle. We were a strange sight.

I lit one of the two Coleman lanterns we found in the chest. Jack noticed something that commanded his full attention: a bottle of Tom Slick's Hennesy Five Star Brandy.

"Too bloody good to leave behind. We shouldn't give the Wai Wai any bad habits." With a pixie-like glint in his eye he held the bottle up, made a sign of the cross and broke open the seal. "What do you think, mate? We deserve it, right?"

I agreed. He took a sip and passed it to me. It went back in the trunk. The temperature fell further, necessitating another *drop* of Hennesy. Several more ins and outs occurred before we placed it between us for convenience. We exchanged war stories on our respective bush-flying experiences, which improved exponentially as the evening progressed.

We attacked the bottle in earnest, now only half full. I thought I better clear up the subject about no baggage on the last trip. I had mentioned it to everyone except Jack and thought I should address it before he packed a suitcase. I reminded him that rescuing people was one thing, but on this strip the risk was too high to take off with any extra pounds.

Donald Haack

I told him about Leonard's objection and that before he boarded I made him pee to help lighten the load. Jack thought that was hilarious and fell off his Wai Wai chair thinking about the pompous Leonard Clark being made to pee before boarding. When he got over that, he took umbrage about not being able to carry out his personal belongings. That provoked an argument. Brandy will do that.

Jack said they had valuable things in their packs including this Hennesy. I stood fast. Jack quickly solved that problem.
"Waste not, want not," he muttered, or something to that effect, suggesting we drink it instead. He wasn't completely placated. He had forty pounds of personal gear he wanted to take.

"I put my neck on the line three times and once again tomorrow, but for people only," I stressed. "Nothing will convince me to do a baggage run. All gear stays behind."

Staring into the Tillie lamp, he seemed to ponder on it. A few minutes later, he was sound asleep. I covered him with one of the blankets and turned out the lamp. There were no sounds other than the whisper of wind rustling the leaves around us and the chirp of tree frogs down below. I fell into a sound sleep dreaming of flying between trees and narrow rivers.

Jack was shaking me vigorously. It took me a moment to realize where I was. "Mate, I got a problem. I gotta pee."

I looked at my watch—two o'clock. This presented a serious problem. We were over 150 feet up in the trees. The urgency in his voice was a cry of desperation. I tried to think. No way could he navigate that ladder in the dark and certainly not in his present condition. Probably fall down the hole before he put a foot on the first rung. In retrospect, drinking the Hennesy didn't seem like a very good idea. I struggled with the option of peeing down the hole. I didn't want to open the trap door for fear of him falling. I could hold him but the idea of pissing all over the ladder turned me off. We still had to climb down in the morning. We could handle the smell, but not the slippery part. That option was out. What else, I wondered.

I checked the open window with my flashlight. The bottom of the window was five feet, chest high, built so you wouldn't fall out—but too high to pee out. There might be one solution: a rope I found in Tom's chest. I tied it around Jack's waist and anchored the other end to the bamboo wall on the far side of the room with enough slack to reach the window. I tested it and shortened it so he wouldn't fall out. At least I didn't think he would. I pulled the locker box directly below the window. It was still too low. I climbed on it and knelt on my hands and knees.

"Jack, climb on my back. If you hold onto the window frame you should be able to pee out the window. For God's sake, be careful. Remember, I'm right below you so make sure you lean far enough out. Better you fall out the window than pee on me 'cause if you do, I'll throw you out anyway," I quickly added. "The rope is short enough so you can't fall out," I reminded him, hoping it was true and would hold his weight.

Not too steadily, he maneuvered onto my back, partially leaning out the window. I tried not to think of the black void hundreds of feet below. He started peeing. He gave an audible sigh of pure relief but moments later it was followed by ungodly screams and shrieks from the jungle below. The *black hole* suddenly came alive.

It took a moment before I realized where the screaming came from. "Jack, stop, for God's sake, you're pissing on the Indians who tied their hammocks down there."

He stopped. The angry shouts and screams quickly sobered him up. Seconds later, we heard chopping sounds and felt shock waves vibrating our house. I understood immediately what the *groundlings* were doing—cutting down the trees of our house with their machetes. In minutes we would plummet to the ground. I considered climbing down, but the idea of confronting angry machete-wielding savages just after they were pissed on in their hammocks was quickly ruled out.

We were running out of options. Hoping they would understand, I yelled down in my best Brazilian though I doubted they could hear me over the chopping and shouting. Then suddenly…nothing. Total quiet. That was more unsettling.

"Total silence," Jack said. "They're coming up after us, that's what they're doing."

For a moment I thought the same. Then I heard a different noise, rising like a swell of a beach wave before it crashed. It grew louder and louder. It was peals of laughter. The Wai Wai with their fantastic sense of humor took a few minutes before they could find it, but they did. I shouted down apologies and thanks, but I don't think they heard or understood. I could visualize the slapping, rolling on the ground, and wild peals of laughter that obliterated my feeble attempts at communicating.

They probably will tell this story to their children, as I will to mine, about the two white men up in the trees thinking they were going to die. It would be described and embellished many times. I hoped I would be around to tell my story, but the way things were going, I wasn't sure.

We survived the night. At first light, we carefully climbed down the ladder. No Wai Wais were in sight. We picked up our few personals and found our way to the airstrip where most of the Wai Wai were waiting to send us off. It was a cool wet morning, the kind we needed for a safe take off.

Before I departed, I explained what the airstrip needed so we could return safely. I promised to bring my family and more tools. Jack and I did a thorough preflight, and then double-checked to make sure we didn't miss anything. With the help of the eager Indians, we pushed the plane back to the edge of the runway and lined it up. I cranked up the engine and checked the mags. With a good push from the now experienced Wai Wai, we rolled on our way for a near perfect take off. We circled, made a pass, and dipped our wings to say goodbye. In turn, they waved. Those on their way to hunt waved their bows and arrows. The Wai Wais were fascinating. I wanted to return, spend more time and learn more about them.

I kept my promise and returned three times.

Donald Haack

We arrived at Lumid Pau just as the rising sun burned off the last of the clouds and mist. Tom, Leonard, and Dick were there to greet us. After refueling, I flew the three to our Marquis house and came back for Leonard in the afternoon. He suggested I drop him at Lethem where he would spend the night. That would save me one trip shuttling the other three to Good Hope where they would meet the DC-3 to Georgetown. I agreed.

That night after dinner, Tom Slick asked me where I obtained the mining map he saw hanging in our library. I explained it was from a Venezuelan expedition years earlier and the part we played in assisting the Kennicott company assaying a gold mine in the Amacuro basin.

From the intensity of his questions, he obviously wanted more information. I was reluctant. Several times in the past week, I asked how they happened to be in Wai Wai territory. There was no reply, only an embarrassing silence. I could play that game too.

He wasn't to be put off, though. Finally in frustration, he blurted out. "Look, I know we've been less than open with you. We owe you big for the rescue you did for us. I doubt if anyone else could or would have gotten us out. You asked why we were in Wai Wai country. Clark was going on a rumor of diamonds in that area. Frankly we found absolutely nothing to substantiate it. Leonard didn't want us to say anything about it. Now, after the fact, I really don't know why...except Leonard was with the Office of Strategic Services, OSS, during the war. That organization eventually became the CIA, and honestly, I think he never got over that cloak and dagger stuff." He glanced back at the map on our wall. "The reason I'm interested in the map...Look, this is more than just a small coincidence. I don't know how to even explain it, but I've been interested in that particular region on the La Paragua River for several years. I couldn't find out who held those concessions and now that territory shows up on a map in your house." He was confused.

"That is some coincidence," I said slowly, "particularly since my brother and I have title to those concessions." He looked at me in disbelief.

A year later we had a joint mining operation going on the La Paragua River that included Tom Slick, my brother, and me. Leonard Clark and Dick Macklin elected to come along and watchdog the operation, a decision that would cost them their lives.

It was indeed strange to have read Leonard Clark's books, rescue him, and later close out the last chapter of his life.

SABOTAGE

It had been a few weeks since the Wai Wai rescue and life was once again settling into a routine: I restocked most of the trading stores up and down the border, our camp had supplies, and the dredge and prospecting crews were back at work.

We weren't expecting the next blow so quickly. On a routine call to B.G. Airways, I was informed there was a telegram urging me to call our Georgetown office immediately. It was from Tom Slick and *urgent*. I was to call his office in Houston, collect, as soon as possible…a life and death matter. It sounded ominous. I was stunned and showed the message to Jan.

"I can't imagine what in the world Tom Slick is calling us about. I knew he was working with Bob on our joint venture on the Venezuelan claims, but I'm at a loss what could be so important to send us this life and death message."

Jan wanted an answer. I didn't have any.

"There's so much work here, the last thing I want is to go to town, but I guess I'll have to. Something strange is up."

I went alone. It took three hours to make the connection while

I sat in the stark offices of Cable and Wireless, Ltd. We finally connected. After a minimum of pleasantries, Tom went right into the reason for his telegram. The ten-minute conversation with Tom left me completely stunned.

"Leonard Clark, through his OSS connection in World War II, found the file in the State Department, actually the CIA, on why our Helio Courier went down. It wasn't an accident, it was sabotaged, exactly the same way yours was. And it was done by the same people: the Russian Polish group headed by Joe Tezarek and Caesar Gorinsky whose job it was to buy up all the rough diamonds in the area and ship to Russia," Tom explained.

I knew that since the start of the Cold War, the U.S and its allies had boycotted industrial diamonds to Russia. Tom continued. "So Russia organized small groups throughout the world to secure their own supply of rough diamonds. Tezarek and Gorinsky operated the one in South America. Seems that when you built your home in Marquis you were right smack in the middle of their territory and apparently were seen as a threat. It wouldn't be long before you found out what was going on at the borders of the three countries, particularly, since you had the only plane other than Tezarek's." There was a pause as he let that sink in.

"When we came into Guiana, we were a bit secretive, but someone must have informed the Tezarek- Gorinsky group about Clark's OSS background and assumed the CIA was on to them. We didn't have a clue and were strictly prospecting, but by happenstance we wound up in the middle, like you. They thought we were a threat that had to be dealt with so they took us out."

I was too much in shock to reply.

He continued, "Did Gorinsky have any access to your gas supply? And who was the last person who fueled your plane before the crash?"

"My gas supply was at the Good Hope airstrip and Caesar was with me when I refueled," I heard myself say as if the voice didn't belong to me. I felt like a robot. There was no immediate response from Tom and I realized he was expecting me to say something else. I didn't. I was still in shock. Eventually I broke the long silence. "Are you still there?"

"Yes, but from what you told me that pretty well confirms Clark's report."

"You don't understand, Tom," I said. "The Gorinskys are the closest friends we have down here. We lived in their house for six months. We are like part of the family."

In my mind this was so far fetched that it simply couldn't be true, and I told him so.

He persisted. "Listen, Don, I have to impress on you that you and your family are in immediate danger. They sabotaged your plane. That was to discourage you. They didn't expect that you would continue and bring another plane in. Since you did, they evidently feel you'll find something out and they can't afford to risk that, so it's much more serious. You've got to think of your family. Just get out of there. The situation's life threatening so the sooner the better. If you want, you can move to Venezuela and run the La Paragua operation, only don't stay where you are. You and your family are in danger."

After I talked to Tom, I called my brother and explained the whole episode. He, too, was dumbfounded but said he would get in touch with the CIA for clarification and to see what they could recommend. He thought it wise for us to return to the States immediately, find out the all details and then regroup.

Back at Marquis I repeated the conversation to Jan who reacted with as much disbelief as Bob and I did.

"Don, Nellie is like a mother and a sister combined. I've never had so close a friend. This simply can't be. I know Nellie too well." There were tears in her eyes.

"I know, I feel the same way about Caesar. None of this makes sense. Tom certainly wouldn't have warned us if he didn't think we were in danger. Sometimes men do strange things and get involved over their heads. If that really is the case, I doubt seriously if Nellie knows anything about it," I said. But that didn't sound logical either. Everything in our world was suddenly topsy turvy.

"Come to think of it, Caesar asked to come up to Marquis this weekend. He wants to see Karona Falls. It's been twenty years since he's been up and if the hike from our house weren't too bad, he would like to bring Pixie and Nellie. He's talked about it all these years and now that we have a plane it would be the first opportunity to actually see it. I told him fine, I would pick him up tomorrow." I looked at Jan to see what her reaction would be. There was none. She was too much in a state of shock to answer.

Caesar flew back to Marquis with me the next evening and we set out early on the hike to Karona the next morning. We both wore pistols. Not unusual. They were used for protection and hunting. When Jan saw us leave, she was fit to be tied. It had been tense all night and that morning. Caesar remarked about it, attributing it to the fact that we were settling in with a new plane after the trauma of our recent plane crash. We agreed. I slipped a round into the chamber of my pistol and checked the safety before putting in my holster.

The trip to the falls was uneventful except for the small talk about the beauty of the river and the reminiscing of prospecting years earlier. The one disconcerting comment came from Caesar. "You know how remote this territory is. No one around for miles. A perfect place for a murder and no one would ever know."

The hair actually stood up on the back of my neck and a cold shiver shot through my body. I tried to ignore his statement and didn't answer. Instead, I said, "Look, I'm tired of breaking trail, you go forward and I'll bring up the rear." I stepped aside so he had to walk in front. My nerves were too much on end to be in front of him and maybe a sitting duck. The rest of the trip I made excuses to keep him in front of me. Nothing was said about his comment about the perfect place for murder.

On the return as we were crossing the Tipuru River, we chased up a small herd of Capybaras.

"Dinner," is all Caesar said as we both slipped our pistols out. "We'll take the small one, it'll be more tender."

He shot twice without slowing it down and it headed for the safety of the water.

I grabbed Caesar's pistol hand to restrain him from firing again. As the Capybara came from behind the tree, I pointed between his ear and eye and fired once. He dropped in his tracks. We walked over to him and Caesar was going to fire again to make sure he was dead.

"No need," I said as I pushed his gun down again. "He's not going anywhere." He bent down for a closer inspection. A few drops of blood marked a neat hole half way between the ear and the eye. Caesar was visibly shaken.

"Where did you learn to shoot like that? You hardly aimed. And you knew he was dead?" He waited for an answer. I didn't give him one, just shrugged my shoulders. Domingo would understand, but no one else would. And besides I didn't feel like talking.

"We've got work to do if we intend to bring him back for camp meat. You gut him and I'll get a limb to carry him on." I said, backing into the bush. I returned with a stout limb and vines to tie him up. With both of us working, we took the head, lower limbs, and skin off. It would be heavy enough without carrying extras. In less than a half hour we were on our way, the sapling on our shoulders with the carcass swinging between us.

It was dark when we arrived at Marquis. Jan was waiting with a flashlight. I noticed she was wearing her gun and the thong was off the top, ready to draw. The light flashed on to the carcass swinging between us and there was an audible gasp. The light quickly blinded us both as it went from one to the other and there was a sigh of relief. I knew what her first thoughts were when she spotted the white carcass. She hid her feelings well.

"I heard three shots and I worried that something had happened. I guess wives always think the worst." she said, trying to make light of the conversation.

I flew Caesar back the next day. Back at Marquis we tried to analyze what occurred. We couldn't. We again read the cable from Tom Slick and mulled over the ensuing telephone conversation with him.

"Don, I can't make any sense of any of this, but my nerves are just about shot after this last incident. We were going to go to the States in two months. Why don't we just move it up and leave this weekend?" I knew how she felt. I was just as confused and stressed.

We flew into Detroit's airport where Jan's parents greeted us. Jan and Diney would stay with them and I would go on to Milwaukee, where I spent the next few days vainly trying to verify the report from the CIA. Finally in frustration, we called a fellow marine, Senator McCarthy in Appleton, He assured us of immediate access to any files. Knowing McCarthy's proclivity to cut through red tape and assault the bastions of congressional bureaucracy, it wasn't surprising to hear back from him with the results.

"Boys, let me tell you, I went through each and every archive on this diamond story and I can assure you, nobody but nobody in the CIA knows anything about this South American diamond group. There's not a profile on either Tezarek or Gorinsky. So I checked the FBI. Same thing. Absolutely no record. They both told me to get the copy of the report your friend has and send it to me. We can trace it backwards to make sure, but the consensus is that there's nothing in any of the departments on this. Get me that report, and we'll put this to rest quickly," he assured me.

I got on the phone with Tom Slick and told him what happened. We talked for over an hour.

"Clark was in my office when he told me about the report. He had it in his hand waving it between us as we talked. There was some kind of seal on the bottom."

"Did you actually read the report?" I asked.

He hesitated as he tried to recall the exact sequence of events.

"He started to hand it to me, but then he read from it instead. It sounded like an official report, but no, thinking back, I never did hold the document. I didn't think anything about it then. It just seemed logical since he was reading from a CIA document.

The details were all there on our crash along with some pretty descriptive details on yours. It never occurred to me that he made it up, particularly after you said the fuel was stored at the Gorinsky airstrip and Caesar helped you refuel on your last flight." He was quiet and apparently thinking.

"We can find out about this quickly. Don West is in my office. He just returned from the mine site and brought Leonard's trunk, also in my office. If there were any report it would be in there. I'll have Don go through it now and I'll call you back."

Two hours later, he was on the phone again.

"Don and I went through everything of Clark's and I must say, he had some weird writings in that trunk. The whole thing was spy stuff, a lot about your brother, about the natives, and worse how he was planning to have our pilot, Ernie, fly him to the top of Angel Falls so the world would wonder if Leonard Clark was alive or dead...dramatic publicity for his new book. Dick Macklin told me Clark was drinking constantly and living in another world of cloak and dagger fantasies.

"Back to your problem, no, there was no CIA report but some of his rambling writings alluded to plots he made up of people trying to kill us and diamond smuggling rings were the focal points. Don, I can't tell you how sorry I am for all the anguish I caused you, but I really thought your lives were in danger. All the while, Clark was attempting to make his novel take on a real life. I don't think he ever got over his OSS work in World War II."

"Don West and I have decided to either go down there or fly him up here to explain himself. We're all owed an explanation, but particularly you and Jan. If he's gone that far off the deep end, I really don't want him on the mining site anymore. We'll resolve this immediately and I'll keep you posted."

I told Jan about the conversation with Slick. She was visibly relieved and I was glad since it was her last few weeks of pregnancy. She stayed with her mother and father in Birmingham where her parents enjoyed having Diney and her.

A week later Jan was in the delivery room of Beaumont Hospital and *our* Tom arrived as scheduled. He was healthy and fine, Jan was doing well and we were again proud parents. My mother and father flew in from Milwaukee to see their new and only grandson. It was a fine reunion.

Until we learned the truth of the Leonard Clark intrigue, we didn't know if we were going to return. All plans were up in the air and for a while we didn't know if we had a home or a job to go back to. Now with the good news and the happy arrival of our Tom, we made arrangement for our return trip to Marquis

Five years later over a couple of beers in the Tower Hotel, I related the full story to Caesar. He asked several question. I filled in the blanks. He even remembered the part about his comment that *it was a great place for a murder*.

"I thought it was just a thought-provoking comment." he mused. "Sometimes we have no idea what we say to someone can be perceived so differently. Hmmm." He nodded, acknowledging the understatement.

"Leonard Clark" he repeated. "Some story. I met him in Lethem when you dropped him off from the Wai Wai country. He was waiting for the plane at Teddy's bar. Thinking back on our conversation, I shouldn't be surprised by what you just told me. He was strange." He paused for quite a while. "What an asshole thing to do."

JAIL

It was Friday, the week we did the Lethem mail run. Jan packed a day's supply of Diney's and Tom's nappies and baby food for her stay with Nellie at Good Hope. Caesar had arranged to fly with me. When we landed at Good Hope, Nellie informed me "C" had to leave the night before. I dropped Jan and family with Nellie and continued on the twenty- minute flight to Lethem, the government's largest interior station and an abattoir for shipping beef to Georgetown. The DC-3 brought supplies and mail from Georgetown every Friday, the social day of the week.

On the approach, I noticed the DC-3 hadn't landed yet so I skipped the long approach, overflew the runway to assure there were no cattle, landed, and taxied to the unpretentious two-story Lethem Hotel.

"Doc" Doug Diamond approached before I shut down my engine. He must have been waiting for me on the airstrip. A tall imposing man dressed in black towered above him. Ordinarily, that wouldn't get attention but because Doug was quite short, but this guy was really big. I hadn't met Padre Marco, the Brazilian priest, but from the stories and descriptions, it had to be him—wild unkempt bushy hair as if it had been struck by lightning, and a huge beard to match.

As I stepped out of the plane, both men talked at once. I gave Doug a greeting pat on his shoulder while reaching out to shake hands with the giant.

"You must be Padre Marco," I said slipping my hand into his big paw, amazed at how big it was. I'm six-one and he was taller. "I'm Don Haack," I continued, while his deeply set black eyes bored into mine. Thick black eyebrows that matched his beard and hair framed his eyes. I thought of Rasputin, the Russian holy man who had a life of debauchery in Tsarist Russia. Any similarity stopped there. Though a bit unorthodox, Padre Marco's reputation for doing good was legendary

He was momentarily taken aback by my greeting and recognition. He straightened up to an even more imposing full height and his face softened. Smile wrinkles spread from underneath the wild eyebrows. He squeezed my hand. I had the feeling that Padre Marco could crush coconuts one-handed if he wanted to. The feeling of great strength surrounded him like a suit of armor. The thought entered my mind that it was a good thing Padre Marco chose to be a priest. He would have made a formidable enemy.

"I'm sorry," he blurted in Portuguese, "pardon my bad manners. Yes, I'm Padre Marco. Happy to finally meet the Americano I've heard so much about. You have helped my people along the frontier many times. I feel I know you, though we've never met." It was as if he were seeing through me, not at me—an unnerving feeling. The Padre had a powerful presence that was felt as well as seen. "My friend," he continued in his sonorous voice of authority, "I understand you once were of my faith, a Catholic."

Oh, my God, I thought. Caesar has been talking. In a weak moment after a few drinks, I related the story to Caesar, who must have repeated it to Padre. Now there would be another effort to convert me back to Catholicism. My thoughts were instantly interrupted by the Padre's commanding voice.

"Fear not," as if reading my mind, "I have no intention of trying to reconvert you. I will leave that to God if he so desires. You have your reasons for leaving the faith. I respect that," he whispered almost as if we were in a confessional.

His change in voice and demeanor put me off balance, a technique, I suspected, he used often to good effect. I had a new respect for this padre. Perhaps, too, because my uncle Max, a Catholic priest whom I liked very much, had said the identical words to me shortly after I left the church.

"You have helped many people here. I have known many *good* Catholics who have not done as much in a lifetime as you have in the time you have been here." He continued holding my hand in more of a grasp than a handshake. He gave a gentle squeeze now with both hands.

A warm feeling spread throughout my body as if I had been anointed. Padre, I thought, if nothing else you exude an intense sincerity accompanied with a reinforcing hands-on manner.

Apparently there were two emergencies: a twelve-year old Brazilian girl had contracted malaria and needed medical attention. She had been visiting relatives near Lethem when she fell ill. Her family and doctor were in Boa Vista, the Brazilian outpost seventy miles west across the frontier. Padre Marco brought her to Lethem hoping I would fly them both to Boa Vista. Evidently word of my mercy missions was common knowledge even in Brazil.

The second crisis concerned Doc Diamond, our local veterinarian, who discovered a Brazilian outbreak of dreaded hoof-and-mouth cattle disease. For decades the main livelihood in the Rupununi was cattle. Doc said it was imperative he contact his counterpart in Boa Vista to establish a quarantine buffer zone along the frontier, a necessary precaution to keep the disease contained. Doc wanted to fly on the same flight with Padre Marco and the sick girl.

Boa Vista, a Brazilian town and army post, had a long history of being harsh on airplanes. Obtaining a permit was a long procedure starting with contacting the Brazilian Consul in

Georgetown, if and when he was in, filing a request which could take days, then awaiting a cablegram from Boa Vista via Rio de Janeiro. With luck, this process could take two weeks. This emergency could not wait that long.

They walked me to the nearby fence where the young girl in a semi-conscious state lay on a blanket. An Indian woman knelt beside her, wiping her forehead with a cloth she dipped in a bowl. The child's sunken eyes and dry yellow-tinged skin told me all I needed to know. "A few days ago," the Padre said, "she alternated between shivering and fever. Yesterday and today she has cramps and is vomiting. Probably malaria originally, but now other complications have set in." She was indeed very sick.

Padre Marco convinced me that under these humanitarian conditions, there existed a "bonafide" mercy mission. Red tape should be no problem.

"You could be in and out in less than two hours," he assured me.

He personally would be responsible. Boa Vista was his parish. Everyone knew him. They also knew Doc Diamond and that hoof-and-mouth was a serious crisis—and the justification of an unscheduled flight. I didn't know better. The padre played on my conscience. I didn't have anything else planned except to be back at Good Hope for afternoon tea.

Padre, Doc and I carried the frail Indian girl on a makeshift stretcher, a double-wrapped blanket between two poles. Her cloth travel bag and hammock provided a pillow. In obvious pain, she was carefully lifted through the cargo door and eased onto the floor. Padre Marco jumped in, sat alongside, and bathed her forehead with water from a Bank's Brewery bottle. Doc Diamond climbed in the right seat.

Boa Vista, a mere thirty- minute flight directly west of Lethem, was new to me. I drew a line on the map, started the engine, and taxied up to the fence in front of the adobe two-story Lethem Hotel. After scanning the gauges, I pushed in the throttle. For the girl's sake, I tried to find the smoothest part of the not-so-smooth grass airstrip and used half flaps to shorten the takeoff run. Seconds later we were airborne and I climbed to 2,000 feet.

Twenty minutes later, Padre pointed out the palm trees of Boa Vista. A few miles north, the airstrip. We were right on course. The runway ran east-west. I continued our straight in approach. The 6,000 foot airstrip had a single building alongside. Even though I didn't expect traffic in this god-forsaken place, I still scanned the horizon and made the customary low-level pass to chase off cows, sheep, or anything that might be on the nice, level area with invitingly good grass.

The airstrip was approximately three miles north of Boa Vista. The town had two main streets lined with palm trees, mud houses, and numerous paths or jeep trails extending out like spokes in a wheel. After the pass, I made a 180 degree turn, pulled back power, extended full flaps, and without the slightest bump touched down onto the Boa vista airstrip. I hoped my first visit here would be a good one.

I braked short and taxied alongside the only building. That was the last sane thing I did for the next five days.

We were immediately surrounded by small excited brown men with big automatic rifles pointed close to our faces. This was not a cheerful welcoming party. I quickly pushed Padre Marco out the door, hoping he could explain to the soldiers why we were here, and that this wasn't a smuggler's run or an invasion. It was a mercy mission.

As far as the armed rabble were concerned, Padre Marco did not exist. They neither listened, understood, nor attempted to. We broke the law: without papers we landed a foreign plane in a Brazilian army outpost.

We were literally dragged from the plane and not allowed to park or tie it down. Our armed captors removed the keys, jabbed rifles in our ribs, pulled the almost unconscious girl out, and pushed us into an open jeep. Along with three guards, the three of us held the sick girl and hung on precariously while the driver took off in a roar almost running down the guard who barely got the gate open as we sped through. This did not bode well.

It was a wild, wild ride. The terror caused by driving recklessly at speeds way too fast on the rough roads was second only to the fear of being hit by the rifles held inches from our faces. I was convinced that one of us would wind up with a rifle barrel jammed up our nose before we arrived wherever we were going. Miraculously that didn't happen and we were able to prevent the girl from being catapulted out of the jeep. We were the enemy as far as these soldiers were concerned. They didn't smile or speak.

If anyone knew Padre Marco, he hid it well and treated him with indifference. I had the feeling these guys were cloned in Rio and sent up here with no clue of any formal religion. Doug Diamond was scared shitless, as he put it. He said absolutely nothing. He let Padre Marco do the talking. We both hoped that "Vaya con Dio" might somehow prevail and left Padre to explain. Anything we said could trigger a disastrous response. I tasted bile in my mouth.

At first, Padre became indignant, then plain mad. Priests aren't supposed to get angry, but he did. He raged, invoking the power of the devil, the will of God, and excommunication—individually and collectively—to no avail. In between invectives and breaths, he assured me that all would be straightened out the minute we saw the capitan of police, the justice, the mayor or the governor of the district. He had more optimism than I, yet I hoped he was right.

We went straight to jail. It was, we discovered, Carnival week and all offices were closed. The police capitan, the justice, the mayor, the governor, and every other official were all in Rio celebrating. The government had flown a DC-3 to Boa Vista transporting the officials to Rio for the week-long Carnival celebration, the biggest event of the year—similar to our Mardi Gras. For those living in the interior, it was manna from heaven. If invited, no one would miss the event. Apparently everyone of importance was invited. Great timing on our part.

We pulled up to the jail, a one-story mud building that had small windows and bars. An old sergeant who must not have been important enough to be invited to Rio stood in the doorway. We quickly determined he was not the smartest individual but might just be the highest-ranking official in town.

The sergeant was frightened enough by Padre Marco's exhortations to grant him two small concessions. I thought it might be more to shut the Padre up than out of mercy or gratitude. The sergeant, pressed by Padre, had the sense to send the girl straight to the hospital. Padre also put enough doubt in his mind that he was making a grave mistake by placing the Americano in jail. After listening to Padre, he instructed his men to put me in the Boa Vista Hotel under house arrest with two armed guards.

Doc had a permanent visa for Brazil so he didn't break any laws. Padre was Brazilian and lived there. He was okay. But I presented the big problem: not only a foreigner without papers, I was the *piloto* who landed an airplane illegally. I was the big criminal.

If one came by boat, jeep, foot, or donkey that was okay. But Brazilians have this "thing" about airplanes. An unauthorized landing in Brazilian territory warrants the book being thrown at you. Mercy missions and emergencies are not in the vocabulary of the Brazilian army. Padre tried to assure me that even though I was inconvenienced and might have to spend the night, God was with me, and the girl and her family were grateful. Padre was heading straight to the telegraph office to cable the governor or capitan in Rio to extract my immediate release, with proper apologies.

Padre soon discovered that the *jefe* of the telegraph office was also in Rio. His assistant, now unsupervised, couldn't be found.

The sergeant made a big deal about placing me under house arrest in the hotel. First he wanted a jeep to take me to the hotel; ridiculous since the hotel was less than a hundred yards away. We could have walked several times while we waited for a jeep. But the sergeant insisted on doing it his way. We remained silent. Padre felt he had won the important issue. They in turn saved face by maintaining their control over a confusing situation.

Apparently there were only four jeeps in all of Boa Vista, none belonging to the police. The army jeep had returned to the airport. An hour passed before they "borrowed" one from a reluctant villager who at first refused. When the no-nonsense army men unslung their automatic weapons, his wife quickly pulled him back. No more was said, but if looks could kill, the sergeant and two soldiers would have been dead.

I was unceremoniously pushed into the jeep by the army thugs. The sergeant, who obviously had never been introduced to a clutch, threw the jeep into fits and starts and we finally raced off in a dust cloud from the screeching tires and skidding rear end. Fortunately he found the brake in time to avoid slamming into the front door of the hotel.

The Boa Vista hotel, a two-story adobe structure with cement floors, small rooms, and one large shower that occasionally had water, stood on the highest point in town. The central reception room doubled as the dining room. Chairs were stacked on top of each other in the corner. Even as a prisoner under house arrest, I had to sign into the hotel and pay. The guy behind the counter appeared as if he hadn't washed in a week and when I approached him at the desk, I was convinced by the smell that he hadn't.

"I'm the *jefe*," was all he said. *Jefe* was a tall, skinny, seedy character, with a yellowish, pocked-marked pasty face, long uncombed hair, and a greasy thin mustache twisted into points. I felt sure it wasn't waxed, just greasy. His once white linen suitjack now emblazoned with gray and brown mud, red tomato paste, and purple wine stains had probably never been washed. The knees and elbows were layered sagging bulges, the sleeves much too long. But what the hell, this wasn't the Ritz. I wasn't sure this was an improvement over the jail.

His lips barely parted when he mumbled, "Trente cruzieros."

I unfolded thirty cruzieros, which evoked the first sign he was alive. He grinned, exposing brownish teeth, two of which were missing, and muttered something that sounded like "boa" (good), I guess. He rattled off a string of Brazilian Portuguese. I caught "numero cinco," my room number. Before I could react, one of my two armed henchmen shoved a rifle in my side with a "Va,va." I understood *go*.

I went up the stairs into a room that was more of a cell than the one in the jail. It was ten by twelve feet. A small table without drawers leaned against the wall on the left. There were no chairs. Along the right wall, a cot covered by a couple of dirty rumpled sheets completed the decor in this less-than-appealing layout. No sign of a bathroom or basin. The only frills in this stark room were dark red curtains framing the one window that provided light. No rugs. This was going to be a great holiday. Earlier, I had hoped Padre would clear this up quickly, but now I was certain I would have to spend at least one night in this place. I tried not to think about Jan back at Good Hope.

Reluctant to lie on the bed, I was sure the sheets had never been washed. Eventually, I sat down to take stock of my situation. The situation appeared dismal. I went to the window. The sun was setting. In equatorial regions, darkness comes quickly. I tried the lights. Nothing. Either no electricity or no light bulbs, I didn't know which, but I was too exhausted to care. In spite of being dirty, smelly, and in a dreadful space, I lay down and fell sound asleep. I tossed and turned and awakened several times. Daylight finally came along with Padre Marco pounding on the door. The guards let him in. The good news, he said, is that he could clear this up immediately. The bad news was that he was still unable to find anyone in Rio to respond to his telegrams.

The first day was boredom and frustration. Nothing happened since no official could be found. The guards brought in some stew, which was terrible, but I managed to eat a little. Padre Marco brought fruit, papayas and mangoes, which never tasted so good and I ate too fast. Depression set in. I had expected to be on my way by early morning but I was spending another day, which seemed like forever. That second night I hardly slept.

Padre Marco burst in early the next morning with maracusha, passion fruit pulp steeped in water. It was pure nectar. Maracusha, first introduced to me by the McTurks in Karanambo, became my favorite drink but now it tasted like the nectar of gods. He returned at noon with more fruit and coffee. He was angry. I wearily asked what was happening. At first he didn't want to say, but in his frustration it came out. He searched everywhere for the assistant telegraph man. The *jefe*, manager, left on the Cruziero de Sol flight to Rio. Padre explained that ten people more or less run this town. They had been among the twenty-five on board. Now I understood why Padre couldn't get anyone to take action on my plight. And of course, when the head people were gone, "the mice will play," Padre added.

The telegraph office remained open but no one was there. In desperation, Padre left a message to be sent to the governor and attached thirty cruzieros, hoping that when the assistant finally returned he would send it. That was Padre's hope. Reality was quite different. When he returned two hours later, he discovered it had still not been sent. Hernando, the assistant, told Padre he found the cable but no money so he couldn't send it. I asked Padre what happened then.

"I told him to send it, and he did, but we lost a whole day."

"Just like that he changed his mind and sent it?"

He hesitated. "No, I convinced him to do it."

Now I was curious because Padre was obviously not relating everything. I questioned him again. "So what did you tell him that changed his mind?"

"I told him he was wrong for not being in the office all day when he is getting paid to be there to do a service. Then I told him I didn't think anyone took the money off the telegram, which was on his desk behind the counter, and that it was a double sin to steal from the church. I told him I was excommunicating the person who stole from the church and I would specifically excommunicate him if he didn't send the cable immediately because he was responsible for the problem in the first place by leaving the office unattended. That worked. The cable went out at five o'clock. We should hear back by morning."

"You play hardball, Padre."

"No, it is a double sin to steal from the church. You can be sure he will be the first one in chapel on Sunday. His wife will not have to drag him."

Donald Haack

"God works in mysterious ways," was all I could think to say. Padre raised his eyes to mine. There was a hint of a smile.

We had a minor crisis the third morning. Frontier hotels don't provide the usual services and amenities. They provide rooms, period. The guest brings sheets, blankets, soap, toilet paper, towels; in short, everything. Since my visit was unplanned, I had nothing. Padre Marco, who never stayed in a hotel, was unaware of all this. He brought food and drinks. The maracusha fruit juice did what it usually did. I had an urgent need.

I quickly made it known to the guard outside my door I had to go to the bathroom. He led me down the hall, down the steps, and into the public bath. Up to that time I wasn't concerned with the lack of amenities because I didn't expect to be here more than a couple of hours.

The stark bathroom had no toilets only a hole in the ground with two handles on the wall so you don't fall in. Worse yet, no toilet paper. I could manage squatting over the hole, but I couldn't do without toilet paper. I returned to the front desk. The manager was nowhere to be found. I needed toilet paper quickly.

"*Jefe*," I called out. No answer. I ran back up to my room with my no-smile guard tagging right behind. I ran to the window, reached up, unhooked one red curtain, continued down the steps, and back to the still empty main desk. Dragging the curtain, I stepped behind the desk into the adjoining room where the startled "manager" sat up on his cot not sure what to expect.

I showed him the red curtain. In my best broken Brazilian, accompanied by explicit graphics, I demonstrated how I was going to use the drape if I didn't get toilet paper. His eyes widened, his jaw fell slack. Before he could utter a sound, I retreated towards the bathroom, dragging the curtain behind.

That got the *jefe's* undivided attention. Toilet paper appeared miraculously at the same time I reached the bathroom. He actually sprinted. He handed me the paper in one hand and took the red drape in the other. Not a word exchanged.

"Obrigado," thanks, I said. He didn't acknowledge it. He was out of the bathroom in a flash. I glanced at my trusty guard.

Instead of his usual stone like countenance, he broke out in an ear-to-ear grin, which immediately turned into a scowl after realizing he was being observed by me. He turned away while I did my ablutions. He wore a permanent scowl for days and never uttered a word. Pleasant fellow.

Padre Marco brought me soap and a towel. After several false alarms, I discovered the water was supposed to come on three times a day for fifteen minutes. Problem was, you didn't know what fifteen and couldn't count on an uninterrupted shower, which often lasted only five of the alleged fifteen. The first time, I was all soaped up and the water stopped. I wore the dry soap for hours until the water came back on. After the rinse I felt a bit refreshed, but without a change of clothes I still smelled like a locker room after a football game.

Padre Marco congratulated himself on being able to send off the telegram on day four. No word that night. No word the next morning. I wasn't sleeping and started hallucinating. I was alternating between deep depression and furious anger. I made up my mind. When Padre and Doug came to my room that evening I told them what I was going to do. They listened. They weren't happy with what they heard.

I planned to get out tonight and find my way to the airport to fly the plane before daybreak. I passed on my concern to Padre that after five days of house arrest there was a strong possibility the plane could be permanently seized. Without it our company was out of business and we were out of our home—a disaster.

The mining operation depended on a supply of food and equipment and moving men around. There were no other small planes within 200 miles. Even if I were released, without a plane our home in the mountains was inaccessible. With no roads or navigable waterways it would take five days of hiking on the savannah, fording deep rivers, and going through the last fifteen miles of rough jungle trails only to be stranded at our home without supplies.

Just thinking about it enraged me. I was fit to be tied. I left Jan and the children five days ago for what ostensibly was going to be a ninety minute mail run. I left Caesar at Lethem. He would know I had flown to Boa Vista on a mercy mission and would have explained it to Jan when he returned to Good Hope. But without communication from Boa Vista it was anyone's guess what had happened. They would be worried sick by now, not knowing if I crashed or what.

Padre and Doc tried to talk me out of what they termed "my crazy plan" and to wait yet another day. The silence from Rio puzzled Padre. He had no explanation and it blunted his argument to wait. He knew this back country and the critical role of our plane, and understood the anguish my family would be experiencing. He relented. I asked him for a small flashlight. I kept a spare key to the plane in my leather folder. Within the hour he returned with the light. After many *Our Fathers* and *Hail Marys,* he assured me Doc and he would continue praying all night until they knew I was safe. They left at dark with many blessings and brazos. For the first time I felt very lonely…but I had work to do.

My door had a bolt on the inside. There was no reason to use it before, but now I didn't want anyone coming in to discover I wasn't there. I slid it quietly to lock and waited until 10:30 p.m. As quietly as possible, I moved the cot to the window, removed the sheets and tied them together. Despite a scraping noise, I eased open a window, probably never opened before. It sounded terribly loud to me but apparently no one else heard. There was no pounding on the door. The guard was probably sound asleep in the assurance I couldn't get through the outside locked door without him knowing.

I waited a couple of minutes to be sure no one stirred. I double knotted the sheet to the bed, tucked my leather folder into my shirt, grabbed the sheets, tested the weight, turned on my stomach on the window sill, and eased myself down hand over hand. I came to the end of the sheet without reaching the ground. I had miscalculated the distance. Earlier, I estimated it to be seven or eight feet from the end of the sheet to the ground. Since I'm over six feet and with arms extended, I should have touched the ground. Being dark it wasn't easy to see the ground and didn't give me a great feeling of confidence. The terrain appeared to be level when I checked earlier. I held my breath and let go. I hit the ground with my legs taking the initial shock. I rolled back and sat up. No damage. Fortunately, my fall was less than two feet.

I stood up. No moon, pitch black. The stars were bright and after a few minutes of getting accustomed to the dark, I saw trees silhouetted against the sky. This was my first time in Boa Vista. It had been a seven or eight minute drive from the airport heading southwest to town. Traveling at thirty-five miles an hour would place the airport approximately four miles from town. If I headed north and east on that airport road, walking and running should put me there in about forty-five minutes.

I didn't dare use the flashlight now—too suspicious walking on a deserted road in the middle of the night, heading for the airport and army base. In a few minutes I found the gravelly road and started out jogging.

Ten minutes out I had an uneasy feeling of heading west on the wrong road. I could make out a long row of trees ahead, only there weren't any trees to the airport. *I must be on the road heading west out of town and the airport road must be to my east going north.* I somehow miscalculated where the airport road started.

Time being critical, I was both angry and frustrated with my mistake, even though there was no way I could have known. That didn't help. Half- running and stumbling, I double backed until I could see the lights of town, and then took a small jeep path to the left. It was full of ruts making even slow walking difficult. After a hundred yards, I intersected a major road I hoped would lead to the airport. It headed north and to make up lost time, I broke into a half-run. I glanced at my luminous watch—11:15. Still plenty of time for contingencies *if* I could find the airport and plane.

I didn't want to take off before 4:30. Five would be ideal. To reduce some risk, I would have to make a night takeoff when they couldn't see and therefore couldn't shoot at me, at least in theory. I planned to slow-flight on instruments in an easterly heading, which should put me well north of Lethem and then until daylight circle above the flat part of the savannah. The Kanaku Mountains were south of Lethem and I wanted plenty of distance from them in the dark. I rehearsed this mentally but the road had ruts and large clumps of clay that demanded more attention than I was giving.

My running was peculiar at best: high stepping followed by a half skip. It was peculiar but there was madness in my antics. If I stepped in a hole, my weight was partially shifted to the next foot. A sprained ankle would be catastrophic. My one-two shuffle caused a mild pain in the calf muscle, but it was good insurance. The North star was ahead, a little left and low in the horizon. This was the right road. Orion, my favorite constellation, was positioned in the east halfway up in the sky and provided a comfortable, familiar companion in this hostile territory.

I heard it long before the lights pierced the darkness…a jeep. Living in the bush you attune to nature. Civilized sounds are intrusive. Scanning the road I saw nothing but in a few seconds the wildly dancing lights lit up the road. I had to get out of sight. I didn't expect traffic this late at night. Without shrubs or trees anywhere near, I had to run far off the road beyond headlight range or jump in the ditch.

The ditch accommodated me first. I jumped in. It was deeper than I expected. Fortunately it was dry season with no water and I lay flat on my stomach and hopefully safely out of sight. The jeep shot by and quickly became a small erratic light down the road. I checked to make sure there wasn't another one coming before I returned to my strange skip-shuffle.

Twelve, midnight—Orion almost overhead. There were lights in the airport building where the army was garrisoned and probably had guards on duty, if for no other reason than to keep them busy in this god-forsaken place. On all fours the last few yards, I cautiously approached the fence and gate, then sprawled flat out on my stomach and waited. Against the starlit sky, I could see if anyone were on patrol. I didn't have long to wait. A guard with a rifle slung over his shoulder patrolled the inside of the fence. He passed the gate and was out of sight a few seconds later. He wasn't quiet and I heard his receding footsteps. I crawled to the partially opened gate and squeezed through.

The light from the building illuminated the road and if the guard came back now, I would be silhouetted against the building. I hurried across the road and crept onto the field to the right. I didn't get very far before all hell broke loose: four or five big dogs and several small ones barking and running towards me from the building,. They either heard or smelled me. This was something I didn't expect and hadn't prepared for. I knew it was all over. If I stood up I would be a silhouetted target for the trigger-happy guard who just passed.

I didn't have many options so I lay on my back, curled up, put my folder over my face, and slipped out my Swiss Army knife. I opened the blade and waited for the first dog to attack.

A split second later, I reconsidered, closed the knife and jammed it into my pocket. Even if I were lucky enough to kill one or two dogs, the killing would make a bad situation worse. The guards might overreact at their dogs being killed. The best tactic might be to bluff it out, yell loudly and then use a dumb excuse like coming here to turn the propeller to keep the engine lubricated. Better than killing their dogs and getting shot, I hoped.

They were on top of me before I could change my mind—four large dogs arrived first. I curled up, took a deep breath, and waited for teeth to sink in. A few seconds later I realize this wasn't an attack. I had four dogs licking and jumping on me, nuzzling their noses under my arms. They were whining with joy to find someone to play with. The smaller ones just ran around barking, happy to be at the party.

Dogs licked my hair, ears, face, and neck, nudging me with their noses. It happened so quickly I didn't shout out. Now I didn't have to, but the barking and frolicking shattered the silence on this otherwise quiet night and I knew I'd be caught.

I lay there whispering to the dogs, scratching their stomachs, and waiting. Someone came to the door and shouted at the dogs. Nothing happened. He shouted again, louder, and that got their attention. They stopped licking and ran back to the building. I was alone again lying on my back staring up at the sky. Total silence. No one came to find out why the dogs barked. I was thankful and didn't move for several minutes. I checked to make sure the guard was not behind me, and then started my crawl towards the hangar. I passed directly below the lighted window where I heard shouting and the slamming down of dominoes, a favorite Latino pastime. When they played dominoes, their emotions ran high. With the force they slammed pieces on the table I was surprised they didn't shatter. Now I was glad for the noise. The soldiers might not hear me.

I crawled to the side of the hangar below the lighted window into total blackness and waited until my eyes conditioned to the dark. I continued half way down the side of the building before I saw the plane's outline. I ducked under, checked the wheels, removed the chocks, and made sure it wasn't chained. But what I found was worse—a bulldozer parked a foot in front of the propeller. With the plane backed up to the building, the only way out would be sideways. That meant I would have to move the plane forward and backwards a foot at a time, turn the nose wheel on each cycle and hopefully gain a few sideway inches each pass. Fifteen feet would free it from the bulldozer. Here was a major project I hadn't anticipated.

If I could get it out, I could use the puller in the luggage compartment to pull the plane to the airstrip a couple of hundred yards away, not an easy task, but possible. The bulldozer created the major problem that I had to tackle immediately. I hated to think I got this far for nothing. I checked my watch, one o'clock. I rechecked the side of the plane, all clear. If I maneuvered it forward and backwards for the next three hours, there might be a slight chance to position it fifteen feet to the left to clear the bulldozer. If there were even the remotest chance, I knew I had to take it.

I stripped off my shirt and started. *Steer the nose wheel, and turn the wheels by hand until the prop touched the bulldozer blade.* I rolled up my shirt and put it in front of the tire as a marker. *Then realign the nose wheel and inch the plane back until the tail almost touches the hangar.* The leather case went behind the main wheel as a marker of my rear limits. The night was quiet and the sloshing gasoline in the tanks broke the silence. It seemed horrendously loud to me. I moved the plane slower so it didn't sound like big breaking waves. I couldn't take a chance.

Using my knife, I made a mark in the dirt to measure side progress. By two o'clock the plane was slightly over three feet to the left. In two and a half hours it would have to move eleven feet further. I worked faster and ignored the noise. The deadline to be out from the bulldozer was 4:30 a.m. That left twenty minutes to pull 36 Bravo down to the airstrip, do a quick inspection, drain and check fuel for water, rotate the prop to lubricate the engine, and take off. Within seconds of hitting the starter, I had to be moving down the runway. The roar of the engine would break the silence like a thunderbolt. Guards would come out running and probably shooting. No time for niceties like checking magnetos and plugs.

A takeoff in total darkness with no reference lights was an experience I would rather do without. I had read up on the WWII aircraft lost on takeoffs from unlighted fields and crashing within seconds after lift-off. Without reference lights, vertigo occurs. The split second transition from visual to instruments is short and critical. I quickly wiped away those thoughts and concentrated on the task at hand.

By three o'clock I had moved the plane five more feet. I needed another seven feet to free it up. There wasn't a dry spot on me. My shirt was soaked in sweat, my hands ached from turning the wheels, and my pants were wet from drying my hands on them. I was an apparition covered in mud from head to toe. At 3:45 a.m. I checked the marks again...another three feet. Reality set in—it was over, impossible to make the next few feet by deadline.

I reviewed my situation. Not a good option to be caught out here. I had to cover my tracks. I used my shirt to wipe out the telltale marks on the ground. Exhaustion was taking over. I wondered if they would notice that the bulldozer or the plane mysteriously moved sideways during the night. It would give them something to think about. The picture of them standing there trying to figure it out was the only amusing incident of the night. I smiled at the image. I stopped smiling when I thought how I would return to the hotel undetected.

Donald Haack

After smoothing out the tracks, I put on my filthy shirt, my folder tucked inside, and on hands and knees crawled towards the gate. All lights were off. I found the gate this time without disturbing the dogs. I was thankful they were asleep. A few yards from the gate I waited a moment to be sure there was no guard. After hearing nothing and seeing no movements, I wiggled through and onto the road. I crept quietly for a few minutes before I broke into a run.

I had another deadline: to return to the hotel before light. Finding it should be easier if I stayed on the main road, eliminating the detour I took coming out. After a few minutes I saw the hotel outlined in the distance. It wasn't as dark now and would be light in less than fifteen minutes when I had to be *in* the hotel. Throwing caution to the wind, I ran faster. The consequence of being caught out of the hotel by my unfriendly armed goons was not something I wanted to experience. I circled far to the rear of the hotel in case they posted a guard in front.

As I approached the back of the building, I easily found my room. The white sheets hung from the second story like a finger pointing out a bad deed. As I came closer, I thought of another problem I hadn't anticipated—the sheet was farther off the ground than I realized. When I crawled out of my room and slid down the sheet, I wasn't concerned about having to drop a couple of feet to the ground. I hadn't planned on going back up. Now it was a different matter. How to grasp the sheet hanging two feet out of reach? I quickly searched the area. Nothing to stand on.

I checked to make sure my folder was securely beneath my shirt, backed up and took a run for the building, jumping onto the lower window sill with one foot and grabbing wildly at the bed sheet. After several bad attempts, I connected and held on precariously, one hand clutching the sheet, both toes on the windowsill. I hung there motionless while I caught my breath and steadied myself until I had both hands on the sheet. I couldn't afford to slip off now. Through sheer will power I pulled myself up a few inches at a time. There was no crevice for a good toehold on the window. After several pulls I was high enough to wrap my legs around the sheet to give my arms a much-needed assist. It seemed an eternity before I reached the windowsill. I barely had the strength to pull myself in. After moving the cot back to its original place, I made a half-hearted attempt to unknot the sheets but gave up and flopped onto the bed and into a nightmarish sleep.

Pounding on the door woke me up. It was light. I recognized the voice of Padre Marco and didn't bother to close the window and hide the knotted sheets. I struggled up, unbolted the door, and flopped back on the bed without fully awakening.

Doc was with Padre. They quickly closed the door behind them. They saw me sprawled on the cot and were visibly disappointed because they didn't expect to find me here. I struggled to get up. Both began talking at the same time.

I could understand Doc better. "We had an all-night prayer vigil for you, your safety, your safe journey. For what? Here you are sound asleep while we stayed up all night praying."

I painfully pushed up on my elbows. They saw it all: the mud, the dirt, the knotted sheets, and the open window. They understood.

Padre Marco glanced down at the twisted bed sheet still tied to the cot. He told Doc that if the guards saw the sheets tied to the bed they would know what happened. He eased me off the bed.

The three of us grabbed the sheets and tried to undo the knots. It took the better part of an hour before we finished. The sheets were a mess, streaked in sweat and mud from my climb back up. Padre, worried the guards would find out, quietly said *Our Fathers* and *Hail Marys*." I made up the bed using my best marine corps training to tighten the sheets. A quarter could bounce off the cot. That helped hide the worst wrinkles but not the strange knot-induced mud streaks. I tried to smooth out the worst streaks but suddenly Padre stopped me.

He had a strange hint of a smile while he stared at the bed. His beard twitched. I thought he was losing it, cracking up. I'd seen it happen before to people under stress and I didn't know the Padre that well.

Donald Haack

I wasn't prepared for what happened next. Padre glanced around the room confirming nothing was out of place. He went to the window, quietly closing it to an inch from shut and scraped the mud off the sill.

He appeared to be in control but what happened next overturned that image—he flipped his lid. He yelled loudly. It took Doc and me by surprise. We tried to stop him. The last thing we wanted was the guard coming in. The more we tried to restrain him the more vocal he became. The guards would have to be deaf, dumb, and blind not to hear the ruckus Padre was making. They responded quickly by pounding on the door and nearly succeeded smashing it before Padre opened it.

Everything was in chaos. The guards carried rifles and were prepared to shoot but didn't know what the targets were. They were shouting, Padre was shouting. I was wide awake, no longer in a sleepy stupor. Everything appeared to be in slow motion. I moved to the side and leaned against the wall. Doc sat on the floor next to me. Padre stood tall, his arms up in the air, and the center of attention. He shouted and talked fast. I couldn't understand a word. Our priest and friend had snapped from too much strain, I thought.

I couldn't catch the gist of his rantings and mime. He raised his hands as if to heaven, and then bowed his head, hands pressed together in prayer. Much to my horror, he pointed to the sheets. Now I knew he'd lost it. Two minutes ago we frantically tried to hide the sheets, now, to the contrary, he brought it to their attention. I had enough. I was tired, dirty, and I really didn't care. I slowly slid down the wall alongside Doc and I glanced over to see what he thought about our mad priest.

Doc understood Brazilian better than I. He was intent upon what Padre was saying. Seeing my confused expression, he pursed his lips and raised his finger to quiet me. I frowned. He repeated his gesture pointing at Padre with his thumb. Doc was smiling. Maybe they both flipped their lids. I strained to understand what Padre was saying and what, under these circumstances, could possibly be amusing. I obviously missed something. Gradually, I understood our mad priest's message.

Donald Haack

God forgive us, I thought. I glanced to where Padre pointed at the sheet. The guards were walking around the bed in awe scrutinizing the sheets, the supposed miracle sheets. He elaborated the story of the Americano, who without pay flew this mercy mission to save the life of our own sick girl and how did our army thank him? By putting him under lock and key and keeping him from his family. What kind of thanks is that? But God, yes God, knew and made a sign where the senhor slept, a sign for all to see. I glanced again at the sheet. It was a strange design.

Twenty years later it would become a fad in the states known as tie dying: rays emanating from a point, like rays of the sun. It was hypnotic. The more he raved and gesticulated, the more mystical it became. The thought crossed my mind that I felt better that I didn't charge even for the gas on this mercy mission. It's not every day one gets involved in a miracle, much less be its source. He even had me caught in the spell he was weaving.

The guard called in the other guard, the manager, and two maids who heard the commotion and came running into our cramped room. They stared, kneeled, and crossed themselves in front of the sheet. Padre's performance was grand, worthy of an Oscar. He had us all mesmerized. He directed the manager to hang the sheets up on the wall, never to wash them. It was a miracle, a sign from God, and we should all learn from this.

My God, Padre, I thought, you sure do have chutzpah. Were you a Rabbi in your former life? What would God think about your *stretched miracle?* I couldn't take any more. Too exhausted to laugh, I closed my eyes and slept until I was roughly awakened by Padre shaking my arm. We were alone, the room empty.

"A divine intervention that you didn't take off." he said. "I just came from the cable office, a telegram from the governor. He profusely apologized for the misunderstanding and authorized your immediate release. He returns tomorrow and hopes you will be here so he can apologize in person to make amends."

"Padre, no way! I haven't slept, had a decent bath or change of clothes in five days. I stink like a fish. Jan and my friends don't know whether I'm dead or alive. It's a kind gesture on his part. Please thank him, but I'm leaving immediately."

He smiled. "I understand. Let's go." He helped me to my feet.

I was flabbergasted by the complete turnabout of the guards, the little brown men with scowling faces and big guns; not any more. Guns were out of sight, replaced with big smiling faces. These same men now pushed me with friendly elbows while making jokes I couldn't understand. To them it was like a big joke, an incident to highlight their week in an otherwise dull, boring existence in Boa Vista.

I tried smiling but it didn't come easily. I could barely stand the smell of myself. At least it kept the soldiers at a respectful distance and probably why there were no Brazilian brazos with the exception of Padre Marco. The jeep ride out was dusty, quick, and uneventful. We stopped at the hangar near 36 Delta. No bulldozer in sight. After I completed a thorough preflight inspection and was satisfied all was well, I stepped towards Padre who was walking to me. He came to give me a big Brazilian brazo, hug. We held each other tightly for what seemed a long time but in reality a mere few seconds. He pulled back slightly, our faces a few inches apart, eyes wet.

"Vaya con Dio, mi amigo u obrigado," he whispered. Go with God, my friend and thank you.

I could only nod. We parted and I climbed into the plane.

Twenty-five minutes enroute I spotted the Ireng River and Good Hope. I glanced over to the ranch house, a couple hundred yards north of the strip. Jan was at the house waving, holding Diney's hand. I was "home."

Tacapita, north of the Orinoco. Brother Bob, Blackie Davis and friendly parrot.

Above: Two *druggers* along the trail.

Below: Pulling our boat through the rapids (Ireng River).

Above: Local Diver trying our new equipment.
Below: Harry and Don at the diamond strike (Ireng).

Above: Domingo working the diamond suruku.
Below: Chibi at three months.

Above: Dutch

Below: Don, Caesar, Dutch at Good Hope ranch.

Above: Good Hope dining room. Nellie, Jan and friendly pigeon on Jan's head.

Below: DC-3 Jan bringing Diana to Good Hope, Rupununi.

Above: Brazilians finishing Marquis home.

Below: Good Hope. Nellie, Diana and Chris.

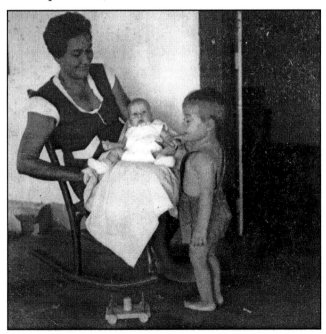

Above: Our house at Marquis.

Below: Marquis valley from the air over Ireng.

Above: Daddy's helper. A smooth martini helps take the edge off even rough days.

Below: Diana in hammock with *attack* cat guarding.

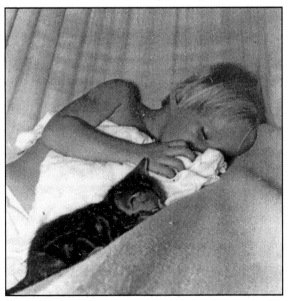

Above: The crew commuting to work.

Below: The "office" Assembling diamond jig, trommel and dredge.

Above: Don and
Harry after big
sale in the trade
store.

Right: The
sad end of 94
Bravo.

Above: WaiWai children.
Below: The old man.

Dinner time with the WaiWai.

Above: WaiWai house. Mother and daughter beside multi-family hut.

Below: Wrestling—their way of settling argumants.

Above: Simuni River. Mother, Dad, 6½foot, 400 lb. arapaima and McTurk.

Below: Our Bambi.

Don and his WaiWai collection.

BAMBI

D utch had encouraged us to establish a trade store and now it was doing a brisk business. When it first opened, it was meant to be for our crew only, which at that time numbered twenty Indians from Karasabai and Tipuru villages. Most of the Indians worked a couple of weeks earning enough to purchase shoes, machetes, pants, fishing tackle, and flashlights before returning to their homes. That encouraged many neighboring Indians to see if they, too, could buy. This gave us a never-ending supply of laborers and customers for the store.

When we couldn't hire all of them, Dutch suggested they bring food or animals to trade. He asked me first if that would be all right, since we could use farine, a food derived from the cassava root and a staple for our Amerindian crews. We always needed chickens for eggs or stew and Jan made great chicken and dumplings. We brought in laying mash from Georgetown. If, in a couple of weeks the chickens didn't lay, *da pot vood get dem* as Dutch put it. We all welcomed the change in diet from bully beef, canned corned beef and jerked beef sun dried in the air.

Donald Haack

Dutch liked to smoke the heavy plug tobacco made by the Indians and he must have dropped the hint to them because soon we were taking in piles of plug tobacco, each plug three feet long and three inches in diameter. The stack extended over half the floor of the shop. Dutch said a half plug satisfied his needs for a year. I was hoping it wasn't only for him, because at that rate it would be a fifty-year supply. Dutch must have been a resourceful trader in a previous life. He suggested we cut the plugs into quarters to carry in the plane, along with five-pound bags of farine, which was also in surplus. He priced them for the trading posts I flew into and to my surprise, everything sold on the first few trips.

When I told Dutch, he gave me a big toothless grin that accentuated his pointed chin.

"Yah, I know vat I had to pay ven I traveled da bush. Dey get a bargain und ve make goot money." He showed me the cost at our trade store. We indeed made *goot money.* Other than chickens, Dutch took in trade a strange assortment of animals. Some became our pets.

"Just how many pets can we have?" Jan reminded me.

We made a cage below our water tower for the tame monkeys, fed them well and they were a source of fun for everyone including Jan. She enjoyed having the various animals and birds and because they responded to her so well, accepted the chore of feeding them. The *acouri* was another matter. The Indians told Dutch it was okay to keep it in the house. We did. It was the size of a rabbit, had reddish brown bristly hair, a head that was indistinguishable from its body and a constantly twitching nose. It had long white front teeth resembling a miniature beaver. We found out from Nellie that the acouri was a nocturnal animal and had a penchant for wood. It barely moved during the day but it didn't take long before we found out about its nocturnal habits.

"Don, what happened here?" Jan pointed to our redwood door and window trim. It had ragged edges as if some big object had crashed against it. "Do you remember any of the boys bringing in heavy objects that could have done this?" she asked.

It puzzled me. "No, I really don't know what could have done that much damage without us knowing about it. And if it happened while Dutch was around, he would've have said something."

Two days later the *damage* was more extensive. The acouri was eating up our house. He left the next day. I didn't ask what Dutch did with him, but I suspect he became lunch for our Amerindian crew. When Jan asked about his whereabouts the next day, I could truthfully say I imagined Dutch gave him to someone to enjoy. Someone who didn't have redwood trim in his house. After that, acouris were put on the list of unacceptable trade items in the store. A few days later Dutch came up to the house to join Jan and me for a drink. He was always invited but seldom accepted.

"Fur special occasions only," he said, sipping his rum and water with the luxury of an ice cube. He swirled the one ice cube in his amber drink, while musing. "Yah, dis is goot living here." He continued swirling the cube till it disappeared altogether.

I wondered what the special occasion was this time. It turned out he wanted to ask us something and wanted to break it gently. I knew he had something on his mind. I waited.

"Vell, I took sompin in trade today," and waited to see if I had any reaction. The acouri story was still fresh in our minds. He knew that. "Vell, I took dis ting und vunder if it's okay. If not, you can take it oot of my pay." He smiled. Dutch wasn't on the payroll. He was a permanent non-paying guest. When he needed money for something, he hinted and we gave him whatever he needed. My curiosity was more than slightly aroused. I was quite certain he didn't take in another acouri. I wondered what would merit this extensive buildup.

"Vait here, I bring." and he got up and left, leaving his drink only half finished. In a few minutes, the door opened, Dutch walked in, then stood back to guide in a newly born fawn. Her spindly legs wobbled. She had a beautiful face accentuated with a jet-black nose and long eyelashes. Her eyes were a doleful, deep brown. Jan melted and knelt down to hold the young deer steady as it slipped hesitatingly on our smooth concrete floor. Jan guided it onto our rug where it could stand more steadily. Dutch informed us the fawn was a *she*. Knowing Dutch, I wondered how he would know. Maybe the Amerindian told him.

Diney ran up to her gently placing her hand on the fawn's neck. At two-and-a-half, Diney was only slightly taller than the fawn. She nuzzled Diney with her wet nose. It was love at first sight. The fawn felt an affinity to Diney and vice- versa.

"Bambi," Diney whispered and the name stuck. Bambi became a part of our family. Tom, not quite one year old, stretched out his arms but he was more unstable than the deer.

Dutch stood back with a big grin on his face. "I guess ve keep her, eh?" he said quietly. I nodded.

We kept Bambi in the house the first couple of weeks. Surprisingly, she was a good house pet, scratching on the door to be let out. Just outside of the door, still walking, she dropped her little round poop balls, which Jan later swept further away from the house. After a few minutes of walking around outdoors, she would cry to come back in. After a few weeks Bambi became restless. She grew and soon lost her spotted fawn camouflage. Growing into a small deer, she went outdoors more often, each time staying longer. We reluctantly agreed we couldn't keep her in the house. Jan bought a red collar for her through our town agent who questioned buying the collar because he hadn't sent up any dog. Jan informed him that it was for a deer. We didn't hear a reply back. He probably was still trying to figure that one out.

Jan decided Bambi needed the collar so the Indians wouldn't mistake her for a wild deer. In the following weeks, Bambi reversed her living habits. She spent most of her time in the bush and returned to the house twice a day. Later, her trips to the house were only nocturnal when we were seated at the dining room table lighted by the gently hissing Tillie lamps. I wondered if Bambi came on cue because of the familiar Tillie lamp noise or the smell of food. She was always home for dinner.

Diney was attuned to the gentle scraping of the hoof on the door, followed by a high-pitched squeal. She would race to the door for first hugs. Now that Bambi was bigger, the hugs were more tolerated than needed. With the dignity of an adult deer, she could now walk gracefully on the smooth concrete floor. After hugs from Diney, she came to the table for food. We had her usual green fare plus her favorite bananas, which she ate last.

Her regular routine was to walk into the darkened kitchen, go through the bedroom and return to us in the dining room. Though when a fawn she had avoided Tom, she now was at ease approaching him. Their first encounters when both were unsteady on their legs, resulted in tumbles to the floor. In their struggle to get up, they would tangle legs and fall down again. Bambi learned to avoid those situations and when Tom approached with his arms open, Bambi would scamper to another room. Tom followed unsteadily calling "Bambi, come!" Bambi wisely stayed one room ahead.

For several weeks Bambi returned almost every night. Later, to Diney's and Tom's disappointment, her visits were less frequent. A week went by without seeing her, then one night as we finished our meal, Diney jumped up.

"Bambi's here," and opened the door for her. We were surprised how big and beautiful she was. Living in the bush gave her an air of alertness. She came to the table to have her head scratched.

"Hey," I exclaimed, feeling around her head with surprise. "Bambi's not a she, it's a *he*. He's growing antlers; they're almost a half inch long."

Everyone felt Bambi's horns. We had a buck not a doe. I thought of Dutch's comment on "her" gender when "she" first arrived. Well, that was in keeping with Dutch's perception of what went on around him. On most things like that Dutch was dead wrong.

We decided to remove Bambi's collar, which could be a dangerous hindrance to him now in the thick bush. We trusted to luck that he could avoid hunters. He returned several times, the last two visits during full moon when we spotted a doe standing alongside of him on the runway near the hangar. Bambi had found a mate. For a long time we speculated whether Bambi raised a family, and if he did, would he bring the fawn to show to us? Many a night we thought we heard his familiar bleat, but to our disappointment, particularly Diney's and Tom's, we never saw him again. We felt a loss when he didn't show up anymore, but we were thankful for the richness he added to our lives when he was a part of our family.

TEZAREK'S LAST FLIGHT

B ad news. I read the message for the second time and
checked it word-for-word as the B. G. Airways radio man
repeated it for confirmation.

"Roger, correct, do you wish to reply now?" he answered.

I was still studying the Director of Civil Aviation request.
More questions than answers ran through my head. "Just tell
him 'affirmative' and I'll get back to him as soon as I have more
information and details."

I would have to think of something in the way of explanation
to Jan, if indeed this message was correct. I had convinced her
that flying in light single engine planes was a calculated risk,
and at worst, we might lose a plane but would always walk away
whole.

I glanced down at the paper again.

Joe Tezarek is five days overdue. He was purportedly on a
flight to an airstrip north of Karona Falls to pick up miners and fly
them to meet the Orinduik plane the following day. They didn't
show up and there has been no message from him. A Brazilian

Donald Haack

along the border heard a rumor about a plane accident four or five days ago. Supposedly, the plane crashed and burned, no survivors. Brazilian authorities have no confirmation. Apparently the short airstrip would not accommodate our twin-engine plane. Can you fly over to check it out and document what happened? We have obtained a special clearance from the Brazilian government to land at the site if it is in their territory. They, too, are interested but have no plane capable of landing on short strips. I'll post this letter on the Good Hope plane tomorrow and you can use it as authority when and if you go. Julian tells me you meet the plane regularly. Good luck. Alex Phillips, DCA.

It was dated yesterday.

Tezarek had the only other plane in the interior. I met him twice—the first time with our mutual friend, Caesar, who gave his blessings about me being an *A-okay guy*. Joe seemed genuinely pleased to have another plane in the area.

"We can always help each other in emergencies and later we may even share gas. Just don't go buying diamonds from my trade shops on the border." He was still smiling but I got the message that he was serious and implying it was *his* territory.

After I shut down the transmitter and generator, I showed Dutch the message. He said he heard rumors from the Tipuru Indians that a plane crashed along the Ireng. He didn't take it too seriously because most bush rumors were just that: rumors.

"Okay, now I ask every Indian who comes to de store. Maybe ve find out someting."

Jan, Dutch, and I poured over our maps trying to pinpoint the area where this might have taken place. I pointed to the map. "If it happened near us, there's only one airstrip between Karona Falls and the Uan Paru Indian village airstrip. It's short with a steep approach in front of a hill with large rocks. The strip ends near the Ireng. There was a barge and diving crew upstream so that's probably the area. If Tezarek went deeper into Brazil, that's territory I've never seen and I haven't a clue of any airstrip. I could land on this one and hike to the barge. Can't be more than a mile. There were foot trails in the area and with luck, I could be in and out in two hours. That crew should know if anybody crashed in the area."

My tentative plan sounded easy, but I knew from experience it wouldn't be without problems. I decided on an early start for any contingencies. The next morning Dutch had the plane out of the hangar and all seats removed. He pointed to a five-gallon can of gas as I approached.

"It looks like you haf quarter full tanks. May be nuff. Brought some extra case you want to add. Tink it is only fifteen minute flight from here and I know you vant to be light as possible first time you land on strip." He waited for me to do the inspection and visually check the gas level in the tank.

"Yeh, that's fine. I'll go with the gas that's in there—more than enough for the short flight."

Seven o'clock, no wind and cool; good conditions for a short take-off. I headed up river and wiggled my wings as I flew over our barge that was already spewing out sand on the right bank of the river. I thought anywhere else in the world I would have made a small fortune moving that much sand. Here, where it was supposed to uncover a *large* fortune of diamonds, it hadn't paid for the gas yet.

I passed Karona Falls where the land above it was flat. At this low altitude, the countryside looked entirely different than flying over at high altitude. I could see every rapid and shallow pool. Not far ahead I expected to see the Brazilian diving crew. I glanced to the left and right sides of the river to make sure I didn't miss any area large enough for an airstrip. Nothing. A few more minutes passed. I saw four men on a pontoon. They heard the plane and waved. I made a low circle and tipped my wings. One of them pointed southwest. I hoped he was indicating where the airstrip would be. I flew broad "S" turns for a better sighting out the side windows. At the eleven o'clock direction I spotted a flat long clearing. That was it. At one end was a crude air sock that hung limp and at first I felt disappointed. I wanted a stiff wind for a short landing. I circled at a hundred feet for a closer look. The hill to the west had high trees requiring a steep approach. Not good.

Better to land from the east where it was flat with no obstruction and ideal for a low, slow approach using full flaps. In this case, no wind meant no tail wind and made it easier to land short.

I pushed in the throttle to climb fifty feet. If there were a plane crash around here, it should be easily seen from this altitude. I circled once, twice, and a third time in ever widening circles. No sign of a plane or burn area. I recalled what one of the Tipuru Indians related. He said the divers on the pontoon heard the plane take off, and when it was overhead the engine stopped, started, then stopped several times, but didn't shut down completely. Tezarek must have turned back to the airstrip. A few seconds later they heard a big noise and saw lots of black smoke. That was the gist of this second-hand message. But it gave me a couple of clues.

I flew over the river to the airstrip's flat approach. From there I could easily see the dredge and they could see me so that couldn't be the crash site. I continued down the strip towards the hill where I no longer could see the pontoon. If there were a crash, it had to be further northwest.

I tried to re-create what happened. He was flying an overloaded plane, presumably four passengers and Joe. His engine sputtered and lost full power. He turned back to land. From his position and under the circumstances, he should have made a straight downwind landing. He might have overshot the runway with minor damage to the plane. Maybe that's what determined his other decision, to come in the way he always did—from the west, into the wind in front of the hill and trees. Without much altitude, in an overloaded plane with partial power and going slow, he was forced to make to make a steep 180-degree turn in front of the hill. Everything was stacked against him... a perfect scenario for a graveyard stall into the hill or the trees.

I gained altitude to clear the trees and circled several times without spotting anything. Then I saw the broken tree and the ragged wood exposing its white scar. It wasn't until after several passes that I was able to maneuver directly overhead to verify there was a burn area below. I was quite certain I had found the crash site, but I would have to make an on-the-ground examination.

Donald Haack

I landed from the other side and, thanks to no wind, I used less runway than anticipated. I taxied toward the hill, turned the plane around, and shut down. When I opened the door and stepped out I had the same feeling I did on so many of the strips here: silence, no animals, no people, and no sign of civilization in any direction. Looking around, I could make out a few paths, whether man-made or animal it was difficult to tell. The feeling of total isolation pervaded the area.

I snapped out of my speculations, took out my leather gloves, machete, water bottle, compass; stuck a pen in my pocket, and stuffed a notebook inside my shirt. I looked up at the hill. From the air, I calculated I would have to hike to the woods, and then turn right to a couple of large boulders. If my compass headings were correct, I had to enter into the woods in a westerly direction for twenty or thirty yards. It looked easy from the air. I climbed to the boulders and up to the trees. It wasn't an open forest but a thick jungle.

After a half hour of hard cutting, I smelled the burned area before I saw it. I cut away a few more vines to reveal an open area no larger than a small room. Everything was black. I looked up. No wonder I couldn't see anything from the air...there was only a sliver of daylight showing through. The plane must have plummeted straight down. That could only have happened if he stalled trying to make an impossible low, slow turn. He must have dropped like a stone, hit the ground, and exploded.

There wasn't much left. I had seen crash sites, some with severe damage, but nothing prepared me for this. What I saw in front of me was no semblance of a plane. The fuselage, which must have been at least thirty feet long, was a mass of blackened aluminum twisted into a five-foot diameter ball. The engine and bent propeller were in the middle of the mass; behind was a compacted tail assembly. The aluminum was partially melted from the intense heat. Pilot and passengers were completely cremated with no sign of skeletons. The scorch marks on trees radiated out over fifty feet in all directions.

Donald Haack

One wing a few feet away was totally blackened but partially intact. The second wing, making a scraping sound, hung precariously in a tree; the only faint noise except for the buzz of insects around the wreckage. The thought of these people who were flying in the aircraft and now totally gone made me feel nauseous. But at least their end came quickly. I thought I should go back for a shovel to bury them properly, but on closer inspection, realized there was nothing to bury.

There were no identifying signs left on the plane. Then I remembered the wing hanging in the trees. The top was scorched. I cut a long branch, reached up and turned the wing over. The remainder of Joe's serial numbers was the identification I needed. I made copious notes, looked down again at what used to be a plane and people. Tears ran down my cheeks, but were lost in my sweat-wet khaki shirt. I closed my notebook and made my way back to the plane. I returned home, typed up the report, and mailed it to Alex Phillips, DCA. It would be up to the DCA and Brazilian authorities to notify families and take care of the details.

After Joe Tezarek's crash, my plane was the only one in the interior. Joe apparently had quite a diamond buying and trading business in B. G. and along the Brazilian border. In the following weeks, almost every airstrip I landed on had a message for me to fly something in. Everyone needed rations, clothing, or tools for their diamond operations. Hundreds of camponieros who depended on Tezarek's transportation were stranded. I inherited his business by default and found I was flying almost full time or organizing cargo from Georgetown to the DC-3 strips where I distributed it to the shops.

Tezarek's crash shook up Jan and me. After I analyzed the scenario and put it on paper, I tried to assure Jan that Joe had made a fatal error in not planning ahead for basic emergencies. It should have been a no-brainer for Joe to have made a straight-in downwind approach with possibly some damage to the plane if he over-ran the airstrip. Instead he went for the long shot, breaking every flying rule...and paying the ultimate price. The explanation helped but didn't dispel all the anxieties she had about my flying.

BUSH FINANCE

With the dredge pumping constantly I had to keep up a regular supply of rations and diesel fuel.

Jan and I calculated our operating expenses and found that our diamond production from the dredge and the prospecting crew contributed only fifty percent of our income. We were advised by my brother in the States that no more funds would be coming from investors so we were on our own, kind of sink or swim.

We weren't about to call it quits, though Jan reminded me that we only drew one month in the last nine months of our agreed-to salary. Our employees were paid weekly and everyone except us was paid up to date. We decided to cut back on some of the staff around the baracoun. We couldn't let Jaime go because his wife, Marie, did our laundry and cleaned up around the store area.

The four-man prospecting crew I'd experimented with proved to be a money-maker. There were no wages for those divers. We made the arrangement on the honor system: a 50/50 split of the diamonds found. In all the time we operated there never seemed

Donald Haack

to be a reason to doubt that it worked. We supplied the diving hookah and Desco mask, the rations, gas, and suruku sieves plus any incidentals such as gravel bags, ropes, hand shovels, canvas for covering the hammocks, and cooking utensils.

Originally Harry wasn't convinced the Amerindians could learn to run the hookah diving equipment, much less maintain it.

"They can't do any serious damage. Just about anything they break, I can repair." I assured him. "We have enough spare parts to rebuild the engine and compressor three times over." He relented and taught them how to check the oil and fuel. It took four men to work the operation: one to dive, one to hold the hose to make sure the exhaust didn't drift back into the diver's air compressor—I let them smell it on dry land and they got the message. Besides, I told them, they would die if they inhaled the fumes. They caught on the first day—the third man handled the suruku, sieving and separating the diamonds from the gravel. The fourth man cooked.

Using hand gestures we explained the diver on the bottom would use the metal scoop to scrape gravel into the canvas sack kept open by a vine sewed into the top. When the sack was full, two jerks on the rope signaled to pull up. An empty second sack was attached to the rope so that when the full one came up, the diver immediately had another empty one with no lost time. They liked the idea of not having to come up each time they had a bag full of gravel, which they had to do when they held their breath and dove down. One jerk on the rope meant you were coming up. Three rope tugs was an emergency, something was wrong and pull up.

I couldn't teach them diving tables. Instead, we worked out a simple method, which worked without fail.

The first diver started when the sun came up above the horizon. He finished his dive when the sun was halfway up the sky toward its noon zenith, approximately ten o'clock. That would be a two-hour stint. Then they rotated. The diver cooked, hose handler dove, etc. They caught on to that by checking where the sun was every two hours, which eliminated teaching them how to tell time and understand diving schedules. In the past without those schedules, hundreds of Brazilians died from the bends. They didn't understand there could be water pressure problems at thirty feet. If they stayed down too long, nitrogen compressed into the blood and when they came up without decompressing, they had a million small explosions inside and bled to death. A horrible way to go.

After we trained our crew, I checked and serviced them once a week, replenishing oil, gas, and rations. I took my pocket diamond balance scale, weighed the diamond production and divided it into two piles. They watched eagerly and since I made the piles, I let them choose which was theirs to keep. Invariably, they asked me to buy their half because we paid more than any of the roving diamond buyers from Brazil.

In the evening by the light of the Tillie lamp, I sorted out the diamonds into several categories: rejects, sands, smalls, quarter carats, half carats and larger. The large poor color or imperfect solid octahedrons were classified as industrials. To determine the dollar value, each pile was weighed separately.

Jan had a list of all expenses. Week after week the only profit came from the prospecting crew's diamonds, one-third of our total production. By contrast the dredge with its small diamond production had produced most of our expenses and showed a substantial loss. It was time for a re-evaluation.

Harry and my brother's theories were based on big pockets of diamonds below sand banks. That's where we differed. They wanted to go for broke rather than build the business a block at a time. We brought in the first dredge and the general rumor was the *big diamonds below the sand* theory. It was impossible to refute and I reluctantly went along. But it wasn't working and we now faced the problem of running out of cash. Going for *the big strike* was costly and we weren't breaking even

By cutting expenses, not taking a salary, flying charter flights, and starting a trade business, we could make ends meet while we waited for *the big strike.*

In analyzing our income, I discovered it would make sense to add more prospecting crews as soon as we could afford it. I figured that six prospecting crews could take care of the complete cost of running the operations. In the meantime, the charter flying contributed the lion's share of income. Jan scheduled three flights a week and almost every company flight coincided with our scheduled charter flights, conserving precious and expensive gasoline.

After we set limits with Dutch on what *pets* could be used for barter, the Indians brought in cattle to barter for trade goods. Dutch's little store did a thriving business, paying a substantial percentage of the mining costs. We soon accumulated a few cattle, more than we could consume ourselves. We sun-dried the meat into jerked beef, which quickly became our number one seller in the mining areas, less than half the price of Georgetown's usually rancid pickled-in- salt- brine meat in barrels. In our new routine, we slaughtered once a week. The extra cattle grazed in our hundred-acre valley.

Then one day, wearing rancher clothes and a cowboy hat, *Toman* showed up at our doorstep. He was medium height, quite good looking—a neatly trimmed mustache, dark eyebrows, and a squared off face. I later learned he was from the Annai village, which had been settled fifty years earlier by African blacks who wanted to leave the confines of Georgetown and try a life in the interior. They went up the Essequiba River where it broke out of the coastal jungle into the open Rupununi Savannah and settled there along the edge of the jungle. They had ample wood for homes and fire, the river for fishing and transportation, and the savannahs to raise cattle. They called their settlement Annai, named after the nearby Annai Macusi Indian village.

After many years of close proximity, many Annai men married Amerindian girls and conversely, some of the black women chose Amerindian husbands. After fifty years, the black settlement and the Indian village were for the most part integrated into one.

Toman was one of the mixed breed offspring. He took an Amerindian wife and had three children, all good looking and intelligent. He brought his oldest daughter, Mariana, to our house on his second trip to help Jan with Tom and Diney and some of the house chores. She stayed with us two years and made Jan's life much easier. Jan had previously brought in several black women from town to help with chores and baby-sitting, but none could stand the isolated bush life. We brought back an East Indian boy, Ramdat who acclimated fairly well but had many lapses of memory. Left on his own for any length of time, he did stupid things like burning down all our producing papaya trees we had planted and nurtured for years. Mariana spoke English, had good common sense and was intelligent. Jan said she was heaven-sent. When Toman first came to us, he simply talked for a long time and I didn't understand why he came or if he was just paying a social call. Eventually, after having lunch, relating stories, and rolling and smoking three cigarettes, he came to the point.

"How would you like to go into the business of cattle and tobacco? I could be a small partner. The villagers have many cattle, more than they can ever use. They would like more of the trade goods you have here, particularly the good machetes. Much better than the ones they bought from John Roth. His were expensive and broke easily. They saw your fishing tackle and liked it…and shotguns, knives like the one you have, and rations to supplement their own homegrown cassava.

"I could gather the cattle for you from all the villages. The Indians grow a little tobacco now, and I heard from Caesar you were interested in growing some yourself. It's hard work. Better let the Indians do the work. You could show them what leaves to grow, how to air dry it, and what you would pay for it and still make a good profit selling it in Georgetown." That was quite a long speech and covered a lot of territory, I thought.

He obviously had been talking to Caesar to know as much about our plans as he did. I questioned him further on how he thought we could accomplish all this and what we would do with all the cattle we would accumulate.

"Once a fortnight I would make a trip to one of the villages and arrange to buy the cattle and bring them here to Marquis. The grass is good enough to feed a hundred head, but that wouldn't be necessary. When we get twenty, I can drive them through Karasabai into the savannah and up to Lethem. You can make arrangements with the abattoir for the slaughtering and B.G. Airways to ship the beef to Georgetown. The price is highest there. With all the gas, rations, and goods you bring up, you could charter the plane both ways and bring down the shipping price."

That was something I had been planning for a long time. The cattle would provide the ideal download. He stayed for three days while we worked out the details. I dropped him at Karasabai on my Good Hope flight where I questioned Caesar about Toman.

"Well, I suppose you know he's a horse and cow thief, at least most of the clan at Annai are. I have my biggest loss of cattle to those people and so does McTurk. Some we catch trying to brand our calves and heifers that were born over the rainy season before we can find them. After they're branded it's impossible to prove they were stolen. McTurk's and my cattle closest to the Annai settlement have the smallest births. It would seem more than just a coincidence.

"So why are you putting him on to me, then?"

"Well, he's another generation and I think he's trying to break out of the family mold and bad name. He's smart. If given a chance, he could do well. And maybe it's better to know *what* he's doing than wondering what he's up to." Caesar was always willing to reach out and help someone.

I made the agreement with Toman. He started immediately and worked non-stop. Every couple of weeks he brought in five or six head of cattle. One trip he and another Indian on horseback brought in over a dozen.

I contacted Nick Daher, the head of the British American Tobacco Company in Georgetown, who supplied me with seeds, three different grades of tobacco leaves and the premium prices the company would pay if we brought the best ones in early. I gave the leaves to Toman along with the seeds and instructions that Nick gave me. Toman took the seeds and leaves with him on every trip, explaining to the Indians in detail how to plant, how to hang and dry and what we would pay for each of the three types of leaves. For the sun and breeze to quickly cure the leaves, he showed them where in their open fields to best position their makeshift covered sheds. The golden brown commanded the premium price, the darkest brown, the lowest. Anything in between would be the second grade. The price difference was a big incentive for quality and early harvest. Three months later, the tobacco started coming in earlier than anticipated. As the Indians brought in the tobacco, Dutch compared the leaf color to our three store samples and paid them accordingly. Most of the tobacco was paid for at premium prices—a win, win for everyone.

The trade store did a booming business and we wasted no time in bundling the tobacco and flying it to meet our DC-3 charter. Because of the transportation advantage our tobacco came in two months before anyone else's. As agreed, the British Tobacco Company paid us the premium price. It was at the time their plant usually stood idle. Later when everyone else's tobacco came in, there was a temporary oversupply causing extra costs of handling and storage. Prices dropped accordingly. The plane became the focal point for quick turnovers in our commodity business.

At first Dutch had the Indians line up dollars on the counter and would point out how many rows it would take to buy certain items. After a few short weeks they learned the system of counting, dollars, and prices.

"Here fi dolla for pants, der" and they would point to pants and hand Dutch five dollars or the green five dollar bill. B.G. dollars were colored for the different denominations. They quickly learned the system. It was common to see Indians passing through Marquis with new Bata shoes and wads of dollar bills stuck in their new khaki pants. Partially due to Toman's activities in the surrounding villages, we became the biggest seller of Bata shoes in the country. After Tezarek's crash, trade stores along the border as far north as Venezuela wanted shoes, pants, and other items. The quality of merchandise and our prices were almost half of what they previously paid. The miners and trade store merchants were happy and we made a good profit.

Well, almost everyone was happy. Dutch came to me when I flew in after being gone for a few days. Something was bothering him.

"What's up Dutch?" He didn't hear but that was his cue to vent his discomfort. He explained we had an unexpected visitor, a Peruvian named Quaziero who claimed he walked across South America from Peru, his home. He needed a place to hang his hammock for the night. He was hungry, asked for a meal, and inquired if we had any work for him. Dutch saw to it that he was fed, then showed him where he could sleep in the hangar out of the rain.

Dutch didn't believe his story and was uncomfortable with him from the first day. He arranged for two Indians to stand watch on him all night. Dutch had lived in the bush a long time and experienced too many surprises, mostly unpleasant. His rule: help a stranger in the backcountry but don't trust him. The second morning Quaziero was still around, busily chopping grass around the hangar. That was the beginning. He worked whenever someone watched. It became a bit of a joke but Dutch didn't think it was funny and kept up his vigil.

Quaziero's *overnight* turned into a week. When I landed, he appeared on the side of the runway, saluted the airplane with a big bow from the waist as he swept off his huge sombrero in an arc. Then he remained motionless, head almost touching his shoes until the plane rolled by. He ran to the hangar, helped push and unload the plane, and disappeared.

As the days passed and Quaziero remained, Dutch's protests about him increased. "Ve're still feeding him, he eats too much und don't do a damn ting."

A week later Dutch informed me, "Dat dam Peruvian moved into da cabin of your old airplane stored near da hangar."

I made a mental note that to keep Dutch happy, I would have to have a talk with Quaziero and hasten his departure. Problem was, he disappeared every time I came looking for him and he extended his stay a couple of weeks. As it turned out, Dutch's sixth sense would prove to be true.

After a trip to the States and Europe, I established buyers for specific qualities of industrial and gem diamonds, increasing our profit by twenty percent. On one trip to Georgetown, I found a note in my box with a name and number to call. I called and within an hour a gentleman met me at the Woodbine hotel where he invited me to the Tower Hotel for lunch. He was an anomaly in the tropics, a Britisher who brings a bit of England with him when he travels. He wore a heavy brown tweed suit, double breasted and not suited for the tropics. His white hair was immaculately combed straight back and he sported a very British bushy mustache. His face was rounded and red. I wondered if the red was from drinking, the sun, or the heat from the wool suit. Nonetheless, his manner was quite proper. He said he wanted to take me to lunch to discuss business, which, strangely was not brought up during the meal. We exchanged pleasantries. He wondered what life was like in the bush, saying his life was normal and nothing out of the ordinary happened to him. He preferred that life and so did his wife who disliked traveling. After lunch he got straight to the point.

"I would like to buy your rough diamonds. I understand you mine a bit, but you do a trading business along the border." He paused a long time. I didn't answer right away because it took me by surprise and I didn't know how to respond.

He took my hesitancy as a negative reaction and continued on, "We would, of course, pay you more than what you're receiving now. To make it easier, all you would have to do would be deposit the diamonds at Barclay's Bank with the carat weight. The dollar amount declared would be paid to you straight off. No waiting. The check would be made out before you left the bank. Convenient, I would think, to help your cash flow a bit, right?"

I was still at a loss as to how to respond and explained I was perfectly happy with my present arrangements.

He continued, "We would be prepared to pay you exactly seven and a half percent more than you are receiving now."

I frowned. " That's quite presumptuous. How would you know how much I'm getting now?" His answer was not what I expected.

"Let's see," he murmured, as he removed a small black well-worn tablet from his pocket. "You sell some of your better diamonds to Harry Winston, some of your three carats to your brother in Milwaukee, your larger industrials to Anton Smit Company in New York, your octahedron industrials to the company in Detroit who is under contract to the Hugh's Tool Company for oil well drills used all over the world. There's more. Do you want to hear it all?" he asked, still holding the book open. It was as open as my mouth from the audacity and accuracy of what he related. It took me a bit to recover and comprehend what he had just told me.

"You must be deBeers." I finally blurted out. "No one else does their homework that well."

He smiled and avoided a direct answer. "My department does buying for many organizations." It was evident whom he was working for.

That began a long-standing relationship. Every few weeks Jan and I came to town with our diamonds, weighed and graded, which I delivered to Barclays and received a check. No more waiting weeks for payments on shipments to the States and London. It increased our cash flow many times over. Every few weeks there would be what they called "an account settlement."

DeBeers was adamant in the premise that the price of diamonds never changed. It was actually an obsession with them. There was a change in the value of each parcel, but to give them their due, it was adjusted up almost as often as down. They called it *grading correction,* moving some diamonds from one category to another. Upgrading or downgrading altered the total value of the parcel.

At first, I thought my grading to be at fault. Later, I understood that it wasn't my grading. What changed was the market supply and demand of certain diamond categories. They simply would not acknowledge a price fluctuation. They preferred to call it *grading corrections.*

After I understood what they were doing, I no longer experienced the personal frustration. I was paid immediately at a price close to seven and a half percent increase. I was happy and so, apparently, were they.

Donald Haack

POTION—STRONG MEDICINE

George, a full-blooded Arawak from the northeast territory on the Venezuelan-Guyana border was the missionary teacher in Tipuru village and became a frequent visitor to our house. Both his parents had been killed and Catholic missionaries raised him. His English at first was barely intelligible but after several visits it improved remarkably. He just needed practice.

He taught in Tipuru fourteen years. Father Quigley rewarded his good work by offering him the one opportunity to visit his home village. Arriving at his village, he recognized very few of his people. His close relatives had left years earlier for better hunting areas. With almost no family he felt like a stranger and chose to return permanently to the isolated Tipuru village.

When Jan and I first moved into our home, the visiting Macusi went back to their village with vivid stories about the strange house and the American family with the golden haired daughter who had deep blue eyes the color of the sky. It piqued George's curiosity enough for him to make the three- hour trek to our house.

Donald Haack

Dutch called me to the store to meet George, who didn't look like a Macusi. He was tall, heavy set, not muscular and had a happy face traced with smile wrinkles. His high cheek boned narrow face was more European than the typical Asian appearance of South American Indians and presented a stark contrast to the squared compressed local Indian face. Another contrast: he had thin eyebrows, the Macusi had none.

Dutch introduced him as Mr. George, the headmaster of Tipuru. I felt I knew him from Fr. Quigley's description and discussions. He offered his hand as he approached.

"You must be from the northeast. I met many Arawaks in Venezuela along the Amacura River." His eyes lit up. I struck a familiar note. When he first spoke, I had difficulty understanding. He apologized, saying Father Quigley had the same problem.

"I no speak English much. Last time Father came he say it take two days to understand my English. It get better," and he laughed. He was right. Within hours his fluency in English improved remarkably and he said that was a special treat for him. That became obvious later—he talked non-stop. Being his only neighbor, I was also his only audience. Father Quigley's occasional visit only teased his need to speak with someone.

"You first person who know I Arawak," he told me one evening.

Arawaks, I had heard were more intelligent than most of the other Amerindians and were proud of their heritage. Because of their intelligence and willingness to learn, they were chosen by the missionaries as teachers to the other British Guiana tribes.

"You only person who know my home in Amacura. I little boy when I fish in Amacura River."

I related my month-long gold expedition on the Amacura and living with Wadi, whom we discovered was his relative. Our guide, Juan, was his boyhood friend. They hunted and fished together. Those coincidences and reminiscences evoked a warm empathy between us. He wanted to know more and I told him everything I could about my stay in his country.

I enjoyed our fortnight meetings. I learned about Indian lore and had a rare glimpse into their unwritten tribal history. I had no premonition that this learning of history, folklore, medicine, and herbs would later save my life. Jan offered him the spare bedroom. He declined, saying it would set him apart from the Macusi. He preferred to sleep in the baracoun with Dutch.

Dutch, when he first came to live with us, moved into our spare bedroom, but his need to relieve himself at night became an esthetic problem. Not wanting to go far in the dark, he urinated outside his room causing an odor problem in the adjacent kitchen. Jan asked me to solve the problem. After I explained to Dutch, he moved to the baracoun saying it was easier to live where he could pee, "Any dam place and no vun care a fart." Though he slept there, he joined us for meals and tea, which he loved and wouldn't miss.

George simply could not hold a conversation with Dutch. It became a shouting match. Even with George shouting, Dutch seldom understood. He resorted to lip reading, which proved impossible in the dark. In spite of my assurance to the contrary, George was concerned about imposing on our hospitality and his visits were limited to one or two nights.

I particularly enjoyed our late night talks. With an attentive audience, George expounded in detail about the Tipuru Indian folklore, a subject he knew better than anyone I'd met. He explained how the tribe functioned, its mores, social laws, the influence and division of power between tuchow, the chief, and peayman, the spiritual leader.

One evening after a long discussion on peaymen, Jan retired to bed. When we were alone, George spoke more freely of tribal intimacies. He explained how they used herbs and pantomimes to create effects in his story telling. At night in the inky darkness of his hut, he rustled grass and leaves and tapped fingers on a branch to emulate a tiger stalking its prey. Blowing air through his lips, clicking his teeth, and rolling his tongue made sounds of water passing over rocks. By softly rustling dead branches and making short staccato grunts, he could imitate an approaching bush hog. The peayman was a master of pantomime and mimic; so much so, he could keep the tribe, including children, totally absorbed with story telling and history. He predicted events, forecast weather and illness in the tribe, healed the injured or sick, and ministered to those in pain. He dispersed special herbs to the hunters to enhance their skills when game became scarce. By virtue of his powers, he was accepted as the most powerful person in the tribe, more so than the tuchow chief.

George went on to explain some of the social workings of the tribe. The tuchow had jurisdiction over family affairs: where to expand the village, where and when to plant fields, who did the work, when and how to store the harvest, when to have fetes, and which hunters to send for game or fish. The tuchow and the peayman worked together on territorial rights with other tribes or inter-tribal problems.

If there were a murder, the tuchow summoned the elders of the village for a judgment, which would be given to the peayman. If the suspected killer was found guilty, the peayman held talks with the victim's relatives assuring them justice by *el tigre,* the jaguar. He worked with one of the male relatives teaching him to acquire characteristics of a jaguar—a day and night vigil until every movement and habit of the murderer was known. The process could take days, months, or even a year. When completed, the relative thought like the murderer, knew where and how much he ate and drank, where he defecated and how often. Every movement was recorded in the mind of the learning *jaguar*.

When the avenging relative was ready, he was summoned by the peayman who gave him a special potion, the same that hunters received to enhance their hunting skills. Then, in his transformed spirit, he was finally given a mummified claw of a real jaguar.

George wondered if I understood all this. He said, somewhat apologetically, that he never told this to anyone before, especially not to Fr. Quigley. I expected him to ask me never to repeat it, but he didn't. Instead, he continued his story.

In the altered state of being the *jaguar*, the relative would pounce on the unsuspecting murderer who later was found clawed to death with large tiger scratches across his face, intestines pulled out of his stomach—ostensibly killed by a jaguar. Justice was served and life went on.

For the most serious tribal problems, the peayman summoned the *Ancients*, the departed souls who oversaw the welfare of the tribe. To do that, he would go into seclusion and take a special potion of herbs that induced an hypnotic-like trance that could last for days. When he returned, the peayman passed on the *Ancients'* Solomon-like wisdom. George explained the need to go to the departed tribal souls was rare.

I told George I appreciated hearing about the tribal customs. I found it fascinating how it contrasted to our so-called civilized way, particularly the manner in which the tribe handled a family breakup. Familial bonds were strong and a man rarely left his wife and family. Infidelity was not taken seriously unless there was a split in the family. Then it was serious. The tuchow, peayman, and relatives of both families would council the man and his wife to keep the family together. If needed, the elders of the village were brought in to add their life-long wisdom.

A deserting husband was forced to adequately provide for his family. If he left the village, he would be an outcast and never be allowed to return—a strong decision and strong deterrent. I related to George how *our* so-called civilized world operated concerning family separations.

"Man and wife each hired an outsider who is paid to fight for them. It may go on for years, which inevitably increases the couple's hostility and reduces any chance of reconciliation. The longer the fight goes on, the more the hired outsiders earn from the couple's wealth and often nothing remains for the wife and family. Those outsiders are called lawyers and live off the income they receive from the people they fight for."

"But that take away what and when they need most. Lawyers no make peace if they get money for fight go on?" he asked incredulously. He waited for my answer. He kept shaking his head. "The Macusi different. They don't take from family like your lawyers. No—whole village shares food, give animals, shelter. Make easy for broken family. You serious?" he asked again.

Donald Haack

I shook my head. "Yes, I'm afraid so, that's exactly the way they do it back there." I sadly admitted.

"Why they send missionaries here? Better we send missionaries your country and stop such bad things. It's bad what you tell me." He glanced at me again for assurance I wasn't making up an unbelievably horrible story.

"Uncivilized? I agree," I added.

I was curious about the herbs. They were secret concoctions of the peayman, passed on from generation to generation. George knew that one consisted of a particular leaf of the bara tree, ground together with other plants. He offered to bring me a bit of it from the peayman if I could give him something in return. I asked him what. He thought for a while.

"You have compass?" he asked. "First time I see compass, I take everywhere. It always point to top of world where they say it always cold and white. Water hard and people walk on it but when sun comes, it goes soft and flows to us here."

There were several inexpensive compasses I wouldn't miss so I gave him one. After a couple of weeks, I forgot the matter entirely. Apparently he didn't. A month later he was at the doorstep. We talked after dinner and he pressed a small package in my hand. It was the size of a package of gum, wrapped in leaves and tied with tiny, flexible vines.

"Good for hunting," George said.

I put it into my pocket. That little *package* would save my life.

"Peayman say thanks. Gives you this for good hunting." he said quietly as if someone were listening. "Put one ball on tongue. It strong. Don't use often. I don't hunt, but it give me strange feelings and keep me awake. Macusi take for hunting and no sleep all night. One ball good for hours. Two and you no sleep all night, but then you must rest. You be very tired. No never take more than two."

I was fascinated about what he said it could do and he assured me it was not dangerous unless too much was taken.

Donald Haack

"Macusi take for hunting, telling tribal history, fighting with other tribes, which no happen often anymore." He said the peayman used a different potion when he contacted their departed ancestors. "*Ancients* have all information from past, like your public library, Father Quiqley told me." His English improved with every visit and I detected an accent that suggested Oxford educated missionaries adopted him.

A few days later when all chores were done, I headed towards the hangar to check on the plane before the next day's flight. I pulled the package from my pocket, untied the vines and opened the leaves. Inside were a handful of small brown balls, the size of BB's. I put one on my tongue. It had a sharp bitter flavor, like an astringent, and made my mouth pucker.

I folded the rest up and returned the package to my pocket. Nothing happened after a few minutes and I decided it was like Harry's stories—more folklore than substance. On the path to the hangar I heard someone following me and expected to see Jan. I turned to greet her. No one was there yet I still heard footsteps, someone walking on dead leaves and twigs. Down the path where the sound came from was Dutch...a good fifty yards away on the path from the store to the house. Each sound matched his footsteps. It was like watching a movie with the sound track turned too high. I could also hear grass moving, though there was barely a trace of wind this late in the afternoon. I watched in fascination as the tiniest of sounds were audible wherever I focused my attention. I bent down to pick up a flat rock along the side of the path. As anticipated, there was a beetle about an inch long with pinchers at the front of its head. Did I actually hear him moving? Or did I sense his movement?

I was awestruck. As I approached the hangar, I glanced to the left at the hull of the Piper Cub that we brought back from the crash site with hopes of restoring; its presence a constant reminder of bush flying hazards. I instinctively felt the presence of the *Mad Peruvian,* as we all called Quaziero, our strange guest who one day showed up for a meal and stayed. He took up residence in the hull of our old plane.

Donald Haack

I caught him unaware. It disturbed him that someone sneaked up on him without him knowing it. What he didn't know is that I didn't sneak up on him, nor did I see him. I just knew he was inside. I tried to recall if there was a movement in the cockpit or whether I heard something that tipped me off. I didn't think so, but felt sure it had something to do with the sharpened perception caused by George's concoction. Whatever it was or did, this was turning into an interesting experiment. I told the Peruvian I didn't need him and left him pretending to clean up dirt around the plane with a plant that he wielded like a broom.

Near the end of the airstrip, my footsteps sounded unduly loud so I reverted to my *Domingo hunting walk* touching on toes before heels. I detected movement near the river. It turned out to be a small pack of capybaras in our cornfield. I could never approach them undetected when I hunted and this gave me the opportunity to observe them for a few minutes. Totally unaware of my presence, they continued eating and I could have easily shot several, but this was not a hunting walk. They were fortunate. I moved closer and deliberately made noise. They were startled and in panic ran in all directions.

I headed home. It was getting dark and dinnertime. I had no appetite. George said that might happen. During dinner Jan again mentioned the rat in the house, a problem that had gone on for weeks. She was terrified the rat would climb onto Diney's crib. There was a persistence in her voice that left no alternative— I had to do something and quickly. I figured this might be a good time to test George's potion.

After Jan retired, it wasn't long before I heard the familiar sounds of the rat making his nocturnal rounds on top of the walls. Seconds later I climbed up and the chase was on. It wasn't long before the usual happened: the rat ran into the peak of the roof into a crevice safe from my butcher knife. I heard him move in his heretofore safe crevice between the upright post and the aluminum roof. Ordinarily this was how the chase ended—a stalemate. Tonight was different.

Without hesitation, I grabbed him from behind and before he could turn around to bite, hurled him to the concrete floor. As he hit, I jumped down pressing the knife through his neck so quickly he never recovered long enough to know what happened. I wrapped him in a paper towel, cleaned up the spot of blood and tossed the remains towards the river. It all happened in seconds yet to me the whole scene proceeded in slow motion. It was so *easy*; I wondered why it took me so long to do this simple task. Or again, was it George's potion?

When I came to bed, Jan asked how I got rid of *Mr. rat*. When I reluctantly explained, she was horrified.

"You didn't actually grab it standing on top of the wall, did you?" she blurted incredulously. "It could've bitten you and given you who-knows-what infection, and you could've broken an ankle jumping down. I can't believe you did that."

In the light of day the next morning, I couldn't either.

It would be a few months later when I next used George's potion—not to do in a rat but to save my life.

THE MAD PERUVIAN

My gun pointed towards him, not at him. He took two steps closer. I aimed the long barreled Targetmaster pistol directly at his head and slid off the safety. He looked at me with that crooked smile, the left corner of his mouth turned as if he were wearing a grotesque mask. He had a flattened nose, straight jet-black hair, pulled into what my mother used to call a bun. His fine-line mustache was impeccably trimmed. His bulging, inky black eyes revealed nothing of his intentions. I felt out of my depth. I certainly didn't want to shoot him, yet, from earlier years of handgun training, I knew the cardinal rule—never pull a weapon unless you are fully committed to using it. So how did I get into this situation, I wondered?

I heard myself saying in a low steady voice that masked the turbulent churning in my stomach, "Quaziero, do not come any closer. I'm not mad at you, but I want you out of here right now. Dutch put your belongings from the airplane hull into a rubber waterproof bag we gave you. There is also some money—fifty B.G dollars and one thousand cruzieros to help you on your way—but you cannot stay here. You're lucky. If you were in Brazil, across the river, you'd be dead."

His expression did not change. He heard me, understood, but there was no reaction. He just stood there.

"Last night when I was gone Mrs. Haack told me you tried to enter the house. Had you entered, she would've shot you. She kept her pistol by her side all last night and did not sleep. This morning when Dutch packed up your belongings, he discovered stolen merchandise from the store, including the missing box of lady's panties in your bag below your hammock. The Indians didn't take them, as you told Dutch."

When Dutch went back to remove the Peruvian's belongings, he came across a thick manuscript in Quaziero's handwriting, captioned *The Autobiography of a Paranoiac*. That was unsettling. The theft was bad, but the thought of Jan, Diana, and Tom in the house all night while he stalked outside in the dark trying to get in was intolerable. That mental image reinforced my resolve to shoot him if necessary.

I continued without raising my voice, "You have two choices. If you don't leave now I will shoot you and let the piranhas clean your bones. Rocks along the river will mark your grave. We might pray for your soul." I had trouble with *soul* in Spanish, but he knew what I meant.

In the unlikely chance I shot him and authorities somehow heard about it, I wouldn't risk putting his body in a marked grave. The river piranhas would do a better job of eliminating any evidence. Authorities never came back here when they were needed. But without much else of importance to do in the interior, they had a notorious reputation of carrying on investigations that went on forever. In this case, even though I could prove self-defense, I could be tied up in red tape for months or years. I really wanted the Peruvian to simply go away.

"Or," I continued, "you can leave now. The Macusi will travel with you as far as Karona falls to make sure you do not return. Then you have your life ahead of you and can do whatever you want. Your family will be proud of you." I picked up my voice to sound more encouraging and friendly.

"You are smart and can do much. Go now", and I pointed to the path with my pistol.

Instead of turning to leave, he approached a step closer. He didn't speak. I don't know if he meant to shake hands or pull a knife. His crooked smile never changed, and like a mask, did not reveal his intentions. I knew he usually carried a long-bladed knife, which we left in his bag, but I didn't know if he retrieved it. Dutch and I felt he would need it to survive in the bush. I glanced down at his hand still at his side. He wasn't extending it open as if to shake hands and I couldn't tell if he was reaching for his knife.

I aimed the pistol down, slightly to his left, and squeezed off a round. The blast echoed around the valley. The hollow-nosed bullet ricocheted off the ground inches from his foot. He instinctively jumped back from the shock of the noise and the dirt hitting his pants. The crooked smile disappeared in an open mouth that looked as if it was going to speak. He didn't utter a word. I couldn't tell what he meant to do. I didn't wait to find out. I raised the gun again, aiming directly between his dark eyes.

"The next shot goes through your head. You leave now or you never will," I added. This time there was no lightness or humor in my voice.

"Adios," I repeated and motioned him on. He stooped down, picked up the rubber bag and heaved it on his back. He settled it on his left shoulder, shifted his feet back and forth like a horse, looked left and right as if he were searching for something or someone, then turned around and started walking.

"Dutch packed two days rations in your bag. You won't starve," I called after him as he moved on. He never answered. In fact he never said a word during the fifteen-minute standoff.

I watched him walk down the path, his strange uncoordinated limp rolling him side to side. It occurred to me that his whole body was a misfit. His unusually large head stuck on his stocky body with no visible neck. His arms were proportionally too long, bowed legs too short. He looked like a cartoon character. I was relieved to finally see him go. So was Dutch.

"Goot riddance" he muttered, as he came up behind me to find out what the shot was. "Spected to see a body, but I see he vas smart enough to leaf."

We stood and watched until Quaziero disappeared past *gold hill*. Three Macusi Indians appeared out of nowhere and followed in his track.

Dutch smiled, "I chust vanted to make sure he don't return. The boys vill make sure dat."

I looked at Dutch and frowned.

"No, no, dey don't kill him, chust make sure he don't turn back. Told dem to go to Karona Falls ver it's open country. Der dey see a long way to make sure he's gone for goot. If he turns back, den...." He ran his finger across his neck. I didn't know what to think, but I supposed Dutch's solution was correct. I didn't say anything.

Three days later, I landed at Uan Paru airstrip, thirty miles north up the Ireng River, two days walking from our house. Two Macusi druggers came to meet my plane.

"Yes, we saw stranger. He attack young girl washing clothes at creek, but she scream. Three boys hunting near, hear scream, come, beat him up, drag him to village. Tuchow tell him move on if he want to live. Man say he go Venezuela. They take him 'cross river into Brazil yesterday. They take his knife, stick him under (he used a word I didn't understand. He pointed to a spot below his chin) 'till blood come out. They wipe it on his forehead as warning. He won't come back."

A month later I flew into a small trading post in Brazil west of Orinduik, twenty miles south of Venezuela. They described a stranger fitting Quaziero's description heading toward Santa Elena, Venezuela. Nobody wanted him around. He hadn't changed.

Quaziero lived a charmed life to have survived as long as he did in the backcountry. If what he did in Marquis was in Brazil, they would have summarily shot him, no questions asked. When he attacked the Macusi girl washing clothes, the boys who rescued her could have killed him outright. Instead they took him to the village where the tuchow also could have pronounced a death sentence. But he, too, did not; instead, he sent him on his way with a warning.

At first I thought the Peruvian was lucky but the more I reflected upon it the more I realized that Indians recognize a basic flaw in people. Quaziero certainly fit that description. His head, legs, and arms didn't seem to match. The twisted built-in grin added to the strangeness. Indians believed that strong spirits live in afflicted people like Quaziero, probably the reason they spared his life.

That was the last we heard of the *Mad Peruvian*.

WHAT'S MY LINE?

O ur monthly trips to Georgetown to sell diamonds and buy provisions were fairly routine. This particular flight turned out to be more difficult. Most of the trip was spent dodging thunderstorms and heavy rain pockets that added an hour to the flight. When we landed, Bertie, our driver was patiently waiting at Atkinson field and rushed us to town. For efficiency, Jan and I split up. I went to bank our rough diamonds and she went to pick up yesterday's telegram. We were advised by radio that it arrived and we hoped it wouldn't be bad news.

We met for lunch at the Woodbine. Jan asked how the diamonds fared.

"First, I want to know about the cable. What's it about? Bad news, or good?" I couldn't tell from her expression, except it didn't appear to be a catastrophe.

She smiled. "Good news. A cable from New York. The national television show, *What's My Line?* hosted by Dorothy Kilgallen and Arlene Francis, wants you to be on their show. They mentioned the unusual profession: diamond hunter and bush pilot." She showed me the cable. "It says, they will pay our airfare up and back, four days at the Waldorf Astoria all expenses paid, including meals and an allowance of $200 per day for miscellaneous expenses *for the two of us*." She emphasized the last part. "It's for next month. What do you think?"

"Frankly, it sounds like fun. We could use the break and I'm sure the business can do without us for a few days. Unless you have some strong objection, why don't you cable them we'll come. And be sure to get the details." I hoped there wouldn't be any objection. Jan's nature was to consider all options before jumping into a project.

"Good." she interjected. "Because, I didn't bother cabling, I called directly. Everything is all set, the hotel is booked, plane reservations made, and they're expecting us on the evening of the fifteenth." She added with a coy smile. "All done. They heard about us from one of their staff members who read the Chicago Tribune Magazine section that featured you last November."

I sat back amused—no, astonished—at the speed of her decision. Living in the middle of the South American bush country takes its toll. It wasn't easy for Jan: running a bush household, raising two children and assisting in the business. With no civilized neighbors to socialize with it was obvious she needed, wanted and deserved a break.

In the next couple of weeks, I made sure all the crews had sufficient supplies. Nellie and Caesar offered to baby-sit Diney and Tom. We departed for the States in anticipation to a welcome break from bush living.

We arrived at the Waldorf late in the afternoon, but in time to clean up. The phone rang. It was one of the producers, waiting for us in the bar downstairs, wanting to meet the *strange couple* who mined diamonds in the middle of South America.

"So, now we're that *strange couple* mining diamonds in the jungles of South America?" Jan mused.

"They're probably expecting us to have two heads, or at best that you'll have long hair, long dress like a missionary. What do you think?"

"I think we ought to dispel that notion and *wow* them," she said as she put the finishing touches to her hair and make-up. I gazed at her admiringly—she could have passed for a model out of Vogue Magazine. Yeah, I thought, that will *wow* them. Not exactly what they're expecting. So much the better.

"Okay, let's go see the big city folk," and I took her hand.

We made the introductions and started our drinks when the producer asked, "You did bring the rough diamonds with you, didn't you? We want to open the show with a close-up of rough diamonds blasted by strobe lights...should be great."

I was taken aback. "Whoops," I exclaimed. "No one mentioned rough diamonds. Did I miss something here?" Jan and I exchanged glances.

"Well, no. We never said to bring them for the show, just thought you would be carrying some and we would shoot those."

I half-laughed, half choked. "We can't carry diamonds between countries...that's called smuggling. Everything is shipped through banks with documented invoices and custom declarations." I thought for a moment after I saw his disappointment of having his brilliant idea shot down so quickly. "Wait, just a minute. I have an idea." and I abruptly left the table. I returned ten minutes later. They could tell it wasn't the hoped for news.

"I called Harry Winston at his home and asked if he could help. He said, 'Donald, I would be glad to help, but it's 7:30 p.m., the shop is closed and no one gets in before 9:00 in the morning, an hour later than your 8:00 shooting. Sorry, I wish I could help you. At least come by tomorrow to see me.'" Not a happy start but we decided we could put on a good show without the diamonds.

Early the next morning as the pre-broadcast shots were rolling, we heard a commotion at the door. Two security guards came in and interrupted the cameramen.

"Sorry to break in but we have a problem downstairs. Is there a Mr. Haack up here?"

"Yes, I'm Donald Haack. Why?"

"There's a scruffy street person downstairs. Says he wants to speak to a Mr. Haack, no one else."

I was confused. "No one knows we're in New York; I haven't even called my family yet. We arrived late last night from South America. I don't know who would know I'm here, but let's go see." We walked together to the elevator.

He assured me as we were going down, "It should be safe. We have several of our security people in the area. Seems that this fellow is carrying his lunch with him."

Standing just inside the door was the *street person*, a sorry sight. I couldn't see his face hidden below a beat up old dirty fedora that had been pushed, pulled and slept on. There was no perceptible shape to it other than just covering his head. The dark wrinkled suit matched the hat: shapeless and baggy. His shoes, slightly curled up from being wet once too often, had never seen polish. He was carrying a brown lunch bag with greasy spots on it. He stepped closer. I stared into an old, kindly, wrinkled face, vaguely familiar, but that was perhaps more in sympathy than reality.

"Are you Mr. Haack?" he asked in a barely audible voice.

"Yes," I answered, not knowing what else to say, or what questions to ask.

He thrust his unappetizing lunch bag at me. I didn't respond immediately. He pushed it towards me again in a couple of jerky motions to emphasize I should take it.

"Mr. Winston told me to give this to you and no one else." he said so quietly I had to ask him to repeat. I reached out, took the bag and scrutinized the face below the hat.

"Are you Mr. Axelrod? I asked incredulously.

He nodded affirmatively and mouthed yes, which I could see but not hear. I thanked him. Before I could adequately express my thoughts, he turned and disappeared out the door.

"That was Mr. Axelrod. He runs Harry Winston's diamond cutting shop," I said as a matter of explanation to the security guards. The security chief and I returned to the studio upstairs.

The producer and cameraman came running over in anticipation. "What was that all about down there? Is everything all right? Who was it?" I placed the paper bag on the table. The plastic bag inside was securely tied by string. I untied it.

"The man downstairs was Harry Winston's head diamond cutter." I opened the string and a stream of rough diamonds poured out onto the table—450 carats of beautiful rough diamonds. We heaped them into an irregular round pile for the camera to zoom in for a close up. The floodlights homed in from all angles to highlight the diamonds in a dazzling array of color and the opening shot for the *What's My Line* program.

Prior to the final shooting, which would be live, we rehearsed a quick run-through so that everyone knew the rules and procedures. They used a substitute panel that completely missed who the real *diamond miner* was. Later, in the real show, the three fake Donald Haacks contrived their answers a bit too much and lost the spontaneity that the rehearsal enjoyed. Arlene and Dorothy concluded that I was the miner, though they admitted I didn't match the part. I'm not sure exactly what that meant.

It was a fun show and afterwards the get-together with Arlene Francis, Dorothy Kilgallen and Bennett Cerf was even more so. They wanted to know all about diamond mining and bush life, but most of all, how someone like Jan could handle living in no-man's-land in the middle of South America. They were fascinated. As it turned out, Jan became the star of the day.

HIJACKED

I had been away from home for two days, one more than expected. Jan worried during these unexpected overnights, but there was no way to let her know I was all right. Bad weather and a flat tire turned what was supposed to be a half-day of flying cargo to Velgrad airstrip into an absence of a day-and-a-half.

I had one more obligation, to pass over King, the small airstrip across from the Brazilian settlement. A white flag in the middle of the strip meant an emergency or a need for rations.

Mervin, pronounced Mer-veen, a Brazilian trader and store owner had arranged to wait on the Guiana side for me yesterday. I didn't show and he probably returned home, which meant I would have to buzz the Brazilian village and then wait for him to cross the Ireng and hike up to the airstrip.

At six feet, Mervin stood taller than most Brazilians. He was a long drink of water, as my father-in-law would say, meaning tall, thin as a rail, and without an ounce of fat. Unlike most miners or shopkeepers, Mervin dressed well. He had a squared face, chiseled chin and nose and a neatly trimmed black mustache. His twinkling black eyes were bracketed by wrinkles, which gave him a strikingly cosmopolitan appearance.

A classic type "A" personality, he was constantly moving, talking, and gesturing with his hands. I doubt he could talk if his hands were tied. He would sit, get up, sit down, walk around, but was never still. It was tiring to be with him for any period, yet it was fun to see him because he exuded happiness and optimism. The gentle attitude was in contrast to his intense drive.

He was primarily a diamond trader although he managed several diving crews, had a store in the settlement, and bought goods from me for his store, crews, and other miners in the area. Diamonds were used as the common currency. He and I became not only good friends but trusted business associates.

Approaching the area, I flew low over the Guiana strip. Someone waved a big white cloth on a stick. It was Mervin. He had apparently waited on the airstrip all day yesterday and today— something important or an emergency. I felt a twinge of guilt.

I side slipped the plane into a steep 180-degree turn, landed, and stopped near Mervin. He rushed to the plane, opened the passenger door, and slid into the seat before I shut down the engine. He was excited and talking so fast I couldn't understand a word.

"Mas despassio, no comprendo," slow down, I can't understand.

In two days Brazil would hold elections, which that country takes very seriously. He explained the candidate for governor waited for me across the river. A chartered plane that flew him here from Boa Vista returned and left the governor stranded. He had visited several mining communities along the border and arrived at King strip yesterday. The opposition party apparently had paid the pilot to abandon him here, hundreds of miles from Boa Vista.

"By law," Mervin continued, "during the polls a candidate must physically be in Boa Vista. Being here without transportation would automatically eliminate him from the elections, which are," he repeated, "only two days away."

Donald Haack

The gist of this rapid-fire dialogue was that Mervin expected me to go into Brazil to fly the governor and aides to Lethem where jeeps could transport them the last forty miles in time for elections.

I explained to Mervin that as sorry as I felt for him and his people, I couldn't take the chance of landing on Brazilian soil without written permission. Brazil takes a dim view of foreign planes landing in their country without prior notice. I told the story how I learned the hard way how that system works when a doctor and a Brazilian priest requested a *mercy mission*—flying a sick Brazilian girl to her home in Boa Vista. I was arrested, placed in a locked room under guard for five days waiting for the red tape to be unraveled in Rio, three thousand miles away.

That argument fell on deaf ears.

"The future governor and the country must be saved," he repeated.

To my surprise, he drew his pistol, pointed it out the door and fired. Inside the cockpit, the shot could be felt as well as heard, reverberating in a mind-stunning explosion. It left us both stunned for a moment. I could only conclude Mervin had gone raving mad. My first concern was the plane. When I looked over his shoulder to see if he hit the wing strut, I found myself staring down at the pistol barrel, inches from my face. The smoking carbide stung my eyes intensifying my anger.

"Mervin, Que the hell passa?" I shouted angrily.

"Lo Siento," sorry, he responded half apologetically. But, he didn't lower the gun.

He's flipped his lid, I thought. This is my friend, Mervin, whom I've known for years? In a forced, reasonably calm tone of voice masking a rising swell of anger, I tried to talk sense into him. Meanwhile my eyes were glued to his trigger finger for any evidence of pressure. There wasn't any. His finger wiggled around the inside of the trigger guard as if to reinforce the point he tried to make.

"Mervin," I said quietly and calmly, "be careful of your trigger finger."

Donald Haack

He looked at it as if he, too, were surprised where it was. He didn't say anything. I waited. It looked like a real Mexican standoff. Suddenly, he grabbed my right hand, opened my fingers, stuck the pistol in my hands and pointed it at *his* head.

I blinked in disbelief, really confused. Now, *I'm* holding the pistol aimed at *him*.

"Mervin, for god's sake…," I said, lowering the pistol. Before I could finish the sentence, he quickly lifted my hand up so the pistol was pressed to his head again. I didn't know what to say. An eternity passed as we stared at each other.

Finally Mervin blurted out, "You must help. Gonzales, this governor-elect is a good man, our people need him. The present government is corrupt and ignores our people on the frontier. The family of Gonsalves came from the *fronteira*. They were poor, honest, hard working people. Now rich and successful, he understands the hardship and wants to help our people here. We want him elected. The present corrupt party knows they cannot win a fair election and will be thrown out of office. If Gonsalves is kept out of Boa Vista during elections, they automatically win by default and stay in power four more years," he continued in what sounded like a campaign speech.

"That cannot happen. That is why you must fly him out. I guarantee your safety. My people here know you were put in jail for that mercy mission helping the Brazilian girl. That was wrong… everyone is sorry about it. They want you to know how thankful they are for what you did," he added. "And," so quietly I almost didn't hear him, "Senhor Gonsalves knows what you did, and is thankful as well. You see why we are desperate? Look, you have my gun. We fly over. If anything goes wrong you shoot me in the head. The people know what I'm doing. They are all for it. They will not let anything happen to you. I am your hostage." He attempted a weak smile. "Let's go," he repeated.

"Mervin, that airstrip is short and not level, low on the ends and high in the middle. There's no way I can land this plane while holding a gun to your head. I'll need both hands and a lot of luck to get down there in one piece.

Donald Haack

Without knowing when the decision took place, I realized we weren't discussing if I was going to go, but how. Mervin quickly solved that dilemma: He took the gun from me, put it in his left hand and put the barrel against his head.

"Good. Now you can fly. We go. If anything happens to you, I shoot myself."

"For god's sake, Mervin—"

"We go!"

We went. What in hell was I doing in this mad scene? Instead of going home, I was sweating out a landing on a new airstrip in a country I shouldn't be in. Beside me was a madman with a loaded revolver threatening to shoot himself. The absurdity of the situation brought the Keystone Cops to mind. But this was real. I couldn't screw up this landing, not even a bad bounce. In nightmare-like fears, I visualized taking a bad bump, causing Mervin's gun to go off. Next I'm sitting in a foreign airstrip with a freshly shot dead body. This doesn't classify as a mercy mission. I envisioned being led away, charged for murder...no one else is in the plane and my fingerprints were on the gun. Great!

Time was against me: 6:15 sundown preceded total darkness by only fifteen short minutes. No twilight this close to the equator. The flight to my house, twenty minutes from here, gave me a mere twenty minutes to check the airstrip, land, handle the formalities that are expected the first time landing in a strange airstrip, gather the passengers, and take off. That time frame left a lot to be desired.

I cranked the engine and checked the magnetos as I taxied to the takeoff area. Just a few feet short, I did a quick turn around, shoved the throttle forward and in seconds we were airborne, heading to Brazil. The Brazilian strip was considerably lower and parallel to the escarpment we were about to go over. To save time, I kept airspeed low after takeoff and stayed a few feet off the ground in a slow sweeping right turn where the escarpment dropped several hundred feet. We took a bump as we hit the upgoing air currents, accentuating the weird feeling of seeing the earth suddenly falling out from under us. Even seasoned pilots get an adrenaline kick from the experience.

Mervin certainly did not qualify as a seasoned pilot. A quick glance at him reinforced my concern that the maneuver was not smart, no matter how many seconds it saved. The gun remained tightly against his forehead, his stupid finger still on the trigger. This scenario wasn't exactly ideal for what was required at this time.

I looked down at the airstrip cut and cleared across a horseshoe bend in the river at the bottom of the narrow Ireng valley. If our Marquis airstrip provided a challenge, I knew this was a greater one making ours a piece of cake by comparison. King's village sprang up along the south side. The short strip stretched from one riverbank to the other with every spare foot utilized. Fortunately it ran east west into the wind. Unfortunately, it wasn't level. With a big hump in the middle, it sloped down at both ends to the water's edge.

With time short, I made a slow 180-degree turning descent, which put me on the downwind leg, the opposite direction to landing. I came in low and slow to examine the area at closer range and clear the strip. On the downwind leg I saw how high it was in the middle and tapered at the ends. I had a sinking feeling at the pit of my stomach.

I could only use the first half for landing. Braking a speeding airplane downhill is difficult if not impossible, particularly when the penalty for not doing so is ending up in the Ireng River. Everyone in the village who turned out for the governor now waited along the airstrip. It was easy to pick out the two dignitaries in their white linen suits. They reminded me of rabbits in northern Wisconsin in the fall. The snowshoe rabbits turned white at first frost, which was supposed to camouflage them in the snow. But if there were no snow, they stood out like a sore thumb, just like the Brazilian dignitaries below

After my low level pass confirmed my fears, I concentrated on the landing. I came in at treetop level with half flaps and half power to examine the terrain. Now I needed more altitude for the 180-degree turn inside this small valley.

Donald Haack

If I were alone I would do a partial Himmelman maneuver: point the nose down to gain speed, then pull up to gain altitude as if going into a loop. Three quarters through the giant loop, almost upside down, hard rudder and opposite aileron flips the plane right side up. That points you in the opposite direction you had been flying. That might be fine if I were alone, but after Marvin's reaction going over the escarpment, I decided it was not a smart option. Instead, I did a very much scaled-down version of the Himmelman so as not to scare the bejesus out of my passenger. Before I made the turn, I motioned with my right hand, and said, "Mervin, for god's sake, cuidado con le pistolo!" careful with the pistol.

He nodded but still had the barrel held tightly against his temple. I discovered that when the adrenaline really gets pumping, action seems to slow down and reflexes speed up. It's one hell of an advantage. Everything worked as planned. I dropped as low as possible after clearing the trees on the opposite side of the river. That put me five feet above the rapids. I used full flaps and ninety percent power to keep from stalling. The stall warning blared. Speed indicated sixty-five knots. Stall speed was sixty- something but the full power provided an extra margin by creating a lift from the prop wash.

One plane length from land I eased the power, pulled up the nose slightly, touched ground and stalled simultaneously. I had just greased it in with all the skill I could muster.

I stood on the brakes. We stopped short of the top of the hill. I cut the motor and collapsed mentally as the adrenaline kick dissipated. We were immediately surrounded by Brazilians: rough looking Garimparos, the miners, many women carrying babies in side slings and hordes of naked children, all ages. I thanked God I shut down the engine quickly. The last thing I needed was a lethal prop turning and churning into a madding crowd. A drunken porknocker walked into my prop years earlier. He lived, but it was not a pretty sight and it was something I never wanted to experience again.

The Governor and aides stayed behind, out of the crowd, to wait our deplaning. Two older men tried to restore order. They waved their arms and shouted for everyone to keep back. They had little success.

I nudged Mervin a couple of times to open the door. I commented that he did quite well in managing to not shoot himself. There was no response but he did open the door. As the crowd thinned, I could see three men, two heavy set and one tall beanpole in white suits. Two of them deferred to the third, who was obviously, the candidate governor. He walked forward very formally talking a mile-a-minute, none of which I understood, and gave me a big *brazo*, the Brazilian hug, which I barely had the presence to return.

Everyone smiled, shouted, and talked at the same time to no one in particular. Mervin had briefed me what was needed so I didn't bother with the usual formalities of translating. No one spoke English. I was on my own and my Portuguese stunk. I raised both arms up in the air to get their attention. To my surprise, the talking ceased, and it was quiet. With my poor Brazilian Portuguese, I didn't want to give a speech, which is what they apparently thought I was going to do.

Instead, I apologized for my inadequate Portuguese. Then went on to say, before they invariably asked, I could not stay for a social cafezinia—the small black coffee, a must in every frontier meeting—because of the urgent need to get the governor to Boa Vista I needed to leave immediately so as not to fly in the dark and endanger his life.

I explained to the village *jefe*, mayor, we had thirty minutes of daylight. Twenty minutes of that were needed to fly to my house where we would overnite. In the morning we would fly to Lethem where a jeep would take the Governor candidate to Boa Vista in time for elections. A big cheer went up.

"So we must leave immediately."

I turned to the candidate to offer a personal invitation. "You will be my guest tonight. Tomorrow at daylight we fly to Lethem where my friends have jeeps. You will have all day to make the five hour road trip."

For me it was a long speech. My grammar and sentence structure were bad, but he understood, smiled and gave another brazo. Two problems remained: their luggage and the size of the three men. I added up the weights—impossible to take all three of them and luggage from this airstrip. They agreed without argument. The governor candidate pointed, indicating that the smaller aide and he would go. No baggage.

It was the correct decision. I later found out from Mervin that two planes, not one, had brought them in and two were supposed to take them out. When the governor chose the smaller aide, I allowed as how they could take one bag. They smiled again. They wanted out…badly.

During this exchange the *jefe* kept looking over my shoulder. I turned to see what attracted his attention. Mervin stood to the side, a big grin on his mustached face. To my surprise and chagrin, he still held the gun to his head. I almost laughed it looked so ridiculous. He must have been caught up in all the action and forgot he was threatening himself.

"Mervin, put the pistol away."

He looked at it as if he were surprised to see it there. He shrugged, grinned from ear to ear, and slipped the pistol into his leather holster inside his pants.

That crisis was over but we weren't out of the woods yet. Time was running out. My two passengers were busy giving *brazos* and *obrigados*, thanks. I pulled them away and hurried them into the plane, while they confirmed their promises of things to come for the village. I checked their seat belts as the politicians waved good-bye. Fortunately, Mervin came to life and had the presence of mind to clear the hordes off the airstrip.

I hurriedly cranked up the engine and taxied downhill to the water's edge. The air sock indicated a light breeze. I hoped for more than that on this unforgiving airstrip. I knew I couldn't abort without winding up in the water. I rechecked my fuel; enough to get home. The light fuel load gave me an extra weight margin for take off. The hot daytime temperatures abated and gave a welcomed and added advantage of cooler air and more lift. I needed all the help possible. First time takeoffs on marginal airstrips were no fun.

Ordinarily, I would've paced off the strip and put a flag where I had to be airborne or abort takeoff. There was no time for those amenities. In the back of my mind lurked the thought: short cuts cause accidents. I tried not to entertain that thought

As I taxied to the water's edge, I double-checked the magnetos. Both up to par. The ground was dry and looked solid right to the water's edge. I taxied as close as I dared, did a 180-degree turn, and pushed the throttle into the full power range. I braked until the engine reached the red line of 3500 RPM, full takeoff power. We started our roll with no flaps for less drag. We moved slowly uphill, gradually gaining speed, but not fast enough to give me a comfortable feeling. Speed at the crest indicated fifty knots, ten short of minimum lift-off speed. I cranked in half flaps for lift and best takeoff configuration for short fields. Halfway down the hill we were indicating sixty-five.

I couldn't afford the mistake of pulling off too soon. I held the nose on the ground until seventy knots, then pulled back slightly. We broke ground just as we reached the end of the strip and the water.

When it looked like we were plunging into the rapids, we cleared with three feet to spare and a good margin of airspeed. The feeling of relief was like a cool beer going down on a hot day. It sort of spreads out all over. We flew along the river down the valley, slowly gaining altitude and cruising airspeed. We were in fat city, as they would say. Time to relax.

My customers were quiet from the time I started the engines. When we reached altitude and they saw me relax, they took the cue, eased back in their seats and broke into rapid-fire conversation; a welcome diversion that kept them from wetting their pants. It was the kind of takeoff that could do that to you.

I pulled out my well-worn map and laid the plastic compass on the round dot that I marked to indicate this airstrip on the map. None of these airstrips appeared on any maps. We built airstrips in a matter of weeks, used them while the crews found diamonds, then abandoned them when the diamonds were worked out and the crews left. The maps were years behind reality.

Few if any of the seventy to a hundred airstrips along the northern Guiana/Brazilian border were indicated on maps. I lined the flat edge of the plastic compass between King and Marquis on a heading of 172 degrees. I mentally added five degrees compass deviation in this longitude, estimated two degrees wind out of the east and set the plane on a compass heading of 178. With luck our 6:15 ETA at Marquis would be ten minutes before dark.

The sun was setting, the panoramic view breathtaking. At a thousand feet, we skirted the mountains directly in the path to our house. The setting sun created a canvas of changing colors forming patterns of lines and swirls across the countryside below. The dry savannas turned red with a faint touch of pink. They were accented by deep shadows racing down the valleys, shifting from light brown to pale blue to deep purple before turning to gray, then black.

As many times as I have seen them, the sunsets always produced a strong, emotional response. This certainly was God's country and His art. There were no signs of civilization in this endless panorama.

The small villages on our left were hidden below the thick jungle canopy. Monkey Mountain, the settlement with eight mud houses controlled by John Roth, the Portuguese trader, perched above the escarpment to our left. At 2500 feet above the Ireng valley, it was well above our present flight path.

It was like being on another planet. My passengers, in awe of the spectacular changing colors and texture of the sunset became very quiet. It was beautiful, but I reminded myself the final change to total darkness descended with alarming speed. The sun disappeared in a short blaze of orange, red, and pink. The few scattered clouds above us at 5,000 feet were splashed in bright red and pink—reflections of a brighter light than we had minutes earlier, and would produce a false sense of security. It would be a matter of minutes before the sun sank further below the horizon, no longer illuminating the clouds and plunging the countryside in darkness as if suddenly covered with a blanket. Not a good time to be in an airplane.

Marquis was the second valley ahead, about five minutes out. I eased back the throttle and trimmed elevators for a gradual, straight-in approach. The mountains surrounding Marquis were 1800 feet high. We continued our descent. Directly below, the white rapids highlighted the Tipuru River coursing its way between the smaller mountains eight miles west of our house.

Descending to 600 feet above the Tipuru and Ireng junction, I banked hard left on my new course over the Ireng and was on the Marquis one mile final approach dead ahead. As I trimmed the plane for landing, I spotted a light, a flashlight—Jan walking from the house to the airstrip. It was a welcoming sight. With only minutes to spare, I was thankful I didn't have need of her flashlight.

We touched down in a gentle landing and taxied to the hangar, where our men helped push the plane into the hangar, then assisted our Brazilians with their bag. I noticed Jan didn't wait, but instead returned to the house.

I wondered if she might be angry with me for being away for two days, or coming home with two unannounced guests, or more hopefully, preparing dinner and in a good mood. Dinners were a challenge in the bush, particularly at Marquis, where we had no goats, sheep, or extra chickens to quickly put on the table. Marquis was so remote, we never expected guests. Well, almost never. But here they were.

I introduced Jan to the governor candidate and his aide before I attempted to summarize my two days of flying, the Brazilian elections, and the plight of the governor-to-be. I didn't mention Mervin and his antics—too unbelievable. I casually spoke of tomorrow's flight to Lethem at first crack of light. I wasn't gaining ground in the family relations department. It got worse. The fact I was leaving again the next morning did not add brownie points. Try as I did to explain the situation, I finally gave up and brought out two bottles of Dewars scotch. One was a gift, the other I broke open to lighten up the party. We had ice in the fridge. Situation saved. Jan struggled in the kitchen without my help while our candidate and I exchanged stories about the interior. Somehow, the three of us we managed to finish the bottle of scotch, before, during and after the meal. As the bottle emptied, there were brazos and back slapping, with elaborate promises. The governor-to-be repeated many times how much he appreciated what we did for him and his people along the border. He would reciprocate by issuing an official document, a *carte blanche* to fly anywhere in the Rio Branco state, an area as large as the Louisiana Purchase.

I figured it was the scotch talking and thought no more about it. The next morning we departed early in a more somber mood. I dropped my passengers at Lethem, with assurances from Teddy Melville, the hotel owner, that he would transport them to Boa Vista. With that accomplished, we had more brazos, along with promises for future meetings. I returned home.

I didn't expect much to come out of this incident. Jan and I didn't discuss it, so it quickly faded into oblivion. Later, I would be happily reminded of the Governor Gonsalves incident.

THE GOVERNOR

Sunday, three months after the Mervin incident. We finished breakfast and Jan and I were sipping coffee and discussing the affairs of the week. Suddenly we stopped talking…and listened.

Living in the bush increased our sensitivity to nature: the wind, rustle of leaves and grass, tree frogs, and distant howler monkeys. Foreign sounds were easily distinguishable. We were sure it was an engine. Our prospecting and dredging operations were shut down. The Ireng River was not navigable by boat, so it was not an outboard. Jan came to the same conclusion I did.

"Is that a small plane I hear?" she asked with her head slightly cocked, listening intently.

"Yeah, it must be, but as far as I know there aren't any other small planes in the country, much less out here." I was confused as she was.

A few minutes passed and there was no mistaking the sound of a small airplane. We watched it circle overhead then fly upriver for a final landing approach. It would be the first time a small plane other than ours landed here.

I told Jan to get her pistol and the rifle from the closet. I strapped on my gun belt and was out the door towards the airstrip. In this isolated and unforgiving bush country, it was best to prepare for the worst. To be surprised could be fatal.

I stopped halfway to the airstrip, a good vantage point, and waited for the plane to land. It returned on a long final behind the mountain on the Brazilian side, where it disappeared momentarily. Well, I thought, can't blame them for playing it safe for a first time landing. The pilot came in high and fast and used most of the runway before stopping and turning. After taxing close to where I stood, he shut down the engine. The identification markings on the plane were Brazilian.

The pilot had two passengers on board wearing tropical linen suits. They apparently recognized me and waved as they debarked and approached. I waved back but it took a moment to realize who it was: my governor friend whom I flew out of a Brazilian airstrip to ensure he arrived in Boa Vista in time for the elections. Recently, I heard, via *bush telegram*, that he was elected governor of the Rio Branco region of Brazil, the expansive territory north of the Amazon.

When I recognized him, I relaxed, hurried forward and exchanged a warm brazo. In broken Portuguese, I congratulated him on becoming governor and was honored to have him visit. He introduced me to his new aide and the three of us walked up the path to the house. I looked back towards the pilot. The Governor shook his head.

"It's okay, he will stay with the plane and check it out while we visit."

When we arrived at the door, Jan had the rifle and pistol out of sight, the table set, and the kerosene stove hissing, making hot water for tea. She was standing at the door welcoming Governor Gonzalez as if she expected him. I was again amazed at her ability to adapt to unexpected situations. Maybe she was making up for the Mervin incident when I not only arrived at night several days late but I brought two unexpected dinner and overnight guests: the governor-candidate and an aide. I loved her for the way she handled that situation and was handling this one.

In true Latin American tradition of socializing before business, we started with an *English tea* hoping it would be a pleasant change from the ubiquitous Brazilian coffeezinia. I was curious what prompted this unexpected visit. As if to answer my question, Governor Gonzales stood up smoothing the wrinkles in his linen suit, reached into his aide's briefcase, and pulled out a rolled up rough-edged parchment— the kind you associate with treasure maps and secret papers. After carefully untying the blue ribbon, he dramatically unfolded the foot-and-a-half-long document that on the bottom had an official stamped wax seal with red ribbon. Impressive.

The governor looked at Jan and me to assure he had our attention. His aide stepped back to give him full stage. Governor Gonzales read the document aloud. It was steeped in official language and word tenses unknown to me. I understood phrases like *the American Piloto, salvation for the hard working miners on the fronteira,* and *missions.* When he finished, he asked if I understood any of the proclamation. I admitted that I didn't.

"Not important," he said. "What it means is that the Government of Brazil is indebted to you for what you have done for its people and for treating them fairly in business. They petitioned the governor's office to give you permission to fly and transact business anywhere in the Rio Branco territory".

I must have looked surprised when he mentioned the Rio Branco territory. It was huge. He smiled and assured me that was precisely the petition. He was happy to announce that as governor and representative of the people, he granted their request. "This is the written confirmation." He handed me the parchment.

"Speaking on behalf of my fellow Brazilians, I thank you for what you have done for us.

I was speechless as I looked at this very formidable document.

"There is one exception, however. It does not include Boa Vista because it is the federal military base of the Rio Branco Territory.

If you cable me at this number in Rio, you will immediately receive clearance from me." He handed me his personal card. "In the meantime I have this written permission granted to fly to Boa Vista in the next month for you and the Senora to be my guest at Government House. He handed me the smaller document as he looked to Jan for an answer. "I hope you will accept."

GUESTS, ADVENTURES, PICNICS

Three years after we settled in at Marquis, my parents thought it would be a good idea to come down to visit and spend some time with their two new grandchildren.

I met them at Atkinson Field and we returned to Georgetown on the thirty-mile, very bumpy road and the horrible fermenting smells from the sugar factories. Not the greatest introduction to the city particularly when you consider mother and dad had been traveling for two days: Milwaukee to New York on Northwestern Airlines, Pan American Airlines from New York to Antigua where they overnighted. Pan Am from Antigua to the Piarco airport in Trinidad where they again overnighted. They were treated royally by Sonny Ramphal, the manager, of the BelAire Hotel, which was close to the airport. With little traffic noise they had a good sleep. At the crack of dawn they were on BOAC's once every three day flight to Georgetown. The flight down was not a trip; it was an expedition and a test of fortitude.

My parents stayed at the Tower Hotel in Georgetown where they could take an early morning swim. We went on a tour around town to the famous Staebroek Market, abundant in local fresh fruit and other assorted eatables; it delighted them. They drank the milk from freshly cut coconuts and ate the milky coconut crème with a *spoon* lopped off the side of the coconut. It was fun to watch because they were adventurous and tried everything offered to them by the vendor ladies. They didn't understand how in eighty-five degrees fish and meat hung on racks without spoiling. Maybe that was why curry powder was invented. It was strong and made it almost impossible to detect if the meat was a bit "ripe"—and no one died from it. My theory is the body adapts to these local customs.

They met Eric Schreier from Switzerland, who owned the *Swiss House* jewelry store, Allan Humphrey, the owner of the *Tower Hotel*, and Louis Chung and family, who did an export tropical fish business to Florida, and whose wife, Winnie, ran our Georgetown office. Mother and Dad's enthusiasm never waned.

After two days we arrived at Marquis and a great reunion with Jan, Diney, Tom, and of course, Dutch, who was now a permanent member of the family. Since I still had to make my usual rounds supplying trade stores and our diving crews, I brought Mother or Dad along on most of the trips. After the first one, I thought they would be glad to stay back to play grandparent or help around the compound, but I found they had an unending enthusiasm for seeing new places and meeting new people or revisiting ones they met on earlier trips.

Mother liked to know how everyone lived. She loved to cook and exchanged recipes with anyone and everyone who would listen. We spent twice the usual time at Velgrad with Joe Tezaerek's brother, Mat, who poured out his Polish history, his escape during the war, and the fact that his family was still there. I learned more about him then, than all the years we were friends. Mother had a knack of being a *mother* figure to everyone she met. She and Mrs. Correia exchanged recipes and all the gossip of the local mining areas. One of Mrs. Correia's girls had a bad cut on her arm. Mother insisted on putting on hot compresses to reduce the swelling and infection. Before she left, she extracted promises they would continue with the hot Epsom salt compresses until the redness disappeared. It did in two days. They were grateful and Mother was a heroine.

We next flew to Kato where Brazao was waiting for us. I delivered his goods that were paid for in diamonds. Brazao, fortyish, was a very fine-looking man who could have come straight out of Hollywood. Mother couldn't understand why someone that good-looking and educated was living in the bush. She noticed the pretty Indian girl who worked with him. I explained she was his *bush* wife and on occasion, he would take her to town with him to stay in the house with his *town* wife and children. The Georgetown wives of bush traders understood their husbands couldn't live without a woman for months at a time. Accepting that, they put their stamp of approval on the Amerindian wives. They all got along well. When his bush wife's children were old enough to go to school, they were sent down to stay with the town wife who took care of them as if they were her own. It took my mother a while to assimilate all that, if she ever did.

Then she met Mervin who couldn't speak a word of English. Mother couldn't speak a word of Portuguese but somehow they held a conversation that lasted over an hour. Mother knew the whole tale of how I saved the Rio Branco territory by rescuing the governor in time for elections. She related the story many times to friends. I never understood how she and Mervin communicated so well.

It was late when we left Mervin's airstrip. Usually, I made five stops a day, but today I was more patient with Mother's socializing so even our four stops proved to be too long. As we took off, dark shadows stretched out across the country like disappearing fingers. There weren't any cumulous clouds to reflect sunlight before total darkness set in.

Minutes after take off, I realized we couldn't reach Marquis in daylight, a tremendous disappointment for everyone. Our evenings at Marquis were the highlight of the day. Starting with pre-dinner drinks, through dinner and dessert and until the kerosene Tillie lights burned low, we recounted the events of the day. It was a very special time for all of us. Worse yet, I could only reach the closest strip, Monkey Mountain; hardly a place I wanted to overnight with Mother. I got stuck there once before in the evening and decided to sleep in the airplane on the cargo rather than sleep in the mud huts with their pungent smells. I was in a quandary. Mother couldn't adapt to sleeping in hammocks and I sure didn't want to ask her sleep on a makeshift bunk in an adobe trading store.

With no other option and using landing lights, we landed at Monkey Mountain with a scant five minutes to spare before total darkness. John Roth was delighted to see us, and offered us food and drink and a place to sleep. It sounded good but I knew the conditions. It didn't raise my spirits. I looked longingly towards Marquis and noticed a light at the top of the mountains to the east—the moon coming up; a beautiful sight. It rose above the horizon to cast a gray glow over the countryside. At the end of the strip, in the dim moonlight, our airplane looked like a bird poised to fly.

As we stood and talked in front of John Roth's store, the moon grew until it was a glorious round white ball. In this clear air near the equator, it was possible to distinguish marks on the face of the moon that seldom could be seen through the pollution and interfering lights of cities. I scanned the sky, not a single cloud in sight.

"Mom, I have an idea. We're in the middle of the dry season, there's little chance of cloud cover, and in another hour the moon will be up and brighter. I've never flown at night before, but we're less than fifteen minutes from home. I know this country like the back of my hand and think we could easily make it back by the light of the moon." I glanced over to see her reaction. If I expected a negative response, I wasn't going to get it.

"If you think you can do it, it's okay by me. The moon here seems bigger and brighter, or is that my imagination?"

Donald Haack

"No, not your imagination. The moon is brighter near the equator. The lack of pollution is a big factor. Moonlight down here is just unbelievable." I wondered if I was reinforcing my argument to go.

In less than an hour we were back in the plane. I double-checked all the lights and instruments. All okay. Since there was almost no wind I decided on a downwind, downhill takeoff. I rotated the plane in a 360 degree circle to make sure there were no stray clouds in the sky. A cloud obliterating the moon in this country would be catastrophic as there were no navigational aids nor lighted fields within 250 miles in any direction.

Not a cloud in sight. I flipped on the landing lights and we were airborne in seconds, gliding over the Monkey Mountain escarpment and heading towards Marquis. Though I knew every mountain, the terrain looked entirely different by moonlight—no depth perception. Unless I flew low, valleys and mountains looked the same.

In the first five minutes over the Echilebar River valley I dropped to a lower altitude where I could distinguish the silhouettes of the mountains ahead. I passed between the first two peaks. It was an eerie feeling not knowing how high above the ground we were and I had to trust my altimeter and calculate minutes elapsed. When I estimated we were over Tipuru village, I couldn't see it and I thought that an airplane flying in the dark should give the Amerindians something to talk about.

The star-filled sky reflected off the water and the rapids highlighted by moonlight gave me a fix on the Tipuru River, a comfortable landmark confirming my position. When I passed the last two mountains bordering the Tipuru, I turned hard left over the Ireng and onto the final approach to Marquis. For a few seconds I couldn't see the river below. I went into slow flight and made shallow 'S' turns for a better assessment of the terrain. I spotted the rapids several hundred yards below our barge. At this altitude I had to make a shallow turn around the Brazilian mountain in front of Marquis. Coming closer I saw the mountain's profile ahead and at the same time the Ireng Rapids became a thousand small lights reflected from the moon. A gradual right turn, and to line up with our airstrip I turned to a 95 degree heading and descended until the altimeter read 450 feet above sea level; hopefully 150 fifty feet above Marquis' elevation.

As I was straining to see our strip, a light flashed on, then a second. Jan and Dad must have heard the plane a long way out and ran to the airstrip with the two Tillie lamps. From pre-planning, Jan would be positioned at the touch down area. I aimed for that point. A hundred yards out I switched on the landing lights. Jan was on one side, Dad on the other and the airstrip extended beyond them.

I cut the power, touched down fifty feet behind them, stopped, turned and slowly taxied to the hangar.

Jan's first comment: "I can't believe you flew at night…in these mountains. You are sober, aren't you?" I assured her I was and that this was only a fourteen-minute flight from Monkey Mountain where we ran out of light. After the full explanation with all the details, the matter was dropped and after a couple of martinis, we had a great evening.

Two weeks later on a Good Hope run, Caesar came out to me. He was barely holding back a smile. Something was up.

"Talked to Tiny yesterday,"—Tiny and Connie McTurk owned Karanambo Ranch, forty miles to the east— " about your mother and Dad. The McTurks thought they might enjoy a picnic on the Simuni. I told Nellie and she's ecstatic and already packed."

I heard stories about the Simuni River from Caesar and Dutch. It was a fisherman's dream. Caesar and Nellie went there several times and fondly reminisced about it. McTurk's friend, Al Pfleuger, of the world famous Pflueger Rod & Reel Company, came to Guiana just for the Simuni expedition and claimed it was the highlight of all his world-wide fishing trips.

"Nellie says we can all go: your family of six, Nellie, the boys, Pixie and me, and Tiny McTurk. Connie's going to stay home. She's been there several times and is going to make tea for us when we return."

I thought that was a strange thing to say, because it wasn't as if we were going on our usual stateside type picnic for a couple of hours. A picnic down here meant five or six days depending on how the fishing went.

It took a few days to work out the logistics. Good Hope was the rendezvous for the Haacks and Gorinskys. We packed food, hammocks, and fishing gear into the plane until I had a full load of cargo and passengers. Caesar took everything else in the jeep. After a twenty minute flight we arrived at Karanambo a little after ten in the morning. McTurk was standing beside the small airstrip Dutch and I had built a few hundred feet from their house and convenient for quick and frequent tea trips. The DC-3 airstrip was several miles away and necessitated first flying over the house and then waiting a half hour for McTurk's jeep and another twenty-minute drive back to the house. That worked only if McTurk was there, and if his jeep, which was a relic even by Rupununi standards, was operable.

We drove down to the Demerara River, a beehive of activity. The Indian boys had the Evinrude on a sixty foot dugout and three smaller dugouts tied off its stern. We brought our Evinrude and two cans of gas as a back up. Caesar had forewarned me the area we were going into was extremely remote and we would have to be totally self-sufficient.

"Even the local Indians rarely get anywhere close. It's just too far to travel from their villages"

Nellie and the Indian boys were rigging something that looked like a double short mast for hammocks and sun shield for the four children. A nice touch. By the time we transferred our equipment Caesar had arrived and drove directly to the boat. Shortly after noon, we were on our noisy intrusive trip down the remote Demerara, enjoying the startled reactions of the animals and alligators along the banks. McTurk pointed out the big, almost invisible alligators too lethargic to move but when our waves hit them, their heads raised as if questioning *who would dare to interrupt our peaceful existence?* We chased up thousands of parrots, parakeets, and the ever-present colorful scarlet and white ibis.

After their sons, Chris and Mark were settled in their hammocks, Caesar and Nellie busily baited fishing lines with chicken innards and threw them overboard. I looked at Caesar, questioningly.

"Fishing for arrawannas... bait," is all he said, and enough to pique my imagination. Arrawannas were a fairly good sized fish, up to two feet long and five or six pounds.

"For bait?" I questioned.

Caesar gave mother and dad each a line and before long they were pulling in nice-sized arawanas. Dad said he hadn't had such great fishing in years. The best was yet to come. After five or six fish, McTurk indicated that would be enough for now.

He slowed the outboard and scanned the banks. We had traveled three hours. By my calculation we should be forty miles downstream from McTurk's ranch. He pointed to the heavy bush on the right bank and to a barely visible tributary marked only by darker water. I wondered where he was going. The entrance appeared to be blocked by overhanging trees. As we approached, he turned upstream, slowed, headed for the bank and when we were close to hitting, turned sharply left into a space six feet wide. It was like entering a cave that meandered between the thick bush.

"Simuni!" Caesar announced above the less noisy low speed engine as we glided through the fairy-like cove. McTurk deftly maneuvered through the passages of low hanging branches, which we instinctively ducked. I looked back. Apparently Nellie removed the children's hammock posts before entering the creek. The river with many turns narrowed. Tiny reduced speed, which enabled us to enjoy the scenery. We talked in hushed tones as if we were entering a place of worship. As we continued, the river widened and divided into several tributaries. McTurk never hesitated as to which one to take. The trees gave us welcomed shade and enforced the feeling we were going down a huge cave. Moments later, he aimed the boat towards a large sand bank, slid onto it and cut the engine.

"We're here." I heard Nellie say. With the outboard shut down, the silence was replaced by a plethora of natural sounds:

birds, frogs, monkeys, more than I could distinguish. We climbed over the bow onto the sand bank, each carrying something until the boat was empty and stowed upstream. There was a flurry of activity as hammocks went up, a fire made, and cooking utensils set on a quickly constructed stick table.

"Who wants to fish?" McTurk called out. "We have to get something for supper."

I looked at my watch. It was four o'clock and we were just going to fish for supper now? I brought two of my brand-new stateside spinning rods and reels, gave one to Caesar and I took the other. Dad and McTurk were from the old school and would use their trusty old reel-type casting rods.

I flipped my plug-bait across the creek. On the first cast a fish lunged at the plug but missed the hook. The second one connected and the fun began. McTurk was more interested in what I was doing than casting himself.

"You'll never bring him in with that line. Doesn't look more than half-pound test. That fish will go three or more pounds." He shook his head. I reeled in a few yards. The fish resisted and took back that amount and more as the reel sang, over-riding the brake that kept the line from tearing from any strain over a half-pound. I reeled in. The rod bent over at right angles. The fish took over and ran out. It was back and forth for several minutes. Almost imperceptibly, the fish's pull became less and less as he tired. When he came up the boat we scooped him with the net. Everyone watched the performance, particularly, McTurk who had never seen that much fun playing and bringing in a fish. It was a beautiful three-pound lukanani, one of the best eating-tasting fish in all of South America. Caesar brought in the second one with just as much fun. McTurk was fascinated and came over to take another look. I handed him my rod and showed him how to use it. Caesar caught another and gave his rod to Dad who also was becoming a believer in the spinning rod. Dad and Tiny were like a couple of kids in a toy store. In no time we had five lukananis. Nellie advised us that was more than enough for dinner, even for our large hungry group.

Donald Haack

She cleaned, filleted, and fried the fish in butter and onions in a big iron pan. A second pan had sliced potatoes. A big pot of coffee hung over the fire. The aroma of coffee and frying fish permeated our little island. We took turns, fishing, eating, cleaning up, and finally settled down around the fire with our coffee and not-so-cold beer and wine. That meal, tasty and surrounded by natural beauty was epic. An auspicious start to one of the most memorable picnics of my life; an opinion, I believe, shared by all.

Early the next morning, Pixie came over to my hammock and shook it gently. "We've been given a job to do," she said quietly.

"Geez, it's barely light out. What are you doing up so early?" I looked around. There wasn't much activity around the camp yet, but I knew that would change quickly. Everyone rose early in the bush. We went to bed a couple of hours after sunset, eight or nine o'clock. I looked at my watch, 5:30. I rolled out and washed. Pixie came back.

"Mom gave us the job of making sure we keep our fish we buried last night in the wet and cool sand. Not quite refrigeration, but better than sitting out in ninety degree heat. They'll keep for one day. Trouble is, the alligators can smell them and they're coming around already." She pointed to a log halfway across the creek.

I looked closer. It was drifting, but not downstream like a log should. It was moving toward our shore and the buried fish. With closer scrutiny, I could make out the two baseball-like eyes, the tip of the snout and part of its back, which looked like a log.

"If you look over there, you can see two more heading this way. Mom says to take your pistol and discourage them, but don't kill them."

I went to the waterside, took aim and shot. A geyser shot up inches in front of the closest reptile, about nine feet long. It didn't discourage him. He kept on coming. Pixie shrugged with a questioning look in her face.

"Okay, I guess it will take a little more to discourage them." I muttered... took aim, and fired off another round, this time popping him on the snout. He came half out of water, thrashed about, slapped his tail loudly, and plunged under the water, heading in the opposite direction. The other logs disappeared at the same time.

"Well, I managed to do our *job* and wake the whole camp at the same time." In response to the shooting, heads popped out of the hammocks like turtles from their shells. Fortunately no one seemed upset. After a hearty breakfast of ham, eggs, and steaming coffee prepared by Jan and Nellie, I joined McTurk who was busy with the arawanas he dug up.

"Getting bait ready for the *real* fishing—arapaimas. Should be ready to go in a few minutes." The two Indian boys brought the three small dugouts and put in several tools and paddles.

"What are the tools for?" I asked Tiny.

"You have your pistol, I heard you shoot. Take it with you, along with that sledge hammer and the small harpoon."

"I thought we were going fishing, not whaling." I smiled

"You'll see what it's for in a minute. I'll explain as we get out in the boats. Here, take these." and he handed me two pieces of bamboo-type cork, each a foot long and eight inches in diameter. It was tied and wrapped with a rope that ended in an enormous fish hook, a four inch piece of bent steel. He cut the arawana bait into five inch chunks.

"Put one on each hook. Let's go." He climbed into one of the dugouts with Dad and pushed off. I took the second dugout. McTurk called to me.

"Sit in front, Jaime will go in back. When you get into the open pond over there, unwrap the line and throw the bait and cork into the water. Make sure you unravel all six feet of the rope. Keep an eye on the corks. You'll know when you get a bite."

I threw the baited lines and corks in the water. I was confused. I didn't have a line attached to the cork but I figured he knew what he was doing. He threw and it wasn't long before the action started. The second bait I threw in went out of sight with a force that left a mini geyser in its empty place.

McTurk called, "Watch around. It'll be up in a few seconds. Follow and try to lasso the cork with that rope at your feet."

I missed on the first and second attempts. It was obvious I wasn't a cowboy. I had Jaime paddle up closer and I slipped the line over the cork just before it plunged out of sight again.

"Keep the line loose." McTurk called. After he settles down, put the line around the bow but don't tie it down. You're about to get a free ride around the lake."

He no sooner said that than our boat lurched forward and was pulled by something *big* down below. We circled the pond several times before slowing. Whatever took that hook was wearing out.

"Keep pulling in, he's tiring. Try to get him next to your boat. Then hit him with the sledge, gaff him with the harpoon, or just shoot him between the eyes. Then paddle back to camp as fast as you can and pull him out of the water. Don't try to get him in the dugout. Too big. He'll swamp your boat. Get him to shore as quickly as possible," he repeated with emphasis.

I didn't understand why until I brought the Arapaima close to our boat. It was the biggest fish I had ever seen: over six feet long with a body bigger than my waist. I grabbed the sledge and slammed it on his head. He didn't cooperate and instead lurched downward. Fortunately I was holding the line loosely and not wrapped around the bow or he would have taken Jaime, boat, and me with him.

This was not the fishing I was used to. It took another fifteen minutes of towing to tire him out again. This time, as soon as he surfaced, I fired two quick shots between the eyes. I didn't think this was a very sporting way to fish, but at the moment, I decided to follow McTurk's advice. I had a subtle feeling this was more of a *survival of the fittest* than a fishing event.

We finally strung the arapaima up on a tree scale—six-and-a-half feet long and 450 pounds. The Arapaima is the largest fresh-water scaled fish in the world. Its natural home is the Amazon River. Its tributaries, including the Rio Negro, Rio Branco and the Mahu (Ireng) flood in the rainy season to join rivers like the Demerara. In dry season, the receding rivers separate and the arapaimas remain isolated in rivers like the Simuni, a tributary of the Demerara.

Donald Haack

After we finished the weighing and took pictures of the fish and my beaming parents the boys quickly sliced off the fillets, then salted and peppered them to hang on a pole in a sunny spot to dry. After a couple of sun-drying days, the dried fish would keep for weeks providing food for the vaqueros on the ranch or for my miners; a welcome change in diet from dried beef.

McTurk later explained the need to rush the arapaima to shore—pirhanis would be attracted and eat the carcass. "You don't want to be in a dugout with pirhanis all around you. Not too good for your health." I thought of Karakarana and couldn't agree more.

JOHN ROTH

Several weeks after I ferried Jimmy Angel's cargo, and as per John Roth's request, I returned to Monkey Mountain. The gold and diamond production had increased dramatically and so did John's trading store, the biggest and best within fifty miles or six days walking. He asked me to supply him with rations and store goods. Like most shop owners, he couldn't afford to charter a whole DC-3 load into Monkey Mountain. The prices I quoted him delivered by my plane were almost half of what it cost to bring goods by bullock from Kato, the nearest regular DC-3 stop. That didn't take into account losses, damage, and spoilage along the way.

I was reluctant to do business with John when I first met him. He came on as the unsavory, unscrupulous, Portuguese trader stereotyped by so many Hollywood movies about Africa. Many of the miners in the area personally asked me to do business with John because it would also help them, and so I did. John was more than pleased to have a reliable source of supplies at fair pricing, something he hadn't experienced before.

Donald Haack

His business prospered and our relationship improved to the point he accepted me as a friend and confidant. I was flattered because as far as I could see, John had no friends, other than the Indian woman he kept as a wife. He treated her respectfully, but everyone else in the area experienced John Roth's short temper and rage, traits that I predicted would one day land him in serious trouble. He was meticulously scrupulous in his business dealings with me, insisting on partially paying in advance, which no one else did.

One Sunday, after we unloaded the last of his cargo, he asked me to come to the back of his store where he lived. He took out a piece of paper, calculated everything I brought, deducted his down payment and asked if I wanted to be paid in dollars or diamonds.

"John, it's all the same to me, whatever is easier for you." He paid me in diamonds before and price was no problem. "Do you have time?"

"Sure. Let's have a look," He beckoned me to a back room. It had a single window and a small table with a sheet of paper and a large 38 caliber pistol. He reached into his pocket and brought out a cigar tube labeled *$2,000*, opened the top and carefully poured rough diamonds onto the paper. They were a better quality than most and apparently were weighed, graded, and valued earlier by John. He spread them with his tweezers and then sorted to one side the bigger octahedral crystals with his little finger's inch-long nail.

I brought out my 8 inch varnished walnut case and pushed open the snap, exposing the silver-plated balance scale. I locked it open, attached the balance and two round dishes, and centered the needle to assure it was in balance. I used my little diamond shovel to scoop up the diamonds and poured them in one of the dishes. Opening three round caps, I extracted measured weights and added them to the opposite side until the needle once again centered. I counted up the weights.

"Looks like eleven carats and thirty points." I looked up. "Does that match your weight?"

"Close enough," as he walked out the door, unconcerned about leaving me with his diamonds.

I divided them into small piles by size and quality, weighed each individually, wrote the value below and the total. "I figure $2,500, John. That's more than it's labeled, but that's what it's worth and what I'm willing to credit you."

His smile broadened, showing off a mouthful of identical white teeth, obviously a denture. "No man in this whole country," and he swung his arm in a big circle, "would give me a price more than I put on that label...except you. That's why I trust only you."

I wondered what he meant by "I trust only you." He wouldn't say that unless he had something specific in mind. John didn't believe in small talk. Everything had a purpose. And it didn't escape me that he knew the value of the diamonds and this was a test of some sort.

There were unwritten rules in the bush diamond trade. For amounts smaller than a thousand dollars, diamond buyers hoped to make 25% profit or more which covered time, risk, licenses, etc. In selling trade goods to shopkeepers, my margin of profit was considerably higher. I bought at bulk prices in Georgetown, chartered the DC-3s to the interior airstrips, and by filling the return flights with my or Good Hope's cattle, I saved considerably on shipping, a big advantage over interior buyers.

B.G. Airways had three airstrips serving the mining area. Their deliveries were erratic and the traders were limited to when they could order enough cargo to warrant a flight, a situation that kept the rates high to small shippers. Goods were lost or stolen because shopkeepers didn't know exact delivery dates. More often than not they had long delays waiting for the plane and then had to carry their goods to their shops several days away, a highly inefficient and expensive method of doing business.

Some shops had small airstrips. Those that didn't were more than happy to construct them with me so I could deliver right to their door. It was a win-win situation for everyone and for that service I charged a good fee. They also had the option to pay in dollars or diamonds at the same value they could receive in Georgetown, where they previously shipped their diamonds several times a year. The profits rose substantially higher for the shopkeepers who bought goods from me. They were excellent testimonials, which led to many more happy customers, including John Roth. So I was curious as to what his charades meant. I didn't say anything and waited.

"There's been some trouble here lately. No man can tell me what to do. No man can tell John Roth how to run Monkey Mountain." To emphasize his point, he reached over for his revolver, picked it up and slammed it down on the table. "This is how I keep order," and he tapped the gun with his forefinger. "There's always someone who wants me dead so they can take over my shop, but this stops 'em," as he continued tapping the revolver.

I didn't respond, but there sat skinny John, knobby knees not quite covered by khaki shorts four sizes too large, sleeveless underwear top, slicked jet black hair, pointed nose, and sunken cold black eyes framed with thin eyebrows. Again the cruel aura emerged, giving me that same strange foreboding feeling about him. He acted like the *god* of Monkey Mountain...no wonder he had enemies, real or imagined, I thought.

"What can I do?" I asked, because this was obviously leading up to something. In more than six months, this was the first time he spoke more than a few words.

"I want you to hold something for me." He reached down, pulled back a faded carpet, removed a stone that blended in with the floor and retrieved a small cloth-bound package. He placed it on the table checking to make sure the string was secure. He pushed it towards me.

"If something happens to me, make sure my Georgetown wife gets this." He specified his *Georgetown* wife.

"Her address is on the paper under the string," and he pointed to it with his long fingernail. As if to answer my question, he added, "Keep the package until I ask you for it. I don't know how long. I'll let you know. Just keep it safe for me. I trust you."

He waited a while before he continued. "I got a lot of credit out, more than ever before but it's okay, 'cause I know they're hitting diamonds. Went to some camps this week. They're workin' day and night. No time to stop and pay off their debts, but they gotta come soon. Rations'll run out. Be getting lots of diamonds then and with what I've given you, it'll be a big parcel. I can negotiate a good price with a big parcel. That's why you gotta hold these for me in a safe place. Couldn't afford to lose that much if some thing goes wrong." I took his package.

Nothing was mentioned in the following weeks, but a month later he came out of his shop as I parked the plane. "Bring it next time." He handed me a pile of money in a paper bag to pay his latest bill and walked back to his shop. I didn't bother counting it. It would be the exact amount he owed. He wasn't in a talkative mood. I figured he meant the diamond parcel by his comment, *bring it next time.*

I brought his parcel on the next trip. I later heard he walked three days to Kato where he delivered his diamonds to B.G. Airways for delivery to his Georgetown diamond buyer, M. C. Correia. I wondered if in his bargaining he received a better price. I would never know.

A week later I landed at Monkey Mountain and before I shut down the engine I knew something was wrong. John was not in his doorway. Indians ran back and forth between the huts. His Amerindian wife came running, waving frantically. As she came closer I saw the pained expression, an emotion seldom seen in Amerindians. I couldn't understand what she was saying until she came up and gripped my shoulder.

"Dey kill John Roth, dey kill John Roth," she kept repeating. "Dey kill my man." She clung to my khaki shirt, eyes red, tears streaming down her face partially covered by disheveled hair usually tied neatly in back. I tried to comfort her. She didn't listen, but pulled me into the store. She pointed to the floor in back of the counter. I looked. The sight overwhelmed me. There was blood everywhere. Two skinny legs stuck out. At the other end of the crumbled body lay what remained of John Roth. A double shotgun blast at close range exposed mostly bone where eyes and nose had been. One ear hung at right angles, the other was missing altogether. There was apparently a second blast in the neck that almost severed his head. I swallowed, trying to keep the bile from rising in my throat. I found it hard to talk. I finally whispered, "What happened, Maria? Who did this?"

It took her awhile to compose herself. "Three weeks ago John pistol-whip the Brazilian boy, Marco, for something he did. But John, he punish him too hard and in front of Indians and Brazilians. The boy, Marco lose face here and swear he kill John Roth before he leave. Yesterday, he steal shotgun from Gomes. He wait down at creek where John bathe every morning. We hear two shots and run down to stream. John lay face down in water all red. Shotgun by John's feet. Girl see Marco running from stream. He gone now. He be in Brazil tomorrow and never come back."

She was right about that—Marco would never again be seen in these parts. "I think you take he body to family in Georgetown. Dey expect dat."

I was surprised that in her grief, she could still think of what his family in town would want. In the past year my extensive flying and trading throughout the interior exposed me to the *real life*. Killings, shooting, drownings or other accidents were commonplace. Requests came regularly to fly the remains back to Georgetown. The first one I carried in a sheet. Tropics are conducive to rapid decomposition. Never again. After that I carried a body bag alongside my emergency ration kit. I brought it from the plane. With the help of two Amerindians we placed John Roth inside. After zipping the bag tightly closed we carried him into the plane. I didn't know whether to go inside the house or not, but was beckoned by Maria to enter. John's pistol was missing. She pointed to the rug. I removed it and the loose stone. The hole was empty. I didn't know the significance of the empty hideaway and maybe she didn't either but for whatever reason she wanted to show me. I took her hand. She stopped crying.

"Goodbye, Misser Haack. You good man to John. You his good friend. Mine, too. You take him to his family."

Donald Haack

"What about you, Maria?"

"Me okay. I go back to family in village," and she pointed eastward towards Paramakatoi Village, three days walking.

Without the irascible John Roth, his shop and rations, the miners soon left. Within two months Monkey Mountain was a ghost town. Not a soul remained, just the airstrip and the frames of the eroding adobe huts. The metal roof disappeared from John's store, the last trace of civilization in a once active trading center.

THE MYSTERY OF THE TWO POLICEMEN

Friday. Mail day. After I landed at Good Hope to pick up mail and cargo, Caesar drove up waving a letter in his hand.

"Was in Lethem yesterday and Eric Cassou gave me this for you, and said to make sure you get it as soon as possible. Sounds like it's very important."

Eric, a good friend of ours, was District Commissioner of the Rupununi Territory. We frequently overnighted at his house for fetes and enjoyed the camaraderie. This, however, was on official stationery. I opened it right away.

URGENT

To: Mr. Haack,

From: Eric Cassou, District Commissioner, Lethem

Dear Don, I've re-written this three times and decided to make it very short. Explanations will come later. I can't adequately do it here.

We have an emergency. There are two policemen stranded and too sick to move, camped out above Karona

Falls, approximately ten miles up river from your house. I understand you have an airstrip nearby. Could you, as soon as possible, bring the two men back to Lethem in your plane? Accept this as full authorization to pay your charter rates plus any extra costs you may incur to expedite this. I really think it is a matter of life or death. Contact me immediately if for any reason you cannot do this.

Thank you,

Your Servant,

Eric Cassou, Commissioner

I was confused and re-read it. I handed it to Caesar. "Can you make any sense of this?".

He read it and frowned. "Two policemen camped at Karona Falls? What the hell are they doing up there?" He shook his head. "Just doesn't make any sense at all. That's no-man's land. Wonder why they were sent there in the first place? You going to pick 'em up?"

"Yeah, and I'm curious what's going on, particularly since he said it's a matter of life or death. It's not like Eric to exaggerate. Most of the Georgetown police have a hard time surviving in outposts like Lethem. But posting them in a remote region like Karona is like signing a death warrant. You remember a couple of months ago I flew out the bodies of three policemen? They drowned in Orinduik Falls…and Orinduik is a big outpost trading center and civilized compared to Karona. Something's fishy. I'll let you know when I bring 'em out. Hope they're still alive. I don't have any body bags at Marquis at the moment."

Caesar grimaced at my remark. I shouldn't have been quite so callous. Those poor guys were probably in pretty bad shape and it sounded serious.

I wasted no time. I did a quick turn-around back to Marquis and gathered Jan, Dutch, and Domingo—whom I pulled off the dredge—and explained what we had to do. Jan brought our first aid kit, Dutch and Domingo fetched blankets and rope to make a pulling stretcher.

"What in the world are two Guiana policemen doing up there, do you suppose?" Jan asked.

I shrugged. "No idea whatsoever but we'll soon find out, either from the police, if they're able to talk, or from Cassou when I deliver them."

In less than a half hour, Domingo and I were on our way. He convinced me he should come along to help transport them to the plane if they were unable to walk. If we placed both policemen in the plane, that would be maximum weight for a safe take off from that short airstrip. Domingo said not to worry; he would walk back to Marquis. Sound idea. I drained ten more gallons from the plane to give us another eighty-pound margin.

Just before landing, I spotted a blue tarp halfway between the falls and our strip, but no sign of life. Not good, but at least we knew where to go as soon as we landed. A few minutes later, carrying the emergency articles we packed, we approached the camp area.

"Anyone here?" I called. An arm extended from under the tarp. Domingo lifted it. One policeman was lying on his back with a white rag over his forehead. I wasn't sure if he was still alive. I noticed the grotesque size of his face—swollen, red, and puffed from scratching. His exposed hands were almost twice normal size, the result of severe cabouri fly bites and the inevitable scratching.

He groaned and slowly raised a hand to his face. At least he was still alive. The other policeman was sitting up but looked no better than the prone one. He tried to talk—nothing intelligible. I came alongside and looked into his face. His eyes were glassy, his skin dry, and his tongue swollen to the point where he had difficulty pronouncing words, even after I asked him to speak slowly. He was in an advanced stage of dehydration. Both of the water bottles at their side were empty. They must have sent the message to Cassou with one of the Macusi Indians a week ago, expecting help in a day or two but not realizing it would take the messenger the better part of a week just to get to Lethem. I didn't understand why they hadn't contacted us at Marquis. They could have been out the next day—another part of the mystery.

Donald Haack

I gave them water to drink from our plane's water bottles and sent Domingo to fill them from the river while I explained we were going to fly them to Lethem right now. They seemed to comprehend, but I knew it would be easier said than done. These were big men, each well over 200 pounds. They didn't look very mobile.

As soon as Domingo returned, we sprinkled their clothes and wrapped cloths around their foreheads to cool them down. The one sitting up we half-carried to the plane. He wasn't able to stand, but once we had him on his feet he was able to put one foot in front of the other, which was better than having to drag 250 pounds. We set him in the shade beside the airplane and returned for the second man. We cut two small trees about fifteen feet long, skinned off the branches and wrapped the blankets around them in stretcher fashion. We tied the ends so the blankets wouldn't come loose and drop our patient. It wasn't perfect—looked like a typical *travois* the American Indians used to haul loads behind their horses.

In this case, Domingo and I would be the horses. We laid out the travois beside the prone policeman and rolled him onto the blankets. We used one end of the rope to tie him in so he wouldn't slide out when we lifted.

Fortunately, even though there wasn't a trail, the country above the falls was fairly open but it was still a major feat pulling him to the plane. We slid one side of the stretcher into the back of the plane and lifted the other end onto the wing strut. Once in place we slid him in and secured him with a seat belt. It took two hours to get both men in the plane.

I ran back to the campsite to see if there were anything we should bring along. I looked around and was appalled at the filth. They must have been here for weeks: opened food tins scattered everywhere, garbage, and dirty laundry. Apparently towards the end, they didn't have the strength to walk, so they defecated right in their camp, big mounds with toilet paper and flies all around. I found their two suitcases, put in their personal belongings, and hurried back to the plane. I resolved to return with a couple of

Indians and clean up this mess. What a terrible thing to do to such a pristine, untouched land, I thought.

Cassou must have heard the plane a long way off or was expecting me to do this flight immediately, because his Land Rover was at the strip by the time we landed and taxied back. He walked up to the plane. I opened the door and greeted him.

"How are they?" were his first words. "Are they going to make it?"

"They're badly dehydrated and weak, but yes, I think they'll do fine if we get them to the infirmary right away." With many helping hands, we had them out of the plane, into the Land Rover, and on their way. Cassou stayed back with me. We were alone on the airstrip.

"Come, let's talk. I'm sure you have many questions and this wasn't something I wanted to do long distance. I wanted to talk to you personally. I owe you that."

I was intrigued by his comments and wondered what it was all about. We went into Teddy Melville's hotel to the back room. Eric ordered two beers.

"Two months ago," he started, "I received this formal letter addressed to the District Commissioner. My name wasn't even on it and a copy had been sent to the Georgetown Department of the Interior, my headquarters. In it was a detailed accusation about how these foreigners, the Haacks, developed a large smuggling ring of diamonds, cattle, and tobacco from Brazil, and were exploiting our country and not paying any Guianese. They built an airstrip near Karona Falls, the focal point of all their smuggling activities." He stopped and waited for my reaction.

I was dumfounded and it must have shown in my face. Then, I was livid. I didn't know where to start it was so ridiculous. I finally found my voice. "Eric, you know absolutely everything I do back there. We have a big trading business but ninety percent of all the trade goes into Brazil...and I showed you the letter from the Brazilian Governor. We get paid in diamonds, which I declared as imported, but Lands & Mines asked me not to list them as imported but rather *from the interior*. The only things imported: hammocks and diamond sieves, were done through your office the first time. You commented that all this stuff stays right on the border between the two countries, nothing ever goes into the interior of the country to Georgetown, and you said please do not go through your office in the future. Interior trading has been going on for over fifty years but we were the first ones to declare anything."

He had his hand up in the air to stop me from going further. "You don't have to convince me. I'm on your side. Particularly since I had reports from the two policemen that during the eight weeks they were there, not one airplane came in and not a single person other than the Amerindians who came to fish passed through. But after receiving the complaint in writing with a copy to the head office, I was forced to make an official investigation by sending in the men to Karona, the so-called smuggling route. It turned out exactly as I thought. I also put my personal comments in the report about the person who wrote the accusation." He smiled. "So that's the end."

It never occurred to me to ask who made the report. I assumed it was anonymous. I looked over to him. "Can you tell me who did this?" I was at a total loss.

"Lorie, your foreman's wife. Harry doesn't have a clue about it. After all you did for him; he would die in shame. She talks bad about everyone and is an incredibly vindictive woman…evil is a better description. Everyone is convinced she is the reason Harry had so many ulcer attacks. Incidentally, I had a long talk with her two weeks after all the reports came back and explained besides defaming you, which under British law is cause for a major lawsuit, the government has spent a great deal of time and money investigating her accusations. I asked her to formally document how and where she had grounds for such an accusation and if there is insufficient evidence, there might be grounds for criminal prosecution from the Crown.

I gave her a week and let her sweat it out before I had two policemen escort her to my office. She broke down completely after a few minutes and pleaded for us to not prosecute her. She admitted her mistake. She had no proof. She only heard rumors and when I pressed her for names, she rescinded even that and said she made it all up herself. She was just jealous of you coming into the country with an airplane and doing well. Plain jealousy, nothing more. I had the whole incident signed and witnessed by my two clerks and we included it in my official report to the Georgetown head office. Case is closed. But you can see why I had to explain this to you in person. I hope you'll forgive me for any inconvenience or bad thoughts associated with this."

I sat there totally dumfounded. "Eric, I'm getting to the point where nothing surprises me anymore. Caesar, Nellie and Jan simply won't believe this could've happened. Even though I know many Rupununi people have little love for Lorie, they would never suspect she was capable of something like this." I reflected for a moment. "Poor Harry," was all I could add.

"Poor Harry," Eric repeated. I stood up to shake hands. He brushed my hand aside and gave me a big brazo hug. For the formal and proper Eric Cassou that gesture was epic.

"Thanks, I guess I needed that."

HARD HAT DIVING

The mining operation was not going well. Harry's excuses varied every day. The river was up, down, too dirty, the current too swift, the divers were sick, the intake hose plugged up, and so it went. Previous divers had used poorly maintained primitive equipment, ran out of rations, and lived in such poor conditions they were unable to sleep or eat properly. Our modern equipment, transportation methods, and concern with hygiene eliminated those problems and we expected success, yet there never seemed to be positive results.

We pumped sand for five weeks, day after day on what Harry described as the *mother lode* sand bank that defied the porknocker.

Divers originally found diamonds along the bank of a pool below Tipuru River. The diamonds were bigger and better as they progressed to the bank, but the massive amounts of sand kept them from hitting the *mother lode*. The sand defeated them and me.

In the past five weeks, we pumped thousands of tons of sand... no diamonds. Twelve barrels of gas without a single diamond. I was exasperated with Harry's vague answers. When he came to the house saying they were getting low on fuel again, I blurted, "Harry, just what the hell is really going on up there? It looks like we have a bigger sand bank below us now than we had above us when we started. Just in different places. We can't keep flying in fuel to move sand banks back and forth. My God, we're supposed to be in diamond mining, not sand relocation business."

Harry didn't have an explanation and finally admitted the divers gave him different answers every dive. I wanted explanations. Harry didn't know because he didn't dive himself.

"That settles it. Before I bring in one more barrel of gas and rations, I'm going to find out what in the hell is going on. I'll dive myself…be there first thing tomorrow morning."

I arrived early. We paddled the dinghy to the waiting men on the barge. There was a Brazilian hardhat diving helmet lying on the deck.

"What's that doing here?" I asked as I stepped onto the barge. "Where's our new hookah mask and equipment?" I looked at Harry.

"Oh, I forgot to tell you, one of the boys broke the glass in the face mask, so we borrowed the brass diving helmet. It's okay, they're familiar with it," Harry added a bit sheepishly.

"Harry, for God's sake, why are we using that primitive, cumbersome diving equipment when we have state of the art stuff here? I have spare parts for the mask. How long have you been using this dumb hardhat?

Harry mumbled something I couldn't hear.

"How long?" I repeated. Harry spoke a little louder.

"About two weeks," he said quietly knowing I was angry. I was so mad I told him I didn't want to discuss it at the moment.

He changed the subject. "I don't suppose you want to use the hardhat to check out the sand bank, do you?" he sounded almost relieved.

"I postponed all my flights today to come up here and I'm not going to do it again tomorrow. If it weren't for the flying charters we wouldn't have an income and this operation would've been shut down months ago. There's been no income from diamonds. And *diamonds* are supposed to be the reason we're here." Harry got the message.

"Okay, we can do this fairly quickly; I want to know what's going on down there."

As the crew assembled the equipment, Harry added, "We have our compressor hooked up to the hardhat so you'll have plenty of air. Just be careful you don't fall over. The helmet is attached to the heavy canvas jacket but water can come in from the bottom and flood the helmet. Other than that it should be safe."

Professional hardhat divers had watertight rubber suits with the helmet sealed onto the suit. A diver could be upside down and no water could enter. This unit was certainly the poor man's version: the helmet attached to a canvas jacket simply to hold it in place while it sat on your shoulders…no seal from the bottom. He helped me put on the weights: thirty pounds tied to my chest over the canvas suit attached to the helmet, and another thirty pounds in the back. I stepped into the weighted boots while they secured the brass bolts and checked to make sure everything was tight. They closed the front mask. Harry pointed to the compressor and to his nose to get my okay that I had enough air. I gave a thumbs up signal as they helped me over the edge of the barge onto a rope ladder anchored to a rock below. He reminded me one more time that they were working downstream from the barge. That's where the dredge intake hose was lying.

I descended three feet below water and waited a few minutes to make sure everything was working all right, no water leaks. All seemed okay. I descended the rope ladder, thinking it was not a substantial ladder to go up and down with this unwieldy helmet, but now I was far too committed to go up and abort. I had to find out the problems before I could make any intelligent decisions.

In less than ten feet down, the light faded quickly. The swirling water from the fast moving current muddied the water to one-foot visibility. My feet touched the bottom. I faced into the current to keep my orientation in this limited visibility and light.

Donald Haack

I tried to keep the two lines—the air hose and a safety line used for signals and hauling up in an emergency—from being tangled. I checked to make sure they were free and clear. They appeared to be. Kneeling, I felt for the rock anchoring the rope ladder. There was a guideline leading to the mouth of the suction hose downstream. I had a secure hold on that rope—my only way back to the ladder.

I wrapped the rope around one hand to let it slide through as I progressed backwards and down the sand bank. At about fifteen feet out, I found the suction hose hanging from the front of the dredge. I followed it to the suction end. The visibility at this depth was zilch and I had to feel around the mouth of the nozzle.

Two large rocks blocked the intake. I tried moving them, to no avail. They were wedged tight. I bent down for a closer look and tilted too far—water poured into my helmet. I held my breath and straightened up until the water level receded. I made a mental note not to do that again. I cursed the crew for this stupid helmet when we had modern equipment. With our facemask I could have gone within inches of the blockage for a visual inspection. It would be easy to remove the rocks and straighten the metal guides. Instead I had to work by feel.

I slid my hands back, feeling for the hammer that should be attached by rope. It wasn't there. I found it several feet back, too far away to be useful when working at the intake. After several minutes of untwisting, pulling, pushing, and readjusting, I had the hammer tied to the nozzle where it was supposed to be.

No one told me about this rock plug up. I wondered if they were even aware of it, and just what the hell were they doing down here if the barge was only working at ten or fifteen percent efficiency? Harry should have noticed the small amount of sand and gravel coming through. There had better be some good answers. In a few minutes of hammering, I had the two rocks dislodged and I straightened the guide bars to their original position.

I felt around the hole under the hose...no rocks, no gravel, just sand. This sand bank had to be more than ten feet deep. At the rate we were pumping sand, we could go on for years and never know what was below. This stupidity made me even more frustrated and I wondered if that's what was causing my difficulty in breathing. I began to sweat and feel hot. Not good. I'd found what I needed and now I wanted out...fast. The rope guided me back to the ladder, which was further than I remembered. Maybe because I exerted myself more on the climb up the sand bank.

I was gasping for breath and felt sweat running down my forehead, stinging my eyes. I blinked to keep them clear, but realized the uselessness of the exercise. I couldn't see anything in this murky water anyway. The urge to get out of here and breathe fresh air was paramount.

That was it—air! It wasn't my exertion. I was moving slowly, conserving energy, and breathing slowly and deeply, but there wasn't sufficient air. I had to get up quickly. Instead of air pouring onto my face, I was sucking in. Something was definitely wrong. The lack of oxygen was causing tunnel vision, the first symptoms of asphyxiation. I jerked on my emergency guideline three times; the universal *Help, Distress*. I yanked hard three more times. Nothing! Where the hell... what were they doing? I grabbed onto the ladder to start my ascent. I wondered if the swift current tangled my lines around the ladder. They seemed heavier than usual.

I didn't have the strength to pull myself up. To stay calm and conserve air and energy, I continued the controlled breathing. Three more pulls on the emergency line... no response! Gasping for air I pulled myself up two rungs. The sweat was pouring down my face.

My eyes burned. I grabbed the third rung and held on for a couple of seconds to conserve strength. Something seemed to be holding me back; maybe the lines wrapped around the ladder. I again tried pulling myself up to the third rung. I had fifteen more to go. I didn't think I could make it, but I had to. I couldn't leave Jan and Diney out here by themselves. I *had* to get back. I pulled up another rung and glanced at the faint light above. I was looking through two narrow lights: tunnel vision closing in fast. I willed myself not to panic. I reached to the back for my belt knife to cut the lines securing my weights, and remove my weighted shoes, jacket and helmet. Unburdened, I could swim to the surface. I moved my hand back and forth before I realized the knife wasn't there. It was left it in the plane in the rush to the barge. A cardinal error. I felt trapped. Stay cool, breathe slowly, I repeated to myself, only there was no air to breathe. I could hear myself gasping for breath and no longer could hear the hiss of air coming in. The hose must be around the rope ladder, kinked, doubled up, and pinched off.

Something had cut off my air supply. I instinctively reached up to trace the air hose. My hand felt the firm rubber hose as far above as I could reach. It hadn't doubled back. Sliding down, my hand hit something that made a metallic click. It took me precious seconds to realize there shouldn't be anything between the hose and the brass helmet coupling. I felt myself slipping in and out of a conscious state as I tried to figure out what I was holding. It was a metal fixture with something round attached to it. What was that doing there? I couldn't think straight and forced myself to focus on what I was doing. As if studying Braille, my hand explored, trying to identify the object. I turned the round piece. It moved. Of course…it was a plumbing fixture, a turn on/turn off faucet. Turning it another 360 degrees, I felt a rush of fresh air pouring over my head. It was a loose plumbing fixture that wasn't secured. It must have been loose at the beginning of the dive. The vibrations of the swirling water and compressed air pouring in had slowly turned it shut.

I gulped the fresh air as my vision came back. My lungs once again filled with air. My thinking cleared. I could get to the top. I continued my climb until I broke the surface. I pounded on the deck of the platform. Two sets of hands quickly helped me up and out of my almost coffin suit. They untied my back and chest weights and helped me struggle out of the helmet. I slumped down on the barge. The lack of oxygen had taken its toll. I was totally exhausted. They handed me a black coffee laced with sugar. It took the better part of an hour before I felt normal again.

I thought there had better be some good answers to all the stupid, careless things I just experienced and yet I realized I would get the same old excuses and explanations, always a reason but never a good one. Life was cheap here, probably the reason why so many died diving for diamonds. I just saw a good example of how easily it could happen. Instead of wasting my time on explanations, I raised hell about no one monitoring the emergency line. I shut down the operation until we had our own facemasks and the quick release weight belts, which were somehow misplaced.

A few days later I moved the dredge off the sand bank and into the adjacent gravel. The crew found a few scattered diamonds, enough to pay operating expenses. I could have kicked myself for being talked into moving the dredge this far upstream. The gravel banks of *Maurice Mines* would have produced several hundred carats by now, and who knows what might be below the deeper pockets the dredge could open? With rainy season only weeks away, it would be risky and time consuming to move the dredge five miles. We would get there just in time to shut down for the season. We stayed and eked out enough diamonds to pay expenses. When Jan and I went over the books, we knew we couldn't go through another season like this one. A move was imperative.

BOX CANYON

Mat Tezarek, Joe's brother, chartered a DC-3 to Orinduik and arranged for me to shuttle the cargo to Velgrad, his home airstrip. Generally that was an easy one-day contract but this time the weather didn't cooperate; a front moved in. An early morning fog covered the ground like a wispy white blanket, clearing only at ten o'clock and delaying my first shuttle trip by two and a half hours. In spite of that, I felt I could complete the seven shuttles by five o'clock, enough time to make it home with a safe daylight margin. Velgrad, directly east of Orinduik, was a mere thirteen-minute flight by plane, but a grueling four days by trail.

A few miles east of Orinduik, the brown open rolling hill country ended and jungle took over. Three escarpments descended several hundred feet to the lush valley where Mat lived near his airstrip. Years earlier Indians had discovered high quality diamonds in the streams that traversed the valley. Mat, encouraged by his brother set up a permanent camp to prospect and trade. He found one hill void of heavy trees in an otherwise

Donald Haack

flat jungle-covered valley. Using local Indians, he built the 700 foot airstrip naming it Velgrad, the city in Eastern Europe where his parents lived. Before he built his house, he planted three avocado trees, which flourished and provided Mat with a super abundance of huge, luscious, avocados. I used any excuse to fly to Velgrad to trade, beg or borrow avocados to distribute among my rancher friends in the Rupununi. This was one of the few favors I could return.

By mid day on my fourth flight, heavy rain clouds moved in causing zero visibility above the last escarpment. The narrow space between land and clouds opened and closed several times, allowing only two flights. The day went agonizingly slow. At 4:30, I loaded the plane for the final trip. The clouds cooperated and lifted. As I taxied to the take off point, I felt a thump, thump, thump. I stopped, unbuckled and climbed out of the plane with the engine still idling. A flat tire! I eased the plane slowly back to level ground and shut down the engine. The two Indians who had loaded the plane, helped to unload the heavier cargo. To expedite the procedure, we lifted the wing until the wheel was high enough off the ground to place a stone below the axle to repair the flat... much quicker than using a jack.

It took the better part of an hour to remove the rim and tire and extract the inner tube. A barbed wire had punctured the tire and sliced a one-inch hole in the tube. If I hadn't stopped immediately, it would have shredded the inner tube to bits. At least I could repair this one with the patches I carried in the emergency kit. When I finished, more clouds had rolled in and light was fading quickly. I couldn't take the chance of making this last trip. I was forced to overnight—the last thing I wanted to do, leaving Jan, Diana and Tom home alone once again. But I had no choice.

Ordinarily I would have slept in the plane, but fully packed, it meant I would have to unpack and then repack in the morning. Without Indians to help, I decided instead to search for a place to bunk down. The small trade store was one possibility. I went in, bought a warm beer, a can of bully beef, an onion and some crackers. I used the key on the corned beef tin to open it, took out my pocketknife and slid the corned beef onto a napkin. I cut a slice of onion onto a cracker, followed by a thick slice of bully beef and lots of pepper. After eating several, I washed them down with copious amounts of beer. They tasted delicious, probably because I was starving.

Mrs. Correia, the storeowner, was asleep in one of the two rooms. Two of her girls tended the counter. I offered to share the corned beef and onions. They accepted so quickly, I had the feeling they hadn't eaten that night. I bought another corned beef and two more beers. My assumption was correct; they hadn't eaten. Mrs. Correia cooked something earlier in the day, they explained, but they thought it was spoiled and couldn't eat it. They had gone without food all day. They thanked me profusely and asked where I was going to sleep.

"I haven't figured that out yet. I have a hammock in the plane but I don't see any hooks in the shop to hang on."

"No problem" one said, "There's a spare bed in the back room and you're welcome to use it." The other nodded her head in agreement.

Following a hard day of flying, loading and unloading cargo, I was exhausted. After two beers and a couple of sandwiches, I could have slept standing up. I accepted their offer and brought my hammock to use as a blanket. The two sheets on the bed would not be enough when the temperature dropped at this altitude. A stiff breeze, humid and cold, came in from the jungle. I took off my shoes, wrapped up in my hammock and instantly fell asleep. The hammock didn't keep in much of the warmth and I slept fitfully. Later, there was a welcoming warmth on both sides and I slept soundly. Just before daybreak I turned on my side and the source of warmth on both sides moved in unison. In my state of half sleep, I didn't quite understand how that could be, but since the warm feeling prevailed, I slept on.

As daylight and light streaks entered through the cracks in the wood window shutters, I awakened to movements in bed. The two *warm objects* quietly got out of bed trying not to awaken me. They were both in the same clothes from the night before with shawls over their shoulders. They were my source of warmth and I realized they had given me their bed. When they knew I was asleep, they crawled in and the three of us shared the bed and warmth. I had to smile because the more I thought about it, the more ludicrous it became. Mrs. Correia brought the girls up here for business purposes. The bed was their place of business. They didn't want to embarrass me by offering to share their bed with them, so they let me fall asleep first, then came in, and left before they thought I had awakened. I reflected on the paradox of the evening. I spent the night sleeping with two *ladies of the night* who were proper enough to not want to cause me any embarrassment. Strange are the ways of bush life, I thought.

I got up, went down to the creek, washed, shaved and returned to pick up my bag and hammock. The bed was made, my hammock neatly folded. The two girls were cleaning the store and they bid me good morning and pointed to a hot strong coffee on the counter. No mention of the night before. I thanked them profusely for the good night's rest and the coffee. I thought I detected a hint of a smile exchanged between them but it was not obvious. Nothing else was said and I didn't want to delay. I needed an early start so I could return home and get back on schedule with the rest of my flights.

Total overcast. Ceiling, zero. No flight to Velgrad in that junk. I waited two hours. Still overcast to the east, but partially cleared to the north. I wondered if it were possible to go north around Kukenam, the two-mile high mountain, and then come into the valley from the east. At ten o'clock, I was totally frustrated. No weather break in the east, making it impossible to get into the valley. I decided a try to the north even though it was unfamiliar territory. I put in extra fuel figuring that if I stayed below the ceiling I might make it clear around Kukenam. The weather to the east was usually better and since Velgrad's elevation was lower, I might get in. I did not spend any time considering the alternative. I took off. Five minutes north of Orinduik, I left the rolling open country. I was over the seemingly endless carpet of jungle bordered by high escarpments that formed the Ireng corridor. If the maps were correct, it went directly north fifty miles before turning west to the tri-boundary of B G, Brazil and Venezuela. I planned to follow the river twenty miles then find a passage east and north of Kukenam. Flying due east for twenty minutes should put me on the east side of the mountain and on the Kaiteur plateau adjacent to the Velgrad valley.

Fifteen minutes up the Ireng, I turned right onto a heading of 90 degrees and if calculated correctly, the backside of Kukenam. The terrain ahead rose gradually and in the limited visibility another mountain appeared to the north. There was no mountain north of Kukenam on the map, but that was not unusual. Few if any maps were accurate in this mostly uncharted territory.

I didn't want to continue on a northern heading because the terrain rose substantially with no apparent space between the cloud layer and the ground. I remained on the easterly course I hoped would get me around Kukenam. I had at least a thousand feet between the clouds and the bush below. The new course, a tributary to the Ireng, put me above a shallow valley with quite visible rapids, which meant I was going up in elevation. This should have been a clear warning signal. Unfortunately I was concentrating on compass headings and elapsed time in case I had to do a *180* and return on this same route. I couldn't afford to be lost in a valley at 3500 foot elevation with two-mile high mountains in the vicinity.

I hugged what I thought was the north face of Kukenam. The river below and on my left wound tortuously with miniature waterfalls everywhere. It occurred to me that this would be a spectacularly beautiful flight in better weather. Too bad I couldn't appreciate it at the moment.

Ten minutes on my new track I noticed the compass heading drifting slightly to the south from 90 degrees to 100 degrees. Looking up ahead was another bend but it wasn't to the east, it was further right to the south. I shouldn't be coming around Kukenam this quickly—it was too big a mountain. I didn't have a good feeling about this. Another five minutes out, the heading on the last turn showed 115 degrees and instead of the mountain on the left receding to allow me to fly east, it was closing in to the south. The thought occurred to me that I was flying in a canyon between the two mountains but it should open up and turn east in the next few minutes. At least that's what I hoped.

In the next thirty seconds the opposite happened. The canyon did not open to the east, instead, on the next turn to the south, it closed in drastically with the terrain rising to near the cloud level. There was less than 500 feet between the clouds and the terrain ahead. The altimeter indicated 3800 feet. Without realizing it, I had climbed 300 feet, the clearance now between bush and clouds diminished rapidly.

The enormity of the problem hit me full force. I squinted out the windshield. I was in a dead end box canyon, a solid rock wall ahead. The river was no longer a river; it was a stream of water falling from the rock face above. I was trapped. The left face was too close to make a turn without going into a stall or slamming into rock. I felt the adrenaline shoot into the pit of the stomach like a bomb ready to explode. The back of my neck felt hot, my hairline tingled and adrenaline kicked in high gear. I knew what had to be done, but the thought of it scared the bejesus out of me. I fought to keep that feeling suppressed. Absolutely no room for negative thoughts in this situation.

My only salvation was a Himmelman maneuver. Going into clouds flying on instruments in a tight space presented the worst possible conditions for this maneuver. But then there was no other choice, a fact that intensely focused my thoughts.

I had practiced the Himmelman maneuver before but never in a fully loaded plane and never under anything but ideal conditions; clear sky, 5,000 feet high with all the visibility I needed in case I messed up. None of those amenities now and absolutely no margins for error. I knew it was possible—if everything was 100 percent correct. The Himmelman maneuver? Dive downward for speed into a loop, pull up and when on the top, upside down, flip the plane upright to continue the down side of the loop. The trick is two-fold: to know when the plane is upside down at the top of the loop, then flip it back to upright position while maintaining a heading exactly opposite to the direction started. Hopefully that would bring me down into the narrow canyon heading the direction I came from.

Before I shoved the throttle in full and pushed the nose down to increase air speed, I noted the compass heading of 160 degrees. There couldn't be more than two, three hundred feet between me and the mountain ahead. I would need that much for the climb out on the way up the loop.

I descended, increasing airspeed to140...150mph. A hundred feet from the ground, I pulled up. The altimeter rose, 3400, 3500, 3600, and at 3800 I was IFR in the clouds, which obliterated all visual contact with the outside. My only world was the array of instruments in front of me. The G force pushed me down in the seat. Completely on instruments, I hoped to break out in the opposite direction in less than thirty seconds— an eternity. Altitude 3850, 3900, airspeed dropped to 110, 100, 90. I held another two seconds, altitude 3950, 3975, another second at 3975, then an almost imperceptible drop to 3950, airspeed 95. The top of the loop, I hoped, and upside down. I eased back on the wheel and felt a light strain further confirming I was near zero gravity, upside down.

I kicked full rudder and opposite aileron. My insides felt like they were falling out. Now I had to ignore all physical feelings and rely strictly on instruments. After two seconds, I should be right side up. My eyes were glued to the turn and bank, the quickest responding instrument that would let me know when the wings were level. When they were I checked altitude—descending at 300 feet per minute. Airspeed: 120. I pulled on full flaps, reduced power to 50 percent and checked carburetor heat to keep it from freezing; a primary cause of engine failure in clouds.

At reduced speed and descending, the plane was in level flight, no turns. The lower air speed gave me a couple of seconds margin like flying in slow motion. The next critical step was the heading. The gyroscope compass came around first indicating 10 degrees north. I hoped it was right. That placed me too far to the right and perilously close to that rock face. I quickly turned, over-correcting and held for four seconds. If calculations were correct, I turned 20 degrees off course in the loupe and my new heading should be 350 degrees. The magnetic compass stopped its wild swinging after being upside down and reversing course and settled at 352 degrees, within 2 degrees of the gyro. Up to that point I could only hope the gyro compass was correct. I quietly thanked the fact that magnetic compasses near the equator correct three or four seconds faster after a turn, than they do in either northern or southern latitudes.

Five seconds passed. Altimeter showed 3800 feet. If everything were correct, I should break out into visual in a few seconds. I had to. I knew it was impossible to fly any length of time on instruments in a narrow canyon. I pushed the nose down further, the flaps held airspeed to 85. I flew as slow as possible allowing extra seconds to make calculations and maneuvers. Every second gave me an extra margin and could keep me from flying into the canyon wall. Another long six seconds elapsed and still not visual. I couldn't wait. I had to make a correction for the next turn to 290 degrees and I better be where I'm supposed to be. No time for doubts, I had to believe my timing and headings were correct.

Altimeter; 3750, 3700, still not descending fast enough. I pushed the nose down further. I had to get visual within seconds. Airspeed still held at 85. In another eight seconds I made the correction of another 10 degrees to hopefully stay in the canyon. It had been twenty seconds and ten seconds on my last two turns entering this canyon, so I had to repeat the procedure in reverse, only this time blind and adding a few seconds for the reduced speed.

Gyro heading settled in at 310, I eased a bit more west to 300. I was more afraid of crashing into the wall on my right. I felt I had a bigger margin on the other side coming in. I hoped I was right. Altimeter 3650. Why the hell am I not in the clear at this altitude? Coming in, I estimated the bush at 3300 feet and the cloud ceiling at 3800. Magnetic compass settled in at 302 degrees, gyro showed 300, not too bad considering the antics I just put them through.

Donald Haack

I eased a couple of degrees more to the left, pulled back on the power, altitude indicated 3600, clouds now a bit wispy. Couldn't see ahead, but the space below revealed the river to the left. I eased a bit more left. Ten more seconds of reduced airspeed and, if I calculated correctly, should be on the reciprocal of 105 or 285 degrees. The gyro indicated 295 degrees, too far right.

I pulled a hard wing-down turn 10 degrees left to get to 285. Now I could see clearly below me and slightly ahead. Altimeter, 3550 feet, which would put me only 200 feet above the bush. The ceiling must have closed in another 200 feet lower. I dropped my wing slightly to the right to check visibility. The canyon wall loomed less than a hundred feet away. I must have been just yards away before my last turn. I shuddered at the thought that if I hadn't pulled that hard turn when I did, I would now be part of the landscape. The knot in my stomach got a bit harder, but I was lucky. I was still up here.

That also answered my question as to why the bush was so close below me. The terrain rose a couple of hundred feet higher at the base of the cliffs. As I eased to the left, the land dropped off drastically giving me the extra couple of hundred feet between the clouds and bush. I trimmed up the plane and pulled up the flaps to retrace my flight back.

Now I felt drained emotionally and only wanted to be on terra firma. I double-checked my compass headings. There was a choice between two valleys up ahead and I realized I wasn't out of this nightmare flight yet. I didn't remember this other valley coming in, but then thinking back, if I came in from the west, unless I looked back, I couldn't have seen the valley coming in from behind. But now, backtracking I had to make a choice. The canyon widened but I had to choose which fork to take…it had to be a course heading downstream. The rapids should help in my decision.

With more maneuvering space in front of the fork, I eased to the right and tilted the wing down where I could get a better look at the river, barely visible in the thick bush. Then I caught a glimpse of white water over rocks, the white being on my side, so the river was flowing downstream toward me. I didn't want that valley, probably another dead end. I took the left valley and in a few minutes, I was over the much larger Ireng and I could see the light of the savannas ahead.

Someone was on my side. I quietly gave thanks for my pre-planning and for having practiced a maneuver I never expected to use. In minutes, I crossed over the demarcation between jungle and open savanna and in the distance I saw the cleared area of Orinduik. As I approached, the airstrip came into full view. With the adrenalin rush over, I felt my body drifting into an oppressive come-down, an overwhelmingly depressed feeling as though the energy fluid were draining out of me like air leaking from a tire. It started with a light feeling in the head, then drifted downward, expanding into the chest and arms, which now felt like lead weights. Everything became a big chore even the slightest throttle changes and steering. I knew I had to get down fast. All I could think of was lying down and sleep. It took every bit of energy just to aim towards the airport.

I approached at twice my normal speed, dispensed with any go-around to clear the strip, pulled back the power to idle, pulled on full flaps for a straight-in landing, undoubtedly the fastest ever. I taxied to the side, shut down the engine, climbed out, chocked the wheels, pulled out a blanket and stumbled along the trail to Orinduik Falls. The spectacular ninety-foot falls dropped in three sections. This trail went to mid-falls following a path between two rock outcroppings and ended at a soft dry patch of grass. I curled up into a fetal position and wrapped the blanket around me. It wasn't cold but I craved warmth. I wondered if I were in the first stage of shock. The normal procedure—keep the patient warm.

With a slight change in wind a light mist drifted over that felt cool on the face. In the background, the tumbling water took on many familiar sounds: the crashing of cymbals opening a symphony score, rushing water cascading over rocks was the violin section moving to a fast tempo. The wind gusted from light to heavy creating the background of oboes, clarinets and flutes, perfectly in harmony and adding depth to round out the score. The maestro stood at the bottom of the falls directing the crescendos then easing into softer sounds, allowing the oboe soloist to emerge. I had the urge to look up to verify that scenario but instead I fell into a deep void of mind-numbing sleep while the symphony continued.

I fell from the sky. I dodged trees in narrow corridors and banked steeply so as not shear off the wings. I flew into black bottomless canyons and felt the airplane disintegrate while I hurtled into space below. The symphony played on flawlessly. Another plane had the front torn off. I hung precariously to keep from falling out while attempting to balance and steer at the same time. Black voids appeared on all sides. I must avoid them lest I disappear forever. The airplane shook violently. It got worse. I awoke. Someone was shaking my arm and calling my name.

"Captain Haack! Captain Haack! Are you all right? Madam Correia sent us to find you and make sure you were okay. She saw you land, leave the plane, and stagger off to the river. When you didn't return in an hour she became worried and sent us here to find you." She repeated again, "Are you all right, you look a bit funny?"

I tried to open my eyes. They felt stuck. I tried to focus, to no avail. I drifted between the vibrating airplane and the girl's hand shaking me. What was real? What was a dream? Gradually, the girl shaking me won out. I opened my mouth and the only words that came out were, "Where do you want me?" I thought about that for a second or two and realized that didn't make any sense. That wasn't what she was asking. "An hour?" I mumbled. "Have I been here for an hour?" I was thinking, *only* an hour? It seemed like days, weeks, an eternity, a different life. Now she stopped shaking and was looking at me a bit oddly.

'You're not okay, are you?" She looked a little scared. "Maybe I should call Madam Correia."

"No, no." I assured her. "I was just in a deep sleep. Pretty tired. It was a bad trip and I needed the rest. I'm okay. No need to concern Madam. I'm getting up." I struggled to my feet. They didn't seem to belong to the rest of my body but they obeyed. I put one in front of the other. The girls walked a few paces behind me. I glanced back at them. They were concerned I wouldn't make it. At the top of the hill, they took the path to the store. I took the one to the plane.

I approached it but did not get in. I put my hand on the wing. It felt cold and foreign and I wondered if I could go back in again. There was a barrier. My hand remained on the wing for several minutes. Then an imperceptible change occurred. It was no longer cold to the touch, no longer a stranger. The plane and I had returned from a strange voyage together. I felt a bonding with this inanimate object. Did it have a soul, I wondered? We survived together. The kinship and closeness was forceful and compelling. I opened the door. It was inviting. I went in and experienced an emotion akin to slipping your hand into a familiar, comfortable, old worn glove. It fit perfectly, I thought.

Donald Haack

TO LIVE OR DIE

The requests for emergency missions escalated to the point where I had to make decisions about which ones I could do. I felt like a triage nurse. Some of the requests were being abused, but there was no way of knowing in advance. The one that proved to be the most frustrating of all involved Toman Davis, who worked for me part time. Toman, working with the local Indians had done an excellent job on the tobacco project. It would be another six months before he would need to work on it again. He told me that in the past two months there had been many requests for him to buy cattle, so many that he couldn't handle them all. He was going to take on his older brother, Servi to help him on the round up.

Toman brought Servi to Marquis on his first run with cattle from Tipuru. He didn't look anything like Toman. It was hard to imagine they were even brothers. Servi could not look you in the eye, he rarely spoke and looked old enough to be Toman's father. Toman was tall and well proportioned, Servi was short and emaciated, probably from his heavy drinking, which everyone knew about. Servi shook hands with me and gave a short speech on how he wanted to *get his life straightened out* and working with Toman would help him do just that. It was a sincere sounding plea and I quietly hoped it would work out. It would be a win-win for everyone.

The first of several calls came from Toman and was delivered by a Macusi from Karasabai village. Toman wrote he had a family emergency: his brother, Servi had suddenly taken very sick and needed immediate attention. Could I come to Karasabai and fly him out? It was written *Friday*; no date but I assumed it was yesterday.

I questioned the Indian. He said Toman gave him the note the day before. I felt more justified about flying to the village today. I gassed the plane and fifteen minutes later touched down at Karasabai.

I spent an hour asking everyone in the village, including the Tuchow and Peayman, about Toman's brother and his illness. The story I pieced together was that, yes, someone was sick. They think it was Toman's brother, but they weren't sure. Yes, he recovered this morning and both Toman and he left shortly thereafter. No, there was no note for me. But they were glad I came. It was always nice to see the Americano land with his airplane on their strip. They were glad they fixed up the airstrip they said as they smiled broadly. Very happy.

Rather than waste the trip completely, I flew on to Good Hope to ferry gas and rations. Even though we were not short on supplies, they would be used eventually and this false alarm wouldn't be a total loss. The next time I saw Toman, I would have to talk to him about emergencies. The *next time* was supposed to be in two weeks but because of bad timing, the shortage of gas and the cancellation of one B.G. Airways charter, we didn't connect.

The following week Nellie handed me another note from Toman.

"Toman arrived yesterday but didn't stay. He left this for you. Apparently his brother had an accident cutting trees near his home. Nellie didn't know whether it was Servi or another of his five brothers. They built an airstrip near the house and they're cleaning it up so you can land today. His brother is bleeding badly and needs to be flown to Lethem. He asked me if I thought you would be there early in the morning or when. I didn't know… only that you were coming today to meet the mail plane and that I'd pass on his message. He left on horseback yesterday morning and should have reached his house by noon. Can you do it?" Nellie knew about the previous false alarms and how scarce gasoline was.

I said, "I know the airstrip; I dropped Toman and Servi there two weeks ago. That's no problem but the shortage of gas is. B.G. Airways is two weeks late in delivering aviation gas and diesel for the dredge. I've reduced the number of trips and canceled several charters. Worse, I can't get to all my trade stores up North and they're holding diamonds for me. To keep their operations going they'll sell the diamonds for rations and fuel at exorbitant prices and then will be hard put to pay what they owe me. I guess this is an emergency, so I'll go for Toman's brother. It sounds serious.

"Do you want me to accompany you in case it's a serious medical problem?" she asked.

"Ordinarily yes, but we may have a stretcher case here and if Toman wants to stay with his brother all the way to Lethem there won't be room for you. Guess I'll chance it and see if we can bring him out."

As I made a pass over Toman's runway, I thought it odd no one was around the strip or near the houses. My thoughts focused to landing on this short strip and not on speculation why there were no people. After taxiing back to the start of the airstrip, I shut down the engine and expected to be met by someone. No one came. I climbed out and looked around. Not a soul in sight. Maybe they were all inside trying to keep the patient alive. I went to the door. It was open. I called. No one answered. I hollered, whistled, and shouted. Nothing.

No one was there. I walked into the two houses next door. A few dogs barked and threatened until I clapped my hands. They ran with their tail between their legs. It was like a ghost town.

Donald Haack

I sat on a chair on Toman's porch and waited. There was barely any breeze and it was hot. My hands and arms were sweaty and the wet marks in my khaki shirt spread out from under my arms and over my back. No one came. I went back to the plane, retrieved my binoculars, and scanned the horizon. I spotted a person about a half-mile out walking this way. *One person...a woman.* I looked at my watch. The brown wet leather band was stained to a dark black color from perspiration. The crystal was a bit foggy from condensation underneath. The Omega was supposed to be waterproof, but in this climate condensation was ever-present.

It took her fifteen minutes to arrive at the house. She spoke to me in Macusi. I answered in Brazilian. She nodded. Her Brazilian was worse than mine but adequate enough to explain that everyone left in the morning.

"There was a drunken party two nights ago...broken bottles, glass, and blood everywhere. One of the men was cut pretty bad. This morning they went down to the creek to wash up. There was more drinking, more fighting. Finally they all left."

"Was anyone left behind—injured or killed?"

"No, they were too drunk to kill each other. They could barely stand. Stupid men. That's the only thing they can do well—get drunk. And they do that well. Look, the house needs fixing, the newborn calves need tending, the fences are down, the cattle are out, and the well needs repairing. So what do they do? They get drunk," she said, spitting out the last words.

She turned towards me again as if she saw me for the first time.

"So what are you doing here, you and your plane?" and she pointed her nose twice towards the plane sitting on the strip.

"Toman wrote and asked me to come. Emergency...to save his brother who was badly injured," Looking around this desolate place, I wondered just what the hell I was doing here.

"Injured? Wounded? Hah, bah. The only thing wounded is their...." she used a word I didn't understand but she tapped her head. I knew she meant brains. "They're all wounded there." she ranted, and shook her head in disgust.

Donald Haack

It seemed useless to spend any more time here. I said good-bye to the old woman. She nodded and turned away. She had said her piece.

Caesar arrived at the airstrip before the engine shut down. He motioned me over to the jeep.

"How did you know I didn't have any passengers," I asked. He didn't look up. The freshly rolled cigarette was held between his clenched teeth. He was half smiling as he spoke so as not to break the rhythm of lighting up in the wind.

"Didn't have to ask. Those Annai guys were always having emergencies and they always survived. Couldn't even do a good job of killing themselves no matter how hard they tried. Like cats, have nine lives. What did they tell you?" He looked over to me after the smoke indicated the cigarette was lit.

"No one was there. Apparently they had a drunken brawl last night and they're all gone according to one old lady left behind." I was about to get back in the plane. Caesar pointed to the jeep instead.

"Hop in, Nellie has tea ready for us." I chocked the plane climbed into the jeep and we lurched off toward the ranch house. Nellie had the tea waiting for us.

"Another false alarm?" she asked without waiting for an answer. " 'C' brought something you might like from town," and she pointed to the platter displaying a large piece of gorgonzola cheese, thick slices of raw onions, and freshly baked brown bread.

"Ah, a feast for a king." A welcome change in diet, I thought, which made me less angry about the false alarm.

A fortnight later after a long day of flying, I picked up Jan and the kids and we flew to Good Hope for the mail pick up. We accepted Nellie's invitation to spend the night at Good Hope. Jan thoughtfully brought avocados and passion fruit for our hosts.

A few minutes later Caesar arrived from rounding up cattle and handed me a note.

Donald Haack

"Your business partner…again," he said in carefully cadenced words, "wants your service on yet another mercy mission. Seems *another* brother is sick with fever and the note asks if you can fly him to Lethem for treatment." He raised his eyebrows waiting for me to respond.

I didn't know what to say. I waited a minute. "I'm in no shape to fly anywhere today. Been to Orinduik and four stops along the way. We really appreciate your invitation to bunk down with you tonight. No, I don't think we'll make that flight tonight or tomorrow. I doubt if it's a real emergency. If we go by past experiences, it probably isn't." I felt relieved at coming to that decision quickly and not having to justify the rationalization behind it.

Two days later we heard that Toman's brother, Servi died from fever—apparently malaria.

AMBUSH

After I completed most of Mrs. Correia's charter flights at Orinduik she introduced me to a guy named Gonzales. "He wants you to supply rations to his Brazilian store. Says he has a good airstrip. Could you do a trip for him tomorrow when you finish your flying here?" she queried.

My first impression of Gonzales was negative and I should have relied on my instincts. Instead, because the flying and trading business brought in substantial income, I got caught up in the euphoria of success and accepted the charter. The next day after I completed Mrs. Correia's flights I loaded up Gonzales, his cargo and took off.

Fifteen minutes out of Orinduik, I was in uncharted territory. The legendary *Lost World*, Mt. Roraima, loomed high into the clouds a few miles north. Its summit wasn't visible but the lower 8,000 feet offered an enormous aura. Gonzales' airstrip was sited on the west bank of the second river coming from the base of Roraima. The airstrip would be easy to spot at a point south of where that creek made a sharp right and then left turn. Creeks were easy to spot: dark green lines etched in a brown landscape. After twenty minutes of flying, I spotted the airstrip right where it was supposed to be.

I made two passes to determine the condition and to chase off the usual chickens and other livestock. It was a typical interior airstrip constructed on a hill facing into the prevailing easterly wind. Flapping lightly, a piece of cloth masquerading as a windsock confirmed a light breeze. On the third pass I landed and stopped short of the Gonzales' mud brick trade store. After we emptied the plane he informed me of an emergency. His brother's Indian wife was critically sick, probably malaria, and was much too weak to walk or be carried out by bullock. Gonzales pleaded with me to fly her to Orinduik to meet the DC-3 to Georgetown. He said he had made arrangements with Mrs. Correia to have his sister-in-law flown to Georgetown. His brother's airstrip was ten minutes further west.

I was skeptical; if Mrs. Correia knew about this, why didn't she tell me? Nothing was said about an emergency. I didn't like the sound of it. This was already far out of my usual flying territory—more than a half-hour into Brazil, southwest of Santa Elena, Venezuela.

He played on my Samaritan emotions and I reluctantly agreed, but the bad vibes persisted. Gonzales offered to show me the way. Fifteen minutes after I took off we landed on his brother's strip. Hernando looked even sleazier than his brother. The two other hombres hanging around his store were no better. All four of them wore guns. There were no introductions. I felt more uncomfortable than ever. I asked Hernando where his wife was and he replied that a couple of Indians had gone for her and should return shortly. He pointed to a well-worn path towards a hill. His house was on the other side.

Waiting a longtime for her was not an option. I had to leave in twenty minutes, two hours before dark. He assured me it was no problem and offered me a drink of his special rum. I refused, explaining I couldn't fly and drink. He insisted I just try a small one. I refused as politely as I could but I disliked his arrogance and insistence.

He kept repeating how sick his wife was and how appreciative he was that I was saving her life. "We have two children and she is a good mother and wife. What more could a man ask for in this world?" he added.

His story didn't sound right, but unfortunately I was caught up in a scenario difficult to exit. If his story were true, leaving now would seem like I didn't care if she died, which they assured me would happen without my flight. A young boy out of breath came up the path and talked to Hernando.

"My wife took a turn for the worse," he translated. "She was throwing up blood and couldn't move but she now can travel to the plane and will be here soon."

These excuses and delays stretched into an hour-and-a-half and too late to fly. They apologized profusely saying they would have her here first thing in the morning. Staying overnight was the last thing I wanted to do, but now there was no alternative. I tied down the airplane for the night.

The offer of food and drinks continued. I didn't trust his food and I certainly did not want to drink rum. I had my own bully beef. I asked for some crackers and a beer. I was thirsty and knew he couldn't tamper with the beer. I sliced an onion I carried with me, layering it between a slice of beef and cracker, and washed it down with warm Brazilian beer... a gourmet meal. Hernando was insistent I drink his rum. There must be a reason and I would find out why.

I ostensibly joined him in several shots, but instead of drinking his rum, I surreptitiously poured it through a crack in the floor. I assured him it was good rum. Truth was, it was lousy. After five or six shots, I pretended to be drowsy. They showed me to a back area of the store where they hung a hammock and handed me a blanket. The building was divided into thirds: the store in front, behind that a room with goods and food, and the third used as their bedroom.

I was to sleep in the one with goods and food. They hung the hammock near a huge open window—for fresh air, they said.

Acting is if I weren't in control, I excused myself and stumbled to the hammock, closed the door and quietly bolted it. A partial moon came up giving enough light to see the airstrip and plane.

I didn't wear my pistol. It was in the flight bag I'd brought in earlier. I checked it, pulled back on the slide and slowly eased it forward to put a round in the chamber. This would be a long night without sleep. I would leave early in the morning with or without his wife. I had a story concocted about how I had to meet the mail plane but would return later. In actual fact, I would never return to this place. My problem now was to get out in one piece. I was thoroughly convinced they had something nefarious in mind: the airplane, money, Gonzales' payment in diamonds, or the diamonds they thought I was carrying from Mrs. Correia.

My feeling was reinforced when I first arrived and walked in the store. All four men wore pistols but no one disarmed inside the store. I learned at Tatahiera's house in Brazil not to carry a gun into a dwelling unless you had hostile intentions.

The "suspects" were talking in low voices in the adjacent room, but I couldn't make out what they were saying. I waited until they thought I was asleep and then lifted one of the one hundred pound bags of flour into the hammock. I placed the pillow at one end and covered everything with the blanket. I hoped it looked like a fair facsimile of me in the hammock. With another blanket hiding me, I took up a position near the window. Now came the waiting game.

An hour passed and nothing happened except I was getting sleepy. The adrenaline that had kept me awake was gone. I remembered George's potion. It might help to stay awake. I removed the small package from my emergency ration packet, unraveled the leaves, and placed one of the little hard round balls on my tongue. I allowed the foul-tasting sphere to slowly dissolve. There was no immediate reaction.

After a few minutes, I could hear their conversation and understood some of what they said, enough to know that Dominic, one of the other two men, was chosen to do something. Hernando instructed him to use the machete, not the *pistola*.

Donald Haack

At this point their intentions couldn't be clearer and I would have to be one step ahead of them. The fourth person, called *Little Pedro* would be a back up to use the *pistola* if necessary. Hernando and Gonzales were to wait in the shop and cover the rear of the building in case I got out. Someone kept saying *cabeza, cabeza,* over and over to make sure Dominic went for the head and not the feet by mistake. They mentioned the word *Jivaro* several times. I knew then what they had in mind and why they didn't want to use a gun—they would blame the deed on the Jivaro Indians who used machetes, not guns.

The killing of an American pilot would cause an investigation by the Federales. Hernando and Gonzales didn't want that and figured they could pull this coup by claiming the Jivaro Indians did it. From their muffled conversation, I heard them repeat the words *Yanamamis* and *Jivaro*, two adjoining tribes. The Yanamamis, a primitive but docile tribe, lived within two hours walk,

The Jivaros, headhunters from the far western territory, seldom came this far east. In the past they came regularly to hunt and trade. They sold black market shrunken heads to the Venezuelans who paid big money. When they traveled, the Jivaros stuck strictly to trade and studiously avoided any conflict. The local Indians took advantage of their presence by murdering enemies, cutting off their heads, and blaming it on the Jivaros in the area. The innocent Jivaros had to flee, fearful for their lives threatened by tribes seeking revenge. Eventually, few Jivaros ventured this far east, but even in their absence they were blamed for the headless corpses. Just the thought gave me a very queasy feeling and the hair stood up all over my body.

The potion took affect more strongly than the first time. My mind raced from thought to thought, unchecked. I wondered why we, a civilized people, think the Jivaros were savages because they adorned their belts with their defeated enemies' heads. After all, our own soldiers do the same thing; wear their trophies on their coat: their medals and ribbons indicating the battles they fought in. The Jivaros may shrink a dozen heads in a lifetime. One soldier's medal may represent two hundred heads or a bomb dropped on a thousand or two thousand women and children. Doesn't this make the comparison of a dozen shrunken heads by Jivaros pale? So why does our society look down at the Jivaros as savages?

Why I was thinking such strange anomalies with all this trouble around me, I didn't know, but it had something to do with the stimulant. I tried to focus my racing wandering mind on the problem at hand. I should've been scared out of my wits, instead was thinking of situations entirely irrelevant to the present problem. It was as if I were a spectator watching an event. I forced myself to concentrate on the four men and what they were doing. From the side of the window I saw two of them approach and heard every whispered word. I understood a little. They assumed I was sound asleep. Little Pedro stepped up to the window a few feet away out of my sight, but not out of my hearing. In his drunken state, he was breathing heavily.

I had advantages: I knew what they were planning; I could hear and see better; I was sober, they were drunk and I felt pretty sure I could shoot faster and more accurately. Most importantly, I had the element of surprise. They were convinced I was drunk and asleep in the hammock. They didn't know I stood stark sober in the shadows, heard every word, and held a loaded semi-automatic with a spare eight-round clip in my belt. Their revolvers were all poorly maintained, typically dirty with rust and mud around the barrels and looking like they hadn't been fired in months. But I learned never to underestimate an opponent, especially four of them, and treated the situation as if they were all crack shots with good weapons.

My over-stimulated mind had already mapped out a plan with several alternatives. As the men came closer, I flattened against the wall and I followed their shadows as they cautiously approached the window, yet whispered drunkenly.

The one called Dominic neared and waited until his eyes were accustomed to the darkened interior. He leaned over the windowsill until his whole upper torso was in the room. Apparently he tried to make out the form in the hammock, but was unsure which end was the head. A flour sack will do that, I thought, in my strange euphoria. He pulled back out of the room to consult with little Pedro. Pedro stuck his head in pointing to the far side of the hammock where I placed the pillow.

Pedro pulled back, and Dominic returned. He leaned far inside, both hands grasping a machete, and slowly and unsteadily raised it. I brought up my pistol. The sights had a touch of white gloss enamel, easy to see in subdued light. It wasn't necessary to be worried about accuracy, however; at this close range it was an easy shot. I pointed and squeezed the trigger. The loud report and the metallic clang of lead against machete blade reverberated throughout the room. Torn out of his hands, the machete bounced off the far wall. Dominic let loose a yelp of terror. In shock and out of balance from the sting in his hands and the noise and surprise of the machete snatched away, he fell halfway into the room, right in front of me.

Change in plans. I expected Dominic to immediately pull back from the window. I intended to fire a second shot at his feet and shout, "Run, run for your lives." That would keep them in a state of confusion.

When Dominic fell in his upper torso was hanging in the room, his feet and legs outside. He was inches away unaware of my presence. I made the best of the situation. Using both hands, I brought down the heavily weighted pistol barrel as hard as I could on Dominic's head. The sound reminded me of a native splitting a coconut with a machete. Without a sound Dominic fell limp over the windowsill. I reached over, slipped off the safety, stuck the pistol out the window, pointed at the ground, and squeezed off another round. I didn't expect little Pedro to be so close—I almost made him a eunuch. He let out a scream, dropped his pistol, and ran. I wasn't sure if he was hit or not, but to add to the confusion, I shouted loudly: not words, inhuman demonic sounds. I almost scared me.

Climbing over Dominic and out the window, I very quietly crept to the front of the shop staying in the shadows awaiting Hernando and Gonzales. They came running out the door with guns ready. Hidden in the darkness I fired two rounds at their feet yelling, "Funcione para su vida. Dominic esta inoperante. Funcione ou voce sera inoperante demasiado." Run, run for your lives! Dominic is dead! Run or you will be dead, too." I counted on complete confusion and I wasn't disappointed. I fired several shots in the air. Other rounds hit rocks, orchestrating shrieking staccatos of ricocheting bullets. I ran behind and stuck in the second clip and fired six of the eight rounds, keeping two back for insurance. The noise was numbing. Fourteen rounds were fired in less than a minute…followed by shouting and running.

I stopped to re-load the first clip. With so many rounds fired, Gonzales and gang probably thought a small army was chasing them and in their panic and haste to escape, no one fired his pistol. Hearing Dominic was dead, they undoubtedly felt lucky to escape with their lives.

I chased them as far as I dared. The last I saw of the three was on the way up the hill before they disappeared on the other side. I fired a quick burst of four more rounds to keep them running.

I waited, listened. Hearing nothing unusual, I headed back to the building to check on Dominic and to ensure no one else was in the area. I heard no movement, no sound other than the distant howler monkeys and the light rustle of grass that synchronized with the gentle trade breeze. I cautiously approached the side of the building. Dominic still hung lifelessly over the sill. I worried that I might have hit him too hard and he really was dead. I lifted him outside. He groaned…a good sign. In the moonlight I saw the lump on the back of his head. It would get bigger. I touched it. It felt wet. There was blood through his hair and down to his forehead. He started to move a bit. I dragged him around the front of the shop, took off his belt and propped him against a main support post. I pulled his hands behind his back around the pole and secured them with his belt.

I looked at my watch, 4:30 a.m. This whole incident from Dominic leaning inside the window until now happened in less than fifteen minutes. I took out my binoculars from the emergency kit and scanned the horizon where I last saw the backs of Gonzales and his two companions. Nothing in the area stirred. The shots caused dogs in the far valley to bark, but now they too were quiet. The stillness of the bush covered the valley like a heavy blanket, as though nothing out of the ordinary had occurred. At daylight, I was sure the three would return, perhaps on another path. I would not be here to meet them.

I looked for paper to leave a note, but thought better of it. They would hear soon enough after I filed a detailed report to the governor about their false emergency and attempted murder. They would have their hands full with the Federales from Boa Vista.

I checked the plane thoroughly. Everything seemed to be in order. I double-checked Dominic. He was groaning louder but still not conscious. I climbed back through the window to the room I was to have slept in, removed the flour sack, and straightened out the hammock. I folded the blanket and left it on the pillow. That would confuse them when they tried to figure out what went wrong—how I could be in two places or who else was there and who shouted, "Run, for your lives. Dominic is dead." But he wasn't dead, only knocked out. It would keep them guessing long enough, I hoped, to stop any future nefarious plans they may concoct.

I picked up my overnight bag and emergency kit, removed the binoculars, and scanned the horizon one last time for any signs of Hernando and his hideaway friends. Nothing. I walked to the plane at 5:30, cranked up the starter, and taxied by dim moonlight to the end of the runway. I looked over to see Dominic rolling and shaking his head. He would have some headache for a few days. Without a wind, it made little difference which direction I took off in. I chose east, directly towards home. I left the lights off, revved up to 3200 RPM. I accelerated down the runway, continually scanning the instruments to avoid vertigo that could occur in those few seconds of transition between a visual takeoff and instrument flying in an area devoid of reference lights.

Airborne, I kept half-flaps and climbed to 4,000 feet, well above any hills in the area and went into *slow-flight:* 95 knots, 2000 RPM, which conserved gas as I awaited daybreak for visual references before crossing the border into the higher mountain country. There was enough light at 5:50 a.m. to see the outline of the Ireng river and Orinduik. I checked my watch. I had ingested George's potion four hours ago and hadn't slept all night. The effects were wearing off. All I wanted was to lie down and sleep.

I didn't tell Jan about the incident other than it was a financial disaster and that I wouldn't go that far into Brazil again. She seemed relieved. I stashed my little pack of George's medicine behind the Collins radio in our library and forgot about it. Weeks later I decided to take it to town and possibly ship it to the States to be analyzed. I knew it had some useful medicinal properties. The enhancing of the senses and the apparent ability to create a slow motion scenario in a crises could be an extremely useful tool.

I looked behind the Collins transmitter. The packet wasn't there.

"Jan, did you see a little leaf-pouch on the desk behind the transmitter?" I asked as casually as I could.

"Oh, yes, it looked like some something the mice dragged in and made into a nest. I threw it out."

"Where?" I asked too quickly.

"What difference does it make? It was just some old leaves."

"Do you know where you threw it? There was something in there I wanted to check out and analyze. It's something the Indians use and I wanted to know if it had any special medicinal value."

"In the trash and Ramdat burned it."

THE FLOOD

W e were still at breakfast enjoying a second cup of coffee. Sunday morning was the only time we could do that. Jan looked outside and stopped talking. I followed her gaze and saw Harry approaching up the path. He wore all his emotions on his sleeve so was easy to read. His gait was troubled, slouching. His hand held the right side of his stomach, an indication his ulcer was kicking in again.

As he came closer, I noticed his face was taut, his eyes on the ground, shoulders slumped. All I could think of was the cartoon character in L'il Abner—Joe Blftsk, the little man who walked dejectedly beneath a dismal rain cloud that followed him wherever he went. All Harry needed was the rain cloud to make the image real. Jan and I exchanged worried glances.

He refused a cup of coffee. "Ulcer's back," was his only comment. We waited. He shuffled back and forth and finally sat down at my urging and seemed relieved to get the weight off his feet.

Donald Haack

"Don, we got a problem. Big one. Equipment's gone." No further explanation.

"What do you mean equipment's gone? The dredge? Tools? Did someone move the barges? What?" I waited for an answer.

"Everything, it's all gone." He didn't know how to explain and I gave him time to gather his thoughts before I asked again. Finally he continued, "The rains must have started way up in the mountains near Mt. Roraima. We saw lightning in the sky a couple of nights ago but didn't think much of it. It must have been a big storm, causing a flash flood. The river came up almost twenty feet last night and wiped away all three barges: the dredge, the dewatering cone, and the mineral jig. They're all gone. No trace. Just the cable hanging on one side of the river."

I sat there dumb struck, not knowing what to say...or ask.
"Let's get in the plane and take a look from above. They must be hung up somewhere along the river. The faster we find them the easier it'll be to bring them back," I said with more hope than conviction.

Harry's face lit up with the anticipation that we would find them and at least there was something tangible to work on. We were airborne in less than ten minutes. I flew upriver to the barge site first. The view was unbelievable. Yesterday, the river was black, almost clear, ambling twenty feet down below the banks, wending its way cautiously around the rocks and narrows. Now it was a monster out of control. Brown, muddy, frothing water charged uncontrolled, flooding over its banks in several places. Spinning round and round in a surrealistic landscape, whole trees were caught in these whirlpools. I was shocked at the power of the river and its abrupt and harsh change on the landscape.

Neither of us spoke. I turned 180 degrees to fly downstream. Even from up above, the speed of the water was frightening. It appeared that nothing could stand in its way, an onslaught that wiped out everything in its path. A few miles downstream we passed Marquis without seeing a trace of equipment. As I turned to go down the pass between the mountains, I pointed out my window. "Harry, down there on the left, just below Maurice

Mines, isn't that one of the barges?" I dropped lower and pulled on flaps to slow down for a better look. The barrels were all intact, the barge was upside down, nothing else around.

We continued down the pass all the way to the Karasabai valley where we could see for miles ahead. But we saw nothing! Nothing but raging water.

"My God, Harry, that must have happened early last night to have carried the barges this far down in a few hours. Wherever they are, they're too far gone to ever try to retrieve them. With the force and speed of that river, I have to believe that most of the equipment was lost immediately after the cable snapped and is in the first mile or two of what used to be rapids. We won't be able to do any searching and diving until the water recedes. That could be months from now." Harry didn't answer. He just stared down at the river in disbelief. The river floods every year but usually it rises a few feet at a time. This was a freak storm that Harry said was greater than anything he had seen in all his years.

Later, when I sat with Jan, I fully expected she would be devastated by the news. Instead, she said, "Do you think the *gods* are trying to tell us something? We've struggled with the dredges and equipment. We were under financed. And if it weren't for your *never-let-it-die* perseverance, the company would have closed down two years ago...or earlier. It never made a profit from day one. The flying, trading, and diamond buying you developed kept the mining company afloat. That and my work on the books, payroll, inventories, etc., were full-time jobs with the company and we didn't draw salaries. All the profits from the other businesses were poured back into the company. It's been like your expression: *water going down a gopher hole*. There is literally nothing to show for all the effort except a pile of accounts the mining company owes.

"I think we should look out for ourselves. We're a family of four now and you're in a high-risk business. Let's look at what it would take to pay off the company debts and start putting something aside for us."

Donald Haack

Her logic and ability to cut to the chase was undeniably accurate, as usual. I had no retort. She was right, of course. I had been obsessed with making the mining company a viable business...against all odds. I looked over at her. She wasn't smiling, but she certainly wasn't devastated either. She was waiting for my response. This *act of God* took the decision-making out of my hands and as it inevitably sunk in, was as if a great weight lifted off my shoulders.

"You're right, of course," I heard myself say. "Let's take a look at what we have, what we have *to do* and get on with it."

EPILOGUE

For the next six months without the burden of supervising and supplying the dredge, other business picked up and we worked seven days a week. I flew constantly supplying the outposts, buying diamonds and collecting old debts. Toman rounded up the last of the cattle for one more drive to Lethem where we made our last shipment. He had made enough profit to continue on his own in cattle trading, a smaller but still lucrative business.

We were sitting down for tea after a hard day when Jan put down her cup and made sure she had my full attention. I had to admit this was not always the case, as she frequently pointed out to me.

"With the sale of the plane, the mining company's local debts will be paid and we've been able to build a small nest egg. It's time to go. I have enough faith in you that I know that no matter where we go or what we do, you'll be successful."

Logic was on her side. I knew these were our final days at Marquis. Jan packed household belongings, clothes and toys to be given to Nellie for distribution to the Macusi or missionaries. The rest went to the Red Cross in Georgetown. We shipped stateside a few of our personal belongings.

It was hard for me to get into the mind-set of closing a business I'd worked to build up. I was severing associations with Indians, Brazilians and traders with whom I'd worked all these years. The hardest of all was leaving our closest friends, the Gorinskys, their relatives and ranchers in the Rupununi who had accepted us as part of their families. It had been a powerful relationship, which I appreciated even more after we left.

Dutch was getting too old to go hiking in the Echilebar mines. He moved back to the Rupununi savannah where he alternated residences between Good Hope and McTurks' Karanambo ranch.

As we flew out of Marquis on our last trip over the bush, I thought back to the Amerindian saying, "Once you have eaten laba and drunk from the Caroni, Senhor, you will always return." The implication being that if you acclimated enough to drink directly out of the rivers and eat local game, you had mentally and physically adapted to local life. *You would return.*

Bush life had become so much a part of us. There was hard work, adventure; we never lacked for challenges. But there was a sense of peace and accomplishment too. Jan and I had participated in the local culture more deeply than either of us could have anticipated. It was as if we had entered into a book I had read in my youth. We met and lived with the characters, become their friends and now it was time to close that book, mindful of the prophecy of the *laba and creek water.*

ABOUT THE AUTHOR

Donald Haack, a diamond broker has been referred to as the "Indiana Jones of the diamond industry." He has diamond experience as a miner, trader, and broker on the national and international level.

Don was born and raised in Milwaukee and West Bend, Wisconsin. He graduated from the University of Wisconsin with a major in Economics and Finance after which he served in the U.S. Marines at Cherry Point, N.C., his first exposure to North Carolina and Charlotte.

Don spent 20 years abroad as manager and consultant of diamond mining companies in British Guiana and Venezuela, a licensed buyer of rough diamonds, and as a pilot with over 5,000 hours of bush flying. He organized and operated "Guyana Wings," an air charter service to remote diamond mining areas of South America. In the 70's, he designed, built, and operated ocean-going excursion boats in Grenada and St. Martin and maintained international gem connections in Europe where he had one of the biggest sales to a royal family.

He has a rare insight of the inner workings of the DeBeers cartel, and many anecdotes concerning his friend, the late Harry Winston, who donated the Hope diamond to the Smithsonian institute.

After two revolutions in third world countries, Don, his wife, Janet, and four children returned to the U.S. in 1981 where they opened, Donald Haack Diamonds in Charlotte, N.C.

Don served as president of the World Trade Association, past chairman of the Better Business Bureau Board of Directors and Chairman and President of the Foreign Trade Zone. He has served as Chairman of the Rotary Foundation, is on the Charlotte Symphony Board of Directors, and is a member of Metrolina Business Council, Chamber of Commerce, NC Wine and Grape Growers Assoc., and NC Writer's Network. He writes articles, is working on a second book, *Diamond Safari,* lectures in the field of world trade and gems, and is designing a hi-speed ocean-going boat.